Teaching Stylistics

Edited by

Lesley Jeffries and Dan McIntyre

palgrave
macmillan

First published 2011 by
PALGRAVE MACMILLAN

Palgrave Macmillan in the UK is an imprint of Macmillan Publishers Limited,
registered in England, company number 785998, of Houndmills, Basingstoke,
Hampshire RG21 6XS.

Palgrave Macmillan in the US is a division of St Martin's Press LLC,
175 Fifth Avenue, New York, NY 10010.

Palgrave Macmillan is the global academic imprint of the above companies
and has companies and representatives throughout the world.

Palgrave® and Macmillan® are registered trademarks in the United States,
the United Kingdom, Europe and other countries.

ISBN 978–0–230–23587–8   hardback
ISBN 978–0–230–23588–5   paperback

This book is printed on paper suitable for recycling and made from fully
managed and sustained forest sources. Logging, pulping and manufacturing
processes are expected to conform to the environmental regulations of the
country of origin.

A catalogue record for this book is available from the British Library.

Library of Congress Cataloging-in-Publication Data
Teaching stylistics / [edited by] Lesley Jeffries, Dan McIntyre.
   p. cm.
Includes index.
ISBN 978–0–230–23588–5 (pbk.)
1. Language and languages—Study and teaching.   2. Style, Literary—
Study and teaching.   I. Jeffries, Lesley, 1956–   II. McIntyre, Dan,
1975–
P53.T36 2011
407.1—dc22   2011004897

10   9   8   7   6   5   4   3   2   1
20   19   18   17   16   15   14   13   12   11

Printed and bound in Great Britain by
CPI Antony Rowe, Chippenham and Eastbourne

Teaching the New English

Published in association with the English Subject Centre
Director: Ben Knights

Teaching the New English is an innovative series concerned with the teaching of the English degree in universities in the UK and elsewhere. The series addresses new and developing areas of the curriculum as well as more traditional areas that are reforming in new contexts. Although the Series is grounded in intellectual and theoretical concepts of the curriculum, it is concerned with the practicalities of classroom teaching. The volumes will be invaluable for new and more experienced teachers alike.

Titles include:

Teaching the New English
Series Standing Order ISBN 978–1–4039–4441–2 Hardback
978–1–4039–4442–9 Paperback
(*outside North America only*)

You can receive future titles in this series as they are published by placing a standing order. Please contact your bookseller or, in case of difficulty, write to us at the address below with your name and address, the title of the series and the ISBN quoted above.

Customer Services Department, Macmillan Distribution Ltd, Houndmills, Basingstoke, Hampshire RG21 6XS, England

Contents

List of Tables, Figures and Illustrations

Tables

Figures

Illustrations

Series Preface

One of many exciting achievements of the early years of the English Subject Centre was the agreement with Palgrave Macmillan to initiate the series 'Teaching the New English'. The intention of the then Director, Professor Philip Martin, was to create a series of short and accessible books which would take widely-taught curriculum fields (or, as in the case of learning technologies, approaches to the whole curriculum) and articulate the connections between scholarly knowledge and the demands of teaching.

Since its inception, 'English' has been committed to what we know by the portmanteau phrase 'learning and teaching'. Yet, by and large, university teachers of English – in Britain at all events – find it hard to make their tacit pedagogic knowledge conscious, or to raise it to a level where it might be critiqued, shared or developed. In the experience of the English Subject Centre, colleagues find it relatively easy to talk about curriculum and resources, but far harder to talk about the success or failure of seminars, how to vary forms of assessment, or to make imaginative use of Virtual Learning Environments. Too often this reticence means falling back on received assumptions about student learning, about teaching, or about forms of assessment. At the same time, colleagues are often suspicious of the insights and methods arising from generic educational research. The challenge for the English group of disciplines is therefore to articulate ways in which our own subject knowledge and ways of talking might themselves refresh debates about pedagogy. The implicit invitation of this series is to take fields of knowledge and survey them through a pedagogic lens. Research and scholarship, and teaching and learning are part of the same process, not two separate domains.

'Teachers', people used to say, 'are born not made'. There may, after all, be some tenuous truth in this: there may be generosities of spirit (or, alternatively, drives for didactic control) laid down in earliest childhood.

But why should we assume that even 'born' teachers (or novelists, or nurses or veterinary surgeons) do not need to learn the skills of their trade? Amateurishness about teaching has far more to do with university claims to status, than with evidence about how people learn. There is a craft to shaping and promoting learning. This series of books is dedicated to the development of the craft of teaching within English Studies.

Ben Knights
Teaching the New English series editor
Director, English Subject Centre,
Higher Education Academy

The English Subject Centre

Founded in 2000, the English Subject Centre (which is based at Royal Holloway, University of London) is part of the subject network of the Higher Education Academy. Its purpose is to develop learning and teaching across the English disciplines in UK Higher Education. To this end it engages in research and publication (web and print), hosts events and conferences, sponsors projects, and engages in day-to-day dialogue with its subject communities.

http://www.english.heacademy.ac.uk

Acknowledgements

We are grateful to the series editor of *Teaching the New English*, Ben Knights, for giving us the opportunity to contribute to the series.

The illustrations in Chapter 8 are by Reg Wilson © Royal Shakespeare Company and we are grateful to the Imaging and Copying Service of The Shakespeare Birthplace Trust for permission to reproduce these.

Illustration 11.1 is reproduced with the kind permission of Doubleday, a division of Random House, Inc. Illustrations 11.2 and 11.3 are reproduced with the kind permission of The Random House Group.

Notes on Contributors

Carol Bellard-Thomson was Director of Language Learning at the University of Kent, from 2001 to 2005. Prior to this she was Director of the Language Centre at Lancaster University and Head of French at the University of Dundee. She is the author of *The Literary Stylistics of French* (Manchester University Press 1992), as well as numerous articles on stylistics and language teaching. She is currently completing a PhD at the University of Huddersfield that is an empirical study of student development in learning stylistic analysis.

Derek Bousfield is Head of the Division of Linguistics, English Language, Literature and Culture at the University of Central Lancashire, Preston. His main research interests are pragmatics, stylistics, context and linguistic approaches to understanding and accounting for aggression, conflict and conflict resolution. His publications include *Impoliteness in Interaction* (John Benjamins 2008) and the co-edited *Impoliteness in Language* (Walter de Gruyter 2008). He is editor-in-chief (with Karen Grainger) of the *Journal of Politeness Research*.

Beatrix Busse is Professor of English (historical) Linguistics at Heidelberg University. She has been a Visiting Fellow of the British Academy at Lancaster University and a visiting researcher at the University of Birmingham. Among her publications are *Vocative Constructions in the Language of Shakespeare* (John Benjamins 2006), the co-authored *Key Terms in Stylistics* (Continuum 2010) and the co-edited *Language and Style* (Palgrave Macmillan 2010).

Anna Chesnokova is Associate Professor in the Translation Department of Kyiv National Linguistic University, Ukraine, where she was Head of the English Philology Chair for several years. She has an MA in English and French Philology from Kyiv National Linguistic University and a PhD in Comparative Literature Studies from Kyiv National Taras Shevchenko University. She has published on empirical studies of literature, cognitive poetics, stylistics and literary awareness. Her specific research interest is Emily Dickinson's poetry. Her latest publications include the co-edited volumes *Acting and Connecting: Cultural Approaches to Language and Literature* (LIT Verlag 2007) and *Directions in Empirical Literary Studies* (John Benjamins 2008), as well as chapters for *Cases on Distance Delivery* *and Learning Outcomes: Emerging Trends and Programs* (IGI Global 2009) and *The International Reception of Emily Dickinson* (Continuum 2009).

Lesley Jeffries is Professor of English Language at the University of Huddersfield. She specializes in stylistics and critical discourse analysis, focusing in particular on the interface between the two. Her interest in these areas is reflected in her book *Critical Stylistics* (Palgrave Macmillan 2010). Her numerous other publications include *Discovering Language* (Palgrave Macmillan 2006), *Opposition in Discourse* (Continuum 2010), the co-authored *Stylistics* (Cambridge University Press 2010) and the co-edited *Stylistics and Social Cognition* (Rodopi 2007). She is Director of the Stylistics Research Centre at Huddersfield and a former Chair of the Poetics and Linguistics Association (PALA).

Marina Lambrou is Principal Lecturer in English Language and Communication at Kingston University, London. Among her publications are the co-edited *Contemporary Stylistics* (Continuum 2007) and the co-authored *Language and Media: A Resource Book for Students* (Routledge 2009). She has a background in Applied Linguistics and specializes in research into non-literary narratives.

Dan McIntyre is Reader in English Language and Linguistics at the University of Huddersfield, where he teaches courses in stylistics, corpus linguistics and the history of the English language. Among his publications are *Point of View in Plays* (John Benjamins 2006), the co-edited *Stylistics and Social Cognition* (Rodopi 2007), *History of English* (Routledge 2009), the co-authored *Stylistics* (Cambridge University Press 2010) and the co-edited *Language and Style* (Palgrave Macmillan 2010). He is series editor for Continuum's *Advances in Stylistics* series, co-series editor for *Perspectives on the English Language* (Palgrave Macmillan) and Reviews Editor for the journal *Language and Literature*.

Nina Nørgaard is Associate Professor of Applied Linguistics at the Institute of Language and Communication, University of Southern Denmark. She is the author of *Systemic Functional Linguistics and Literary Analysis: A Hallidayan Approach to Joyce – A Joycean Approach to Halliday* (University Press of Southern Denmark 2003) and co-author of *Key Terms in Stylistics* (Continuum 2010). She is currently working on a monograph on *Multimodal Stylistics*.

Mick Short is Professor of English Language and Literature at Lancaster University. He founded the Poetics and Linguistics Association and was also the founding editor of its journal *Language and Literature*. He is best known for *Style in Fiction* (Longman 1981, second edition 2007), written with his colleague Geoffrey Leech. Among his significant work on pedagogical stylistics is his edited collection *Reading, Analysing and Teaching Literature* (Longman 1989). The winner of a prestigious UK National Teaching Fellowship (2000), Mick used the prize money to fund the development of a web-based course in stylistics (*Language and Style*, now freely available via the PALA website) and edited a special issue of the journal *Language and Literature* (Vol. 15, No. 3, 2006) in which he and others reported on a series of experiments to test its efficacy.

Michael Toolan is Professor of English Language and Head of the Department of English at the University of Birmingham, where he teaches courses in language, stylistics and narrative. His books include *The Stylistics of Fiction* (Routledge 1988), *Total Speech* (Duke University Press 1996), *Language in Literature* (Hodder Arnold 1998), *Narrative: A Critical Linguistic Introduction* (Routledge, 2nd edition 2001), and most recently *Narrative Progression in the Short Story: A Corpus Stylistic Approach* (John Benjamins 2009).

Willie van Peer is Professor of Literary Studies and Intercultural Hermeneutics at the University of Munich, former President of IGEL (International Association for the Empirical Study of Literature) and a former Chair of PALA. He has been a Visiting Scholar in the Departments of Comparative Literature at Stanford and at Princeton University, and in the Programme of Cognitive Psychology at the University of Memphis. He is also a Fellow of Clare Hall at Cambridge University. He is the author of many books and articles on poetics and the epistemological foundations of literary studies, including *Stylistics and Psychology: Investigations of Foregrounding* (Croom Helm 1986) and *The Taming of the Text: Explorations in Language, Literature and Culture* (Routledge 1988). His most recent books include the co-authored *Muses and Measures: Empirical Research Methods for the Humanities* (Cambridge Scholars 2007) and the co-edited *New Beginnings in the Study of Literature* (Cambridge Scholars 2008), as well as the edited volume *The Quality of Literature: Linguistic Studies in the Evaluation of Literary Texts* (John Benjamins 2008). He is currently working on a rational-critical approach to hermeneutics.

Valentina Yakuba is Associate Professor in the English Philology Department at Borys Grinchenko Kyiv University, Ukraine, and Head of English Philology. She has an MA in English and German Philology from Nizhyn State University and a PhD in Germanic Languages from Kyiv National Linguistic University. Her specific interest is the translation of poetry, and her most recent translations of Emily Dickinson's work into Ukrainian are currently in press. She has published on interpretation and culture, situationally-bound lexicon and stylistics.

David West teaches at Ruhr Bochum University, Germany, having previously been Principal Lecturer in English Language and Literature at Northumbria University in the UK. He has research interests in cognitive linguistics and is currently writing a book on I. A. Richards's work in the 1920s and 1930s in psychology, literature and linguistics.

Sonia Zyngier is Associate Professor of English Language and Literature at the Federal University of Rio de Janeiro, Brazil. A founder member of the international REDES group, she has published widely in stylistics and applied linguistics. Among her pedagogically oriented work are the books *Literature and Stylistics for Language Learners: Theory and Practice* (Palgrave Macmillan 2006) and *Muses and Measures: Empirical Research Methods for the Humanities* (Cambridge Scholars 2008).

Introduction

Dan McIntyre and Lesley Jeffries

Stylistics has a long tradition of research in pedagogy, both in terms of what stylistics can contribute to the teaching of other subjects and how stylistics itself is best taught (classic pedagogical works include Widdowson 1975, Brumfit and Carter 1986 and Short 1989; more recent collections include Watson and Zyngier 2006). The distinction between these two aims is drawn out more fully in the first chapter of this volume, though the book as a whole concentrates primarily on the latter endeavour. The overall aim of this collection is to provide a combination of theoretical and practical advice concerning how to go about teaching stylistics. It is aimed particularly at those teaching stylistics for the first time, which might include PhD students new to teaching and specialists in English literature wishing to integrate stylistics into their curricula, though we hope that seasoned stylisticians will also find this book useful. It is part of a series published by the English Subject Centre (a subsidiary of the UK Higher Education Academy), a body which has been assiduous in promoting the concept of life-long learning; so whether you are new to the teaching of stylistics or an old-hand at it, the philosophy of the English Subject Centre is that we can all develop our teaching through the sharing of ideas about best practice.

The series to which this book belongs is called *Teaching the New English*, and the introduction to the series on the English Subject Centre website explains that it 'addresses the different ways in which the subject now manifests itself in the university classroom, each volume taking as its title a single curriculum area and addressing developments within it'. Books published so far have tended to concentrate on particular authors (e.g., Shakespeare, Chaucer) or genres (e.g., the Gothic, Modernist poetry, Romanticism). Our book is somewhat different in that it focuses on a disciplinary approach to the analysis and appreciation of texts of all kinds, not just literature. Although it is true that literary texts are the object of study for most stylisticians, there is also plenty of work in stylistics that addresses non-literary writing (see, for instance, Jeffries 2010). Nor is stylistics confined to the analysis of English. The techniques of stylistics can be applied to any language (see, for example, Bellard-Thomson 1992) and stylistics has been employed to considerable effect in translation theory (Boase-Beier 2006). In this respect, while this book focuses on the pedagogy behind the teaching of stylistics itself, there is no reason why the techniques of stylistics cannot be employed in the teaching of the other authors and genres covered in the series, nor why they should not be deployed in the study of texts in other languages.

Teaching Stylistics is organized in two parts. Part 1 (comprising Chapters 1 to 6) focuses on theoretical issues that underpin the teaching of stylistics (though there is plenty of practical classroom advice in these chapters). Part 2 (comprising Chapters 7 to 12) is focused more on practical issues relating to the teaching of specific types of stylistics.

Part 1 begins with Dan McIntyre's chapter on the place of stylistics in the English curriculum. McIntyre considers the teaching of stylistics in further and higher education and argues that for students to get the most from stylistics, it needs to be taught alongside core methodological principles from linguistics. To illustrate his argument he provides an analysis of an extract from David Peace's novel *1974*, a fictionalized retelling of the Yorkshire Ripper murders, demonstrating the analytical value of such concepts as objectivity, rigour and falsifiability.

Mick Short's chapter follows, in which he reflects on his long career in stylistics and discusses his personal approach to teaching. Short concentrates particularly on how stylistic analysis can help students to appreciate literature. One of the most gratifying aspects of this chapter for teachers is his discussion of the enjoyment that can be gained from teaching stylistics. In the midst of theoretical discussions about pedagogic practice it is important to remember that teaching and learning should be fun!

Chapter 3, by Carol Bellard-Thomson, reports on a pilot project investigating how electronic corpora of students' essays can be used to gain an insight into students' development in learning stylistic analysis. Her overall aim is to improve pedagogic practice with regard to the teaching of stylistics, and her findings so far suggest that the show/tell distinction that is often popularized in creative writing classes may be a useful heuristic for explaining to students how to write-up a stylistic analysis.

The methodological technique of using students' own writing to gain insights into how they learn is continued in Chapter 4, which focuses particularly on how we might teach literary interpretation. Mick Short, Dan McIntyre, Lesley Jeffries and Derek Bousfield discuss their corpus-driven analysis of informants' intuitive responses to a poem in order to shed light on the interpretative process. From this they draw out the pedagogical lessons we can learn concerning how best to explain to students what interpretation is about.

While the primary objective of this book is to describe best practice in the teaching of stylistics itself, Chapter 5 switches focus slightly to concentrate on how stylistics might be used to teach literature to non-native speakers of English. This is an example of the pedagogical value of stylistics to literature teaching generally, and demonstrates the importance of stylistics and literature in the foreign language context. Anna Chesnokova and Valentina Yakuba provide a unique perspective on this by describing their experiences of teaching stylistics in Ukraine. They contend that stylistics is crucial to EFL instruction and argue their case through the discussion of empirical approaches to stylistic analysis.

Chapter 6, by Willie van Peer, Sonia Zyngier and Anna Chesnovoka, continues the theme of investigating stylistics in non-English speaking countries by reporting on an inter-university project focused on the sharing of good practice with regard to empirical analysis. The REDES project that van Peer and his colleagues describe has had significant success in raising both the aspirations and achievements of undergraduate students in stylistics by developing their ability to carry out empirical research projects of their own. In this respect it is a model of the egalitarian nature of stylistics.

Part 2 of the book comprises six chapters which each focus on a different aspect of stylistics from a practical perspective. Lesley Jeffries begins in Chapter 7 by discussing the teaching of the stylistics of poetry, paying particular attention to where this should fit in the curriculum generally. In doing so she returns to the general principles of stylistics before going on to outline what specifically needs to be taught in order to enable students to analyse poems for themselves from a stylistic perspective. Jeffries includes practical advice on how to teach the concept of sound symbolism in relation to poetry and discusses the tricky issue of how to teach both the linguistic and cognitive aspects of stylistic analysis.

Beatrix Busse's chapter outlines and exemplifies the main issues involved in the teaching of the stylistics of drama, taking particular account of the distinction between dramatic texts and dramatic performances. Through an analysis of *Hamlet* she demonstrates various analytical tools, as well as highlighting the value of using a corpus linguistic approach in the classroom. Busse's analyses can be used as the starting point for a wide variety of classroom activities, some of which she describes in her chapter.

In Chapter 9, Michael Toolan focuses on teaching the stylistics of prose fiction, and chooses to discuss what many students would assume to be a difficult text (George Eliot's *Middlemarch*). Toolan begins by acknowledging the problems that many students experience when reading Eliot and suggests that a stylistic approach can help to overcome these difficulties. In order to better explain what is complex about Eliot's writing, Toolan analyses an extract from the novel syntactically. By doing this he provides an objective perspective on the complex structural aspects of the novel. The chapter serves as a useful case study of how to go about improving students' abilities to deal with difficult texts.

In Chapter 10, Marina Lambrou demonstrates the capacity of stylistics for dealing with non-literary texts. She focuses particularly on oral narratives, a topic which opens up for discussion the nature of literariness, since she demonstrates that the narratological structure of such narratives is in every way as complex as those found in prose fiction. Lambrou describes a methodology for analysing oral narratives as well as giving practical advice on how to incorporate such analysis into seminars on stylistics.

Nina Nørgaard's chapter focuses on teaching multimodal stylistics. Multimodality is a concept that stylistics has only recently begun to deal with in any depth. Part of Nørgaard's concern in this chapter is with the capacity of stylistics to deal with non-linguistic aspects of meaning-making. Key to this is a focus on the key principles of stylistics introduced earlier in the book, namely objectivity, rigour and falsifiability.

Like Nina Nørgaard, David West in Chapter 12 also focuses on what is still a relatively new area of stylistics. His chapter outlines the methodological issues underlying the teaching of cognitive stylistics, and includes a useful discussion of what is meant by the term *cognitive stylistics*, and a strong argument for why cognitive stylistics is a better approach to literary appreciation than the relativist and fragmented approaches that are widely practised elsewhere within English Studies.

The book concludes with five appendices. The first is a timeline of key events in the historical development of stylistics. It is often useful for students to see how a discipline has developed in order to get to grips with why particular analytical and methodological procedures are followed. We hope that this timeline will help them to refine their understanding of stylistics. It goes without saying that this is a selective history and a useful seminar activity would be to have students add to the timeline by incorporating other events and publications that they view as seminal to the development of the discipline. Appendix 2 is a list of key works to which we would direct students (and teachers) new to stylistics. Appendix 3 is an annotated bibliography of further reading and resources in stylistics that can be used as a follow-up to Appendix 2. Appendix 4 lists some key stylisticians and their contributions to the discipline. Again, it can be useful for students, when studying a discipline for the first time, to have some sense of who the key contributors are. This is another necessarily selective list; we have tried to concentrate on those stylisticians who have made key theoretical, methodological or analytical contributions which have had an impact on how the discipline is practised today. Finally, Appendix 5 offers a brief survey of current provision of postgraduate courses in stylistics in the UK and US.

References

Bellard-Thomson, C. (1992) *The Literary Stylistics of French*. Manchester: Manchester University Press.

Boase-Beier, J. (2006) *Stylistic Approaches to Translation*. Manchester: St. Jerome.

Brumfit, C. J. and Carter, R. A. (eds) (1986) *Literature and Language Teaching*. Oxford: Oxford University Press.

Jeffries, L. (2010) *Critical Stylistics*. Basingstoke: Palgrave Macmillan.

Short, M. (ed.) (1989) *Reading, Analysing and Teaching Literature*. London: Longman.

Watson, G. and Zyngier, S. (eds) (2006) *Literature and Stylistics for Language Learners: Theory and Practice*. Basingstoke: Palgrave Macmillan.

Widdowson, H. G. (1975) *Stylistics and the Teaching of Literature*. London: Longman.

Part 1
Theoretical Issues

1
The Place of Stylistics in the English Curriculum

Dan McIntyre

Editors' preface

In this chapter, Dan McIntyre argues in favour of stylistics occupying a more central position in the English curriculum, due to its potential for providing a link between linguistics and literature. For McIntyre, the value of stylistic analysis lies in its capacity for replication and falsification, which makes it possible for critics to argue rationally about the meanings projected by texts. McIntyre analyses an extract from David Peace's novel 1974 *to illustrate the value of the stylistic approach and offers two suggestions for how to teach the novel to literature and language students respectively.*

Stylisticians have always taken seriously the pedagogy of their discipline. In addition to the vast array of analytical work in stylistics there is a considerable and growing body of research that focuses on how best to teach the methodologies and techniques of stylistic analysis (see, for example, Brumfit and Carter 1986, Breen and Short 1988, Short and Breen 1988, Short 1989, McIntyre 2003, Short et al. 2006, Watson and Zyngier 2007). Indeed, this book is one such contribution. This awareness of the pedagogical import of the discipline is arguably one of the greatest strengths of stylistics, since it is through this that stylistics is passed on to the next generation of scholars. Nonetheless, stylistics often struggles to find a place in the English curriculum and one of the reasons for this is that stylistics is sometimes characterized as occupying a middle ground between linguistics and literary criticism. The tension between these two areas then leads to neither perceiving stylistics as belonging to them. Linguists often see stylistics as too subjective and lacking methodological rigour whereas literary critics are apt to view it as based too much on formalist and structuralist approaches to text analysis. Increasingly, though, these are dated beliefs and while there may have been some truth to these positions years ago, stylistics has come a long way since then and neither of these perspectives is representative of most contemporary stylisticians' views.

My aim in this chapter is to outline the place that stylistics currently tends to occupy in English curricula, as well as to argue for where – in my view – it *should* be placed. In so doing I will discuss the teaching of stylistics at university-level and at FE-level (concentrating specifically on the teaching of stylistics at what in the UK is termed A-level) and address some common misconceptions about the aims of stylistics. I want to argue that for students to be successful at learning the techniques of stylistic analysis, stylistics needs to be taught alongside the core principles of linguistics – whether these be delivered as part of a specialist language/ linguistics degree or via supplementary language-oriented modules. I include a brief stylistic analysis of an extract from a novel, and some suggestions for teaching this in a seminar context, in order to demonstrate the value of stylistics to teachers and students of literature.

Stylistics and pedagogy

Before I proceed any further I would like to introduce a terminological distinction that I believe to be helpful when discussing stylistics and pedagogy. As I noted in the introduction to this chapter, there is a long tradition in stylistics of research into what is often referred to as *pedagogical stylistics*. This, though, is different from what I would refer to as the *pedagogy of stylistics*. The difference between the two terms, as I see it, is as follows. The first term, *pedagogical stylistics*, refers to the application of stylistic techniques in teaching, though not necessarily the teaching of stylistics *per se*. For example, pedagogical stylistic techniques can be used in the teaching of English as a foreign language (see Short and Candlin 1989), and in McIntyre (2003) I describe how the principles of foregrounding theory can be applied when lecturing to large groups, in order to make lectures entertaining and memorable. The point in both of these cases is that techniques drawn from research in stylistics can be applied as pedagogical tools in the teaching of (theoretically) any subject, not just stylistics itself.

The *pedagogy of stylistics*, on the other hand, refers to the study of how best to teach stylistics particularly. The case studies in Chapters 7 to 12 in this book are exemplars of this. Each considers what pedagogical techniques work best in the teaching of particular aspects of stylistics.

The distinction between these two terms is worth making, since it separates out two distinct endeavours. Most of the chapters in this book deal with the pedagogy of stylistics, though many will have ramifications for what I have described as pedagogical stylistics. This is true of this chapter. My focus here is on the elements that need to be in place within the English curriculum for stylistics to be taught effectively, though the wider points that I make might well be employed in theorizing the teaching of other subjects too.

Linguistics, literature and stylistics

Many of the old arguments about the value of stylistics centred around a debate as to whether the interpretation of literature was well-served by the application of linguistic analytical techniques. The debate is played out most famously by Roger Fowler and F. W. Bateson in a series of articles and responses reprinted in Fowler (1971). Stylisticians claimed that linguistics provided an invaluable set of tools with which to analyse literary texts, while literary critics were wary of the claims to objectivity made by stylisticians, doubting that scientific rigour had any place in the understanding and appreciation of literature. It is not my aim to restate these arguments here. I will assume that readers see at least some intrinsic value in studying the language of texts from a reasonably objective standpoint (for those who still have doubts, I hope the analysis later on in this chapter will demonstrate the value – and necessity – of a stylistic approach). Nonetheless, I mention the arguments because they raise an issue that I believe has caused difficulties for stylistics over the course of its history. This is the supposition that stylistics is the linguistic study of the language of literature. On the surface, this may not seem a particularly contentious claim. Most stylisticians do indeed focus on the linguistic analysis of literary texts. However, we should not forget that text-type is not a barrier to the practice of stylistic analysis. Stylistic techniques can be applied in the analysis of any texts. Indeed, significant early work in stylistics focused on non-literary as opposed to literary language (see, for example, Leech 1966 and Crystal and Davy 1969). The debate with the literary critics and the focus on literary texts has, I believe, contributed to the sidelining of stylistics within the linguistics community. Too often stylistics is viewed as a soft option, not sufficiently rigorous to fall under the banner of linguistics. Tellingly, stylistics courses are mostly found in English as opposed to Linguistics departments, and this I would argue causes difficulties for students with no background in the study of language. If stylistics is to thrive as a discipline, we need to redress this balance. The typical line of argument made by stylisticians is that we should engage with the objections to stylistics put forward by literary critics (most famously by Fish

1981) and aim to demonstrate the value of an understanding of language for literary criticism. Additionally, however, I believe it is also important for stylisticians to demonstrate the value of stylistics to their linguist colleagues; that is, we need to show that stylistics does indeed proceed on the principles of rigour, replicability, falsifiability and objectivity.

A-level stylistics

In the United Kingdom, stylistics in some form or another has been part of the English Language curriculum at A-level for some time. The phrase 'some form or another' is key, since undergraduate students who have studied A-level English Language, and have thus encountered stylistics, often show no familiarity at all with the techniques of stylistic analysis when they encounter it at university. My criticism here is not specifically of the teaching of A-level English Language (there are good teachers and bad teachers at every educational level) but at the often unrealistic and unhelpful constraints that A-level students (and teachers) are put under by the expectations of the A-level syllabus and exams, which stifle students' abilities to develop skills in stylistic analysis. Davies (2000) strongly criticizes both the length of texts provided for analysis in the stylistics sections of A-level English Language exams and the generic nature of exam questions, noting that in most cases even professional stylisticians would find it impossible to write a comprehensive analysis in the time allotted for completing an A-level English Language exam. Davies also notes that the Examiners' Report for the 1997 paper that he analyses contains the criticism that students appeared to have an 'obsession with "features" at the expense of meaning' (quoted in Davies 2000: 27). Davies then goes on to show convincingly that the exam questions themselves largely predetermine answers which favour the simple identification of linguistic features over a consideration of their stylistic effect. Of course, the exam paper that Davies analysed is now out-of-date, though it is not difficult to find examples of the same preponderance for feature-spotting in the advice given to students in A-level English Language study guides. This quotation from Alan Gardiner's *English Language: A-Level Study Guide* (2003) clearly demonstrates this:

> *Aspects of literary texts – what to look for*
> *Author's attitude*
>
> What is the author's attitude towards the people and places he or she has created, and what attitude does the author intend the reader to have?

Narrative voice

What kind of narrative voice is employed? Often there is a first person narrator telling us directly of his or her own experiences. How does the writer use language to give the narrator a distinctive voice?

Narrators (especially in modern texts) often use informal, conversational language, encouraging a more intimate relationship between narrator and reader.

Alternatively, an omniscient third-person narrator may be used, who may influence the reader's response by commenting directly on characters and events. Or the writer may guide us more subtly, using hints and suggestions.

Characters

How is language used to create the characters? For example, characters may 'come alive' for us through their speech, their actions or the author's descriptions of their appearance.

Rhetorical techniques

These are especially common in literary texts: ask yourself, what techniques are present and what are their effects?

Vocabulary

The connotations of words are especially important in literary texts. How does the writer's choice of words help the writer to develop a consistent viewpoint?

Grammar

Look for ways in which word order and sentence construction are manipulated to achieve particular purposes.

(Gardiner 2003: 78)

The subtitle of the section in which this list of features is included ('Aspects of literary texts – what to look for') may potentially be misunderstood by students as meaning that there is indeed a finite set of features of literary texts, and that identifying these is all that is needed for a successful exam answer. More seriously, Gardiner's list is problematic because (i) it runs together linguistic and non-linguistic features (e.g., vocabulary, grammar, author's attitude) which may well be confusing for students new to stylistics; (ii) it implies that these features are not as important in non-literary writing ('[t]he connotations of words are especially important in literary texts'); (iii) it privileges speculation about author intention; and (iv) it asks questions so broad as to be off-putting for new students. To follow this issue further, while the use of checksheets can be extremely useful for stylistic analysis (see, for example, Short 1996 and Leech and Short 2007), the questions asked by Gardiner above are arguably far too broad for A-level students (or, indeed, undergraduates) to cope with. For example, the question 'How is language used to create the characters?' is intimidating both in its scope and its lack of specificity. This creates a problem both for the student, who is at a loss as to what is required, and for the examiner, since the question is so lacking in specificity that it is impossible to see how an examiner might make a reasonable judgement of the quality of a student's answer. Davies (2000: 29) notes the paradox inherent in the fact that Examiners' Reports routinely criticize students for providing unfocused answers despite the fact that the following is a typical exam instruction to candidates: 'In your answer you should comment on vocabulary, grammar, figurative language, dialogue and *any other linguistic matters you think are relevant to the meaning and tone of the passage.*' (quoted in Davies 2000: 29; my emphasis).

One final issue that Davies (2000) raises concerns the over-eagerness of A-level examiners to reward the use of stylistic terminology at the expense of real understanding. Davies makes the point that a 'sample answer' provided in the 1997 Examiners' Report demonstrates no inherent understanding of stylistic analysis but is deemed successful because the candidate uses an array of stylistic terms. This is problematic because it sends a message to students that stylistics is simply close-reading couched in specialist jargon. This, of course, is not the case. Furthermore, stylistics at A-level seems to disregard methodological rigour, and this has the effect of further distancing it from linguistics. One development that must be made, then, is to make it clear to A-level students that stylistics is not simply an alternative approach to analysing literature, but a sub-discipline of linguistics that focuses on the analysis of all kinds of texts using accepted principles of rational inquiry.

Degree-level stylistics

The problems identified in the previous section are, thankfully, not so much of an issue in the teaching of stylistics at degree level. University tutors are much less constrained than A-level teachers by the restrictions of curricula and are, to a large extent, free to set their own syllabus and exams. And although modularization may sometimes mean that courses are squeezed into one term or semester, by and large university tutors have more resources and freedom to be able to deal with the problems that this can cause (see, for example, the reports in Short et al. 2006 on an experiment to develop a web-based stylistics course to alleviate some of these problems). At degree level, then, the problems with teaching stylistics stem more from the disparate educational backgrounds of the students studying it. For instance, in the United Kingdom, stylistics is largely taught in English departments. It is rare to find stylistics on the curriculum in departments of Linguistics, no doubt in part because of the tensions that have traditionally existed between linguistics and literature. Consequently, many students come to stylistics having only ever studied English Literature. What this often means is that such students have little explicit language awareness. This can create a number of problems. First, such students may well struggle with the linguistic content of stylistics courses. Second, tutors can find it difficult to accommodate the varying levels of ability in a class. These are real issues, though there are ways round them. Breen and Short (1988) and Short and Breen (1988) discuss the revamping of a stylistics course to take into account these difficulties. Their strategy was to drip-feed linguistic information throughout the course rather than to teach it up-front before proceeding to apply linguistic techniques of analysis to literary texts. In this way, literature students with little awareness of language were able to absorb enough linguistic information to undertake stylistic analysis, and language students with little background in literature were able to proceed at an equally comfortable pace. The success of Short and Breen's approach is documented elsewhere (see, for example, McIntyre 2003), and has been continued by Short in his experiments designed to test the efficacy of web-based stylistics teaching (see Short et al. 2006). Nonetheless, such an approach does not solve a related problem that can often arise. Language students taking stylistics courses will inevitably find that their increasing abilities in linguistic analysis will transfer to their work in stylistics. It is often possible for literature students, on the other hand, to take stylistics courses without taking any other language modules. All things being equal, language students should do better at stylistics than literature students because of their extra experience of language study. While this can be countered at first year level (see Breen and Short 1988 and Short and Breen 1988), it becomes a greater problem if students go on to take higher level stylistics courses. As an example, we might consider the possibilities for students at the University of Huddersfield wishing to study stylistics.

Currently, all first year English students at Huddersfield are obliged to take a module called Introduction to Stylistics. This is a genre-based approach to stylistics that covers the main stylistic concepts involved in the analysis of poetry, drama and prose fiction. In line with the Short and Breen approach, the linguistic elements of the module are taught in a drip-feed manner with no prior experience of language study assumed. However, students majoring in English Language also take a module called Description of English, focusing on phonetics, syntax and semantics, as well as a module called Approaches to Language Study that examines key methodological principles in studying language, arguably giving them an advantage with regard to linguistic analysis. This is not so much an issue in the first year, but for students going on to do stylistics in year two it becomes potentially more so. Second-year stylistics students at Huddersfield can opt to take modules in the Stylistics of Contemporary Poetry, the Stylistics of Drama and the Stylistics of Narrative. However, students opting for any of these modules who are majoring in English Literature will not take any other language courses. Clearly this puts them at a disadvantage when compared to their English Language peers, even though it is possible for them to learn enough about language to pass the module. There is a finite amount of material that can be covered within one module and even assuming that literature students engage fully with the course and read widely, their experience of language study will still be much less than that of the English Language students. In many ways, theirs is an impoverished experience of stylistics. This is likely to be the case in other institutions too.

We have tried to counter this to some extent by writing a high-level, research-based textbook on stylistics (Jeffries and McIntyre 2010) aimed at addressing some of the lack of knowledge that literature students will inevitably have if they are not taking concurrent language modules. The problem, though, goes beyond the fact that literature students do not necessarily have the same descriptive apparatus and degree of knowledge about the structures of language that English Language students have. The more significant issue is that language students have a greater sense of the methodological principles on which stylistics proceeds because these are shared with linguistics. These include such principles as objectivity, rigour and replicability. What we might term traditional literary studies does not share such key concepts (see van Peer et al., Chapter 6 in this volume, for further discussion of this issue). English Language students will experience these concepts in other modules. Literature students almost invariably will not. Part of the problem here, I would argue, centres around

Widdowson's (1975) distinction between a *subject* and a *discipline*. In order to make clear why this distinction is important, it is worth quoting Widdowson at length:

> This distinction between a discipline and a subject is, in my view, a crucial one [... and the] basis of the distinction needs to be made clear. I want to define a discipline as a set of abilities, concepts, ways of thinking, associated with a particular area of human enquiry. Geneticists, biochemists, linguists and literary critics for example all follow certain principles of enquiry which characterise their different disciplines. But students are not geneticists or biochemists or linguists or literary critics: they are in the process of acquiring principles not putting them into practice, and some of them (indeed most of them) will only acquire a certain number of these principles and will never achieve the discipline as such at all. This is even more true of schoolchildren. They do not have disciplines like genetics or biochemistry on their timetables but something called 'science'; they do not have linguistics and literary criticism but something called 'English language' and 'English literature'. 'Science', 'English language' and 'English literature' are subjects, not disciplines. Obviously the higher the educational level the more the subject which is studied approximates to the discipline whose acquisition represents the ultimate academic terminal behaviour of the learner. But the majority of learners will, of course, never reach this point. It is for this reason that the terminal behaviour expected of them cannot be the disciplines to which the subjects they are studying are most closely related.
>
> The point I wish to stress is that subject must be defined at different educational levels in terms of pedagogic objectives, whereas disciplines are defined in terms of theoretical requirements.
>
> (Widdowson 1975: 2)

Widdowson goes on to say that:

> There is a good deal of evidence in the form of papers at conferences and articles in journals that many teachers are actively engaged in working out what the aims and procedures of literature teaching should be. What seems to be lacking, however, is an explicit set of principles to which different aims and procedures can be related and which might serve to define the subject.
>
> (Widdownson 1975: 72)

In this respect, whether stylistics focuses on the analysis of literary or non-literary writing, it draws on the discipline of linguistics for the principles that underpin it. Students of language and linguistics are thus at an advantage when it comes to the practice of stylistic analysis, because they will be familiar with such principles from elsewhere in their curriculum. Literature, on the other hand, all too often appears to lack such discipline-specific principles, and literature students are thus likely to be at a consequent disadvantage with regard to stylistics. Literature's relative lack of discipline-specific principles is also discussed by West (2008). Here is his assessment of the methodological problems associated with traditional literary studies, which further highlights why many literature students find stylistics so difficult:

> Lacking their own methodology, English scholars try to base their work on methodologies developed in other disciplines – from psychology, or political science, or sociology, or history. But what they often produce is simply bad psychology, or bad political science, or bad sociology, or bad history. English practioners have never studied psychology, so why should they think it acceptable to teach Wilkie Collins, say, from a psychoanalytic perspective, particularly when psychologists themselves stopped teaching Freud some one or two decades ago? Given a literary text, English scholars will talk about anything but the text, talking instead about the text's socio-historical context, or the text's political unconscious, or what the text tells us about the writer's political stance or psychological condition, or her or his attitude towards women, or imperialism or homosexuality. There is nothing wrong *per se* with such approaches. Again, I do not wish to appear an anti-theory Luddite. Theory has revolutionised the subject to its great benefit, and it still has much to offer. But the basis of literary theory – Lacan's reading of Freud, Jakobson's reworking of Saussure in the 1950s, Derrida's post-structuralism, feminist and Marxist theory of the 1970s, new historicism – is linguistics, and the great leaps in literary theory have occurred when scholars have used the insights of linguistics to enrich their understanding of what literature is.
>
> (West 2008: 138)

Although I think West overstates the value of so-called literary theory (a fundamental problem with it is that its lack of definition and cohesiveness renders it unfalsifiable; there is, then, an issue as to whether it constitutes a theory at all), he is right in pointing to the impact that linguistics has had on the study of literature. The general point that I am making here is that because stylistics has a clear link to the discipline of linguistics, students of language and linguistics should, all things being equal, be at an advantage when it comes to the practice of stylistic analysis, because stylistics proceeds on the principles of linguistics. By contrast, it is often unclear what discipline-specific principles underpin literary studies generally.

The benefits of stylistics: a sample analysis

West's (2008) argument is that contemporary literary criticism all too often lacks a clear object of study. For stylistics, with its roots in linguistics, this is not an issue. The object of study for stylistics is language, and in the stylistic study of literature it is the language of literary texts. For the argument I am making to be convincing, however, it is necessary to demonstrate how stylistic analysis can assist literary interpretation. In this section I will try to do this through an analysis of an extract from David Peace's novel *1974*, the first in his *Red Riding* quartet (a fictional version of the Yorkshire Ripper murders that took place in West Yorkshire in the late 1970s and early 1980s). My aim is to show how stylistics can elucidate our understanding of the passage, as well as to demonstrate that a full appreciation of the text cannot be gained unless we take account of the language. Here is the extract, with sentences numbered for ease of reference:

[Context: Eddie Dunford, the first-person narrator, is a crime reporter with a local newspaper. Jack Whitehead is a fellow reporter. Both of them are chasing the same story. In this extract, Detective Chief Superintendent Oldman is holding a press conference about the latest in a series of brutal murders.]

Wakefield Police Station, Wood Street, Wakefield. (1)
2.59 p.m. (2)
One minute to kick-off. (3)
Me, up the stairs and through the one door, Detective Chief Superintendent Oldman through the other. (4)
The Conference Room horror-show quiet. (5)
Oldman, flanked by two plainclothes, sitting down behind a table and a microphone. (6)
Down the front, Gilman, Tom, New Face, and JACK FUCKING WHITEHEAD. (7)
Eddie Dunford, North of England Crime Correspondent, at the back, behind the TV lights and cameras, technicians whispering about bloody fucking cables. (8)

Jack fucking Whitehead on my fucking story. (9)

Cameras flashed. (10)

Detective Chief Superintendent Oldman, looking lost, a stranger in this station, in these times. (11)

But these were his people, his times. (12)

He swallowed and began:

'Gentlemen. At approximately nine thirty this morning, the body of a young girl was discovered by workmen in Devil's Ditch here in Wakefield.' (13)

He took a sip of water. (14)

(Peace 1999: 35)

There are 142 words in the above passage and 14 orthographic sentences. This gives an average sentence length of 10.1 words. This is not statistics for the sake of it. This figure is way below the average sentence length of 17.8 words (calculated through the analysis of large-scale linguistic corpora; see Leech and Short 2007: 90) and what it suggests is that we are dealing with simple sentences as opposed to complex ones. While simple sentences can be lengthy (a one-clause sentence might well incorporate long pre-modified noun phrases in, say, subject and object position), complex sentences – that is, multi-clause sentences – cannot be short. The next question we might ask is why the author has favoured simple sentences over complex ones. To answer this we need to consider the interpretative effect of the simple sentences in the passage, but before we do this it is necessary to look in more detail at the composition of these sentences.

Above, I said that there are 14 *orthographic* sentences; that is, 14 strings of words divided from each other by full-stops. However, in grammatical terms, many of these vary from the standard definition of a sentence as being composed minimally of a single clause (expressing a single proposition) that is marked for tense. For example, sentence 1 consists of three noun phrases in apposition ('Wakefield Police Station', 'Wood Street', 'Wakefield') with no verb phrase at all. Sentence 2 is composed simply of an adjective phrase (2.59 p.m.). Sentence 3 is another noun phrase ('One minute to kick off'). Sentence 4 begins with a noun phrase ('Me') and continues with an adverb phrase ('up the stairs') co-ordinated to another adverb phrase ('through the one door') via a conjunction ('and'). The remainder of the sentence consists of another noun phrase ('Detective Chief Superintendent Oldman') and another adverb phrase ('through the other'). Sentence 5 has the structure of a post-modified noun phrase ('horror show quiet' modifies 'The conference room'), though in reality what we appear to have is a minor sentence; that is, a sentence that lacks a main verb. It is easy to interpret sentence 5 as a shortened form of the Standard English sentence 'The conference room *was* horror show quiet'). The same applies to many of the other sentences. For instance, sentence 3 can be read as an abbreviation of 'There *was* one minute to kick-off.' Sentence 7 in Standard English would be 'Down the front *were* Gilman, Tom, New Face, and JACK FUCKING WHITEHEAD.' Sentence 6, when re-written in Standard English, becomes significantly more complex, incorporating a defining relative clause (underlined): 'Oldman, <u>who was flanked by two plainclothes</u>, *was* sitting down behind a table and a microphone.' We could go on and analyse the remaining sentences in the extract in this way, and what would become clear is that only sentences 10, 12, 13 and 14 incorporate finite verb phrases. Or, to put it another way, all the sentences in the extract are minor sentences except for 10, 12, 13 and 14.

Intuitively, most readers are likely to agree that this seems significant; that is, the decision to write in this way must have been a choice on the part of the author. Whether or not this choice was conscious at the time of writing is debatable, and to some extent immaterial. What is important is that Peace himself must have realized at some point that he was writing non-standard English. That he chose not to use conventional forms must have some interpretative significance. Having identified exactly how these sentences are non-standard, we can speculate on what this interpretative significance might be.

The first point to note is that the text is reminiscent of spoken English. Biber et alia (1999) explain that spoken English is structured according to a different set of rules than written English and that analysing spoken English in line with the conventions of written English will inevitably lead to analyses that show the language to be 'ungrammatical'. In this respect, Peace's decision to write in a form that for written English is considered non-standard has the consequence of generating the effect of spoken English. This may lead us to view the narrator as a more realistic character than if his first-person narration had all been in Standard English. Some readers might want to claim that it lends the story a gritty edge. Whatever we might want to claim, it is at least clear that the source of this interpretation is the syntactic structure of the text.

In terms of local effects (i.e., the effects of individual sentences), the first two sentences serve to identify the position in space and time in which the events of the passage take place. What is significant here is that only the words that are absolutely necessary to convey this information are used. We might want to link this to a sense of urgency on the part of the narrator (there is no time for extraneous information), or to comment that the style of the text seems sparse. We might also note that these two sentences act almost like stage directions in drama, or initial subtitles in film, and in this respect they give the text a dramatic quality where 'showing' is more important than 'telling'. This interpretation can also be linked to the lack of verbs in the text. The noun phrases give a sense of our being shown a series of snapshots of the scene in question, rather than the narrator describing the scene in retrospect (note how the use of past tense verb phrases would change the style significantly). In essence there is a concentration on individual moments in time, rather than any sense of time moving forwards.

But of course not all the sentences are minor. How are we to interpret those that aren't? Here we can draw on foregrounding theory (see Leech 1969 and van Peer 1986) and note that the continual use of minor sentences up to sentence 10 in effect becomes the norm for the text. The status of sentence 10 as Standard English makes it deviant in contrast to the textual norm (i.e., internally deviant). This has the effect of foregrounding it – that is, making it likely to catch the reader's attention. The cameras flash because the press conference is about to start – perhaps Detective Chief Superintendent Oldman has just sat down. In effect, the foregrounded sentence is indicative of a change in atmosphere, from one of frenzied activity to sudden quiet in order that Oldman might be heard. Sentence 11 reverts back to the internal norm for the text (it is another minor sentence) but from 12 onwards the sentences are all complete. We can note that sentence 12 is foregrounded graphologically by virtue of italicization, and that this might be interpreted as an instance of free indirect thought (in essence a combination of the narrator's representation of what a character originally thought, and that character's original expression of the thought; see Leech and Short 2007: 270). Interpreted this way, as opposed to seeing the sentence as a simple assertion on the part of the narrator, the propositional content of sentence 12 suggests a renewed confidence and calm on Oldman's part that is represented by the change to full sentences from then on.

It should be apparent even from this cursory analysis that there is a lot to be said about this text, short as it is. Nonetheless, this analysis could not have been carried out without recourse to explicit knowledge about grammar. Language is intrinsic to our understanding of the effects of this text, and to analyse it fully necessitates a consideration of its syntactic structure. The more we know about grammar, the more detailed and convincing we can make our analysis.

The brief analysis above indicates what can be achieved through stylistic analysis. However, I would not want to claim that a complete stylistic analysis is necessary in order to arrive at the interpretative conclusions I suggested. Many literary critics would no doubt make similar comments to mine but without having done any grammatical analysis of the text at all. The sceptic might then ask what the point is of going to the bother of a stylistic analysis. There are a number of reasons.

The first is summed up by Leo Spitzer, one of the founders of modern stylistics, who said that 'to make our way to an old truth is not only to enrich our own understanding: it produces new evidence of objective value for this truth – which is thereby renewed' (Spitzer 1948: 38). A stylistic analysis enables the critic to argue from empirical evidence rather than from conviction alone.

Secondly, the value of stylistics lies in the replicability of its method and the potential for falsification that this then leads to. What this means is that a critic disagreeing with the analysis of another critic can demonstrate logically and empirically how that analysis is erroneous. For example, I compared the constituent sentences of the extract from *1974* against the norms for Standard English and found a substantial number of minor sentences. Anyone else carrying out this procedure would arrive at the same results. Notice that this is not to say that another critic would *interpret* these results in the same way that I have done, but we would at least be arguing about the same thing. The source of my interpretative claim is located in the text itself and is therefore recoverable. If another critic could demonstrate that my grammatical analysis was incorrect, then that would inevitably impact on the credibility of my interpretation of the text. Once again, stylistics removes the necessity of having to argue from conviction alone, which, unfortunately, seems to be an approach often taken in more traditional literary criticism. Here, for instance, is an example from a peer-reviewed international journal of this kind of impressionistic discussion:

A special form of masochism hinges on the problem of a reflexive pronoun – in the movement from *I like to be hurt* to *I like to hurt myself*, lost is the logic of intersubjective desire (the implied "by you" of masochism proper), and gained is the signifier that represents me to the statement (my own "myself"). In this movement, a supplement appears: the doubled *I/myself* found only in the second instance. Agent of desire in iteration one becomes agent of desiring annihilation in iteration two, but, significantly, what is effected in the second sentence is a split – the gashing cut of the diagonal slash that forever holds apart *I/myself*. Jean-Luc Nancy's formulation of the *corpus* gives flesh to the latter utterance: 'I am addressed *to* my body *from my body*.' The relational and gendered assumptions in traditional masochistic pathologies (so important for all accounts of the phenomenon, from Sigmund Freud and Richard von Krafft-Ebing to Gilles Deleuze) are infinitely troubled when the violence of the gesture occurs on this primary solipsistic level. What is a masochism, after all, that admits no other parties to its pact because its first wound is to any semblance of the non-otherness of myself?

(Brinkema 2009: 131)

I suspect I am not alone in finding this extract difficult to follow – and this is just the first paragraph of the article. Other stylisticians have drawn attention to an unfortunate pretentiousness that persists in much literary critical writing (see, for example, Short 2001 and Stockwell 2008) and the example above is just one among many instances of what I would call bad writing to be found in journals of literary criticism.[1] To my mind, there are at least two reasons why the above extract constitutes bad writing. First, I would argue that writing in such an obfuscatory style is counterproductive. This is because the difficulty of comprehension that such a style causes prevents readers from being able to engage with the argument that the writer is putting forward. Secondly, Brinkema's claims in the above extract are unfalsifiable. That is, it is impossible to argue against them because it is not at all clear either what Brinkema means by such claims or the method by which she arrived at such conclusions. For instance, what does it mean to say that 'A special form of masochism hinges on the problem of a reflexive pronoun'? What *is* this special form of masochism? Why does this hinge on the problem of a reflexive pronoun? What *is* the problem of a reflexive pronoun? And, more to the point, how did Brinkema discover this? None of these questions are answered in the article, therefore it is impossible to engage with Brinkema's claim and either prove or disprove it. In effect, critical engagement is impossible and this clearly goes against all rational principles of scholarship.

In contrast, what should be apparent from my discussion of *1974* is that stylistics offers a means of analysis that is open to criticism in the sense of being clear, rigorous, replicable and falsifiable. There is no need to argue through simple force of conviction because it is possible instead to form an argument based on empirical evidence. The more convincing critic is thus the one who has accumulated the most convincing evidence, rather than the one who is most able to construct grand-sounding sentences. Critical discussion thus becomes a much more egalitarian procedure than it often is in traditional literary critical circles.

Teaching *1974*

I hope to have demonstrated above how stylistics can be of value to the literary critic. Convincing students of this is, perhaps, another matter, and for this reason I want in this section to suggest some ways in which one might go about teaching this particular text in a seminar. There are a number of potential activities depending on the type of student being taught (literature or language) and whether the aim is to uncover something about language itself or something about the meaning of the literary text. Here are some suggestions:

Introducing literature students to grammar

- Begin by asking the students to read the text and then discuss their interpretation of it in small groups. Ask specific questions such as 'What is your attitude to the narrator?', 'How would you interpret the narrator's character?' and 'What is the atmosphere in the conference room before the press conference begins?'
- Collate the students' interpretations and discuss the extent to which they are similar or different.
- Now ask the students to concentrate on the sentences of the text and to identify any which stand out as particularly unusual or noteworthy. The aim here is to guide the students towards recognizing that the sentences are non-standard. This can be done through suggestions such as: 'Would you write in this way if you were writing an academic essay? If not, why not?' Discuss with them the fact that they are all likely to have identified similar sentences as being unusual.
- Once the students have identified the non-standard sentences, ask them to rewrite them in Standard English (see Pope 1994 for more on 'textual intervention' of this kind).
- Ask them what is different about their rewritten sentences. The aim here is to focus on the additions they have made. Focus on the addition of verbs that are marked for tense, in order to introduce the concept of finite as opposed to non-finite verb phrases (see Biber et al. 1999 for more on this distinction).
- Having introduced this distinction, ask the students how their addition of finite verbs changes the effect of the original text. Through

this the students will be moving towards linking literary effect to linguistic form.

- Now ask the students to work again in small groups and try to identify some other links between form and effect. After allowing time for this activity, discuss their findings with the whole group.
- Finally, ask the students what non-linguistic elements they would wish to add to their analyses (for example, the adjective 'horror-show' alludes intertextually to the language of Anthony Burgess's *A Clockwork Orange* (1962); how is this relevant to our understanding of *1974*?).

Introducing language students to literary analysis

- Begin by asking the students to read the text and analyse the syntactic structure of its constituent sentences.
- Once they have carried out this analysis, ask them to explain the patterns they notice in the structure of the sentences. The aim here is to guide them towards identifying the preponderance of minor and incomplete sentences.
- Have the students complete the same rewriting task as that described above and then ask them what the difference in effect is between the original text and their rewritten version.
- Now ask the students to identify the complete sentences in the original text. Demonstrate the concept of foregrounding by explaining that the complete sentences break the pattern of incomplete sentences and thus stand out.
- Ask the students to consider in groups what the effect of the foregrounding might be on the reader. Can they relate this change in syntactic structure to a change in activity in the conference room of the fictional world, for example?
- Conclude by summing up the value of the stylistic method; that is, its capacity for allowing students to argue about literary effect based on a falsifiable analysis.

The place of stylistics in the English curriculum

I began this chapter by discussing some of the problems and misunderstandings associated with the pedagogy of stylistics. The issues raised in relation to the teaching of stylistics at both A-level and degree level lead to a number of potential solutions. Since stylistics has evolved from linguistics and shares the same underlying principles, it would seem sensible that stylistics should be taught within a linguistics context. More importantly, the analysis of *1974* demonstrates how stylistics is necessary in order to account for text and author style; while stylistics might not provide a full explanation of all of a given text's effects, an analysis will always be incomplete without some consideration of linguistic structure.

The value of stylistics to literary studies is such that its inclusion on a literature degree programme is likely to be of significant benefit to students. However, the concepts that underpin stylistics, such as rigour, replicability and falsifiability, are rarely discussed in literature courses. This suggests that it would be highly beneficial for students of literature to study language alongside the literature elements of their course. Indeed, a strong case can be made for the introduction of compulsory English language modules in English degrees. To some people, this will no doubt seem like an unreasonable suggestion. In answer to this I would point out that currently in British universities (and, no doubt, elsewhere) it is entirely possible to graduate with a degree in English and not have studied language in any form. This cannot be an acceptable state of affairs. To have an English degree but to know nothing about the language that forms literary texts is to have an impoverished understanding of English as a subject (cf. the notion of English as a discipline). By the same token, I would also argue that to have an English language degree but to know nothing about the literature of that language is equally unacceptable. In this respect, stylistics can work as a bridge between language and literature, enabling students with a greater interest in one area to appreciate and respect the value of the other.

The other side of the coin is that stylistics also needs to incorporate more analysis of non-literary texts in order to demonstrate that it is more than a simple methodology for the analysis of literary writing, and to assert its status as a sub-discipline of linguistics. If we can do this then we will be moving towards a new conception of English Studies at university level – one which might eventually see English make explicit the discipline-specific principles on which it is founded.

Note

1. While there is, of course, high quality literary criticism which does not make unsupportable and unfalsifiable claims, the poor quality criticism to which I refer here is all too easy to find.

References

Biber, D., Johansson, S., Leech, G., Conrad, S. and Finegan, E. (1999) *Longman Grammar of Spoken and Written English*. London: Longman.

Breen, M. P. and Short, M. (1988) 'Alternative approaches in teaching stylistics to beginners', *Parlance* 1(2): 29–48.

Brinkema, E. (2009) 'To cut, to split, to touch, to eat, as of a body or a text: *Secretary* and *Dans ma peau*', *Angelaki* 14(3): 131–45.

Brumfit, C. J. and Carter, R. A. (1986) *Literature and Language Teaching*. Oxford: Oxford University Press.

Burgess, A. (1962) *A Clockwork Orange*. London: Heinemann.

Crystal, D. and Davy, D. (1969) *Investigating English Style*. London: Longman.

Davies, M. (2000) *Size Matters: A Critique of the Way Stylistics is Assessed in A-Level English Language Examinations, and Some Alternative Proposals*. Unpublished MA dissertation: Lancaster University.

Fish, S. (1981 [1973]) 'What is stylistics and why are they saying such terrible things about it?', in Freeman, D. C. (ed.) *Essays in Modern Stylistics*, pp. 53–78. London: Methuen.

Fowler, R. (1971) *The Languages of Literature*. London: Routledge & Kegan Paul.

Gardiner, A. (2003) *English Language: A-Level Study Guide*. Harlow: Pearson Education.

Jeffries, L. and McIntyre, D. (2010) *Stylistics*. Cambridge: Cambridge University Press.

Leech, G. (1966) *English in Advertising*. London: Longman.

Leech, G. (1969) *A Linguistic Guide to English Poetry*. London: Longman.

Leech, G. and Short, M. ([1981] 2007) *Style in Fiction*. 2nd edition. London: Pearson Education.

McIntyre, D. (2003) 'Using foregrounding theory as a teaching methodology in a stylistics course', *Style* 37(1): 1–13.

Peace, D. (1999) *1974*. London: Serpent's Tail.

Pope, R. (1994) *Textual Intervention: Critical and Creative Strategies for Literary Studies*. London: Routledge.

Short, M. (ed.) (1989) *Reading, Analysing and Teaching Literature*. London: Longman.

Short, M. (1996) *Exploring the Language of Poems, Plays and Prose*. London: Longman.

Short, M. (2001) 'Epilogue: Research questions, research paradigms and research methodologies in the study of narrative', in Van Peer, W. and Chatman, S. (eds) *New Perspectives on Narrative Perspective*, pp. 339–55. Albany: SUNY Press.

Short, M. and Breen, M. P. (1988) 'Innovations in the teaching of literature: Putting stylistics in its place', *Critical Quarterly* 30(2): 1–8.

Short, M., Busse, B. and Plummer, P. (eds) (2006) *Special Issue: Language and Style Pedagogical Investigations: Language and Literature* 15(3): 219–320.

Short, M. and Candlin, C. (1989) 'Teaching study skills for English literature', in Short, M. (ed.) (1989) *Reading, Analysing and Teaching Literature*, pp. 178–203. London: Longman.

Spitzer, L. (1948) *Linguistics and Literary History*. Princeton, NJ: Princeton University Press.

Stockwell, P. (2008) 'Faultlines: The value of English studies', Inaugural Lecture: University of Nottingham. [Available at: http://www.nottingham.ac.uk/~aezps/research/papers/faultlines.doc]

Van Peer, W. (1986) *Stylistics and Psychology*. London: Croom Helm.

Watson, G. and Zyngier, S. (2007) *Literature and Stylistics for Language Learners: Theory and Practice*. Basingstoke. Palgrave Macmillan.

West, D. (2008) 'Changing English: A polemic against relativism and fragmentation', *Changing English* 15(2): 137–43.

Widdowson, H. G. (1975) *Stylistics and the Teaching of Literature*. London: Longman.

2
A Teaching Career in Three Chapters and Three Examples: Why I Teach Stylistics, How I Teach It, and Why I Enjoy It

Mick Short

Editors' preface

Mick Short's chapter explores the philosophy behind teaching stylistics from a personal perspective. Like McIntyre, Short argues that stylistic analysis ought to be at the core of literary criticism rather than being seen as a peripheral activity irrelevant to the main task of interpretation. Short draws on his experience of teaching stylistics to literature students over a number of years and illustrates how a detailed understanding of language can enhance literary appreciation.

A brief history of a stylistics teaching career

I have recently finished teaching my undergraduate stylistics courses for the current academic year, and am moving towards the end of my entire teaching career, so I am writing at a good time for taking stock. This chapter represents a very personal view of stylistics and stylistics teaching which I hope others will find helpful. I will talk in general terms in Section 1, and then analyse three brief examples by way of illustration in Section 2.

The stylistics courses that my close colleagues and I teach are always among the most popular in our department[1] and, by and large, the students say very kind things about what we teach them and how we do it, even though we work them very hard and expect a lot of them. But the nearer I get to retirement, the more I find myself worrying about, and trying to make clear to my students, some rather basic things: (a) *why* I teach them stylistics (and indeed why I submit myself to the 'extra hassle' of doing systematic and precise analysis rather than just reading texts and commenting on them in more 'intuitive' terms), and (b) why I teach stylistics in the way that I do. A little personal pedagogical history may be helpful in explaining my situation.[2]

Naïve beginnings ('Chapter 1')

When, more than 35 years ago, I started teaching stylistics, I did what most others must do at the beginning of their university careers. In addition to being allocated to a few other courses, I taught the area I was most committed to academically, and at least partly expert in, on the simple grounds that this was what I knew about. Effectively, I knew no better and, though I strived to connect with my students and make what I taught as clear for them as I could, there were no books on stylistics teaching in those days (indeed, there were hardly any books on stylistics itself then!) and no courses in universities on how to teach. So I more or less made it up as I went along. Because I was researching the stylistic analysis of literary texts, like most literature teachers I could assume that my students would enjoy the texts I explored with them and that teaching English literature to students was a good thing to do in general educational and cultural terms. So although I wasn't a brain surgeon, I didn't have to work that hard to believe that I was doing something useful, even if many of my literary colleagues[3] were rather less convinced.

My main focus at that time (one that I signally failed in, I have to say) was on trying to persuade my literature colleagues that stylistics was part of the central core of literary criticism.[4] I argued that, as literary criticism involved interaction between readers and texts, any interpretative critical move should, in principle, involve as a significant component (though not an exclusive or complete one, by any means) an argument that connected the linguistic structure of the text concerned to the critic's or student's interpretative view of it, and that this work would help to distinguish between more and less valid interpretations. This standpoint, which I still hold, in turn led me to the view that it would be helpful for students to know how to do stylistic analysis, so that they could support and/or challenge views of texts more effectively when writing essays or taking part in class discussion. In this sense, stylistics was the language-based logical terminus of the *Practical Criticism* approach of I. A. Richards and other related techniques like American New Criticism and French *explication de texte*.

The point I have just made, although it is relevant to all students, had its most significant effect in relation to my more sophisticated students. They could already read texts sensitively and arrive at interesting general views of those texts and how they were affected by them; but they found it much easier to talk about how they *felt* as a consequence of reading the texts than to describe accurately the language (and other structural features) of the texts which led them to their responses. In other words, they could describe their own responses quite well, but struggled when trying to describe the texts themselves and how their understanding related to those texts. Stylistics provided an essential bridge (though not the only one) between text and response.

I also felt that it was important educationally to help students who were not quite so adept at responding to, or talking about, literature, so that they could join the 'elite' who seemed so naturally good at understanding and responding to literary texts and who did so well in their assessed literature work. As a working-class student myself, I could remember struggling at grammar school to come to terms with literature, even though I loved to read it. My school teachers were very supportive but they assumed a level of cultural sensitivity and an understanding of how to go about discussing literature which was familiar to students from more advantaged middle-class backgrounds, but which was not available to me. But taking stylistics as an undergraduate had helped me immensely in understanding the critical 'game' that was being played, and so the best way I knew to help my own English students who were not performing to the best of their critical abilities was to analyse carefully with them the language of the texts they were studying, in order to show, as explicitly as I could, how the texts worked and how I got from those texts to my responses to them. This seemed preferable to the advice I often heard given to students if they couldn't see what their literature teachers were wanting them to see in some text, namely that they should re-read it, more carefully (a piece of advice I can remember getting myself on more than one occasion when I was an undergraduate). To use a golfing metaphor, this 'one club' approach seemed unlikely to help much and also seemed rather demeaning in terms of the attitude towards the students involved.

In many countries in the world, English language and English literature are taught side by side and are assumed to be integrally related. So it is natural for the discussion of the language of literary texts, and so stylistics, to be part of critical discussion. However, the English-speaking world has developed a lack of interest in its native language over the last 50 years (something which seems very strange to speakers of other languages) and most of the native-speaking literary critics I knew thought that stylistics was largely irrelevant to their endeavours. I felt, and still feel, that this attitude led them to miss out on an important and valuable connection which academics in other countries were benefiting from. My literary colleagues were not just very adept in responding intuitively to what they read. They also assumed (a) that there could be as many understandings of texts as there were readers, and (b) that the best students came up with inventive new views of texts, which were in turn prized for their novelty and freshness whether or not, from my point of view, there was much legitimacy to be found from the text for the interpretative view expressed. In turn, not surprisingly, the best UK English literature students also felt that stylistics, and language description more generally, was largely irrelevant to them. For them, the language of the text was rather like a pane of glass which they looked through, without noticing its presence or its effect on their perceptions, and so arguing for and against their intuitive interpretations or emotional response seemed irrelevant in their continuing quest for new ways of looking at literary texts.[5] It is this general view that seems to have led to the approach to writing critical works (and so student essays) which currently dominates literary studies, whereby one states a preferred 'reading' and quotes an illustrative example or two to exemplify that reading, without going on (as I would) to analyse the language and so show exactly how the quotations count as exemplifications. On the other hand, my view, then and now, is very similar to that of Geoffrey Leech (2008: 204), who argues that '"linguistic text" and "literary interpretation" are not opposing sides in a tug-of-war, but two cooperative endeavours of comparable value.'

Methodological middles ('Chapter 2')

The struggle to get English students to 'see the point' of stylistics led to a new phase in its teaching, which began in the 1980s and continues today. We needed to develop techniques to persuade students who were often resistant, at least initially, to feeling its value. This led to a concentration on (a) how to grab student interest and keep it, (b) how best to achieve an understanding and appreciation of what we were trying to teach them, and (c) how best to help them employ our analytical techniques successfully on texts. Effectively, this led to a concentration on curriculum, general teaching methods, particular teaching techniques and appropriate text selection.

When I first taught stylistics I believed, along with all the other linguists and stylisticians I knew, that 'logically' I needed to teach various methods of analysis (e.g., phonetic analysis, grammatical analysis, discourse analysis, pragmatic analysis) to students before they could apply those techniques to texts. But this turned out to be an unhelpful pedagogical tactic. Most of them found learning phonetics, grammar and so on boring, and so by the time we had gone through those phases they had become 'switched off' and we found it difficult to reawaken their interest in stylistics later in the course.[6] This led my colleagues and I to change the 'order' of teaching, so that we started with the (extracts from) poems, plays, novels and short stories (what most English students are most interested in) and would 'drip-teach' the relevant linguistic knowledge needed to describe each text effectively, in order to help students explore the interesting properties of those texts (see Short and Breen 1988). We then tried to show them that the analytical techniques developed could be used on a wide range of texts, not just the one they were exploring at the time.

The main criteria for text selection, apart from what interested the students, were (a) that the texts should be relatively easy for students to understand (we did not want to overtax them interpretatively while concentrating on teaching them how to *analyse* texts), and (b) that the texts chosen should exemplify as helpfully as possible the usefulness of the particular analytical techniques we were trying to teach. This approach, which is explored in more detail in Short and Breen (1988) and Short (1996b), is one I still largely follow, even though it is sometimes more convenient to teach some of the straightforward linguistic information in small mid-course chunks rather than in tiny text-specific chunks, as I sometimes do, for example, in my freely available web-based introductory stylistics course <http://www.lancs.ac.uk/fass/projects/stylistics/index.htm>.[7]

I have tried to introduce into my web-based course the features which I have incorporated over the years into my face-to-face stylistics teaching. The first of these is the general notion that, wherever possible, learning should be fun, and that concentration is also enhanced by brief mental rests. So my web-based course contains lots of cartoons and amusing visual illustrations to illustrate points, and 'smileys' leading to jokes and odd facts providing a bit of relief from text description and analysis. I also use jokes in my traditional teaching; for example, those with a three-part structure to teach parallelism and internal deviation (for the web-based equivalent, see http://www.lancs.ac.uk/fass/projects/stylistics/topic3b/5dream.htm). My first year lecture on sound symbolism and other forms of iconicity/appropriateness/enactment involves plastic hammers with 'arbitrariness' written on the side, which I bash over students' heads (and my own, I hasten to add) from time to time, to help them remember that most linguistic signs are arbitrary and conventional, not iconic (otherwise, they 'see' iconicity where it does not exist). McIntyre (2003) has described this sort of approach, which has an electronic equivalent in my web-based course (see http://www.lancs.

ac.uk/fass/projects/stylistics/topic5a/7symbol.htm), as a way of using foregrounding theory for pedagogical gain. It is not always possible for everything to be fun, of course. Sometimes we just have to bend our heads and work hard at something, whether we like it or not, in order to get it to work and students have to face up to that fact just as much as academics do. But I think that my students are more likely to accept the 'tougher stuff' if I make learning fun whenever I can.

I also think that I teach my students more effectively if they feel a personal bond with me. To this end, I always try to take their arguments and concerns seriously and straight on. At the same time, I am always prepared to make myself look silly in class if it can be used to cement my students' bond with me and/or bring home a pedagogical point. For example, I send myself up with illustrative personal examples, dress up in lectures, sometimes in drag, to act out dramatic extracts (in which I get students to participate too), tell personal anecdotes about mistakes I have made to illustrate theoretical points, and so on. If my students like and connect with me, they are more likely to like what I am interested in teaching them. This approach, along with the fun element helps them over that initial 'learning hump' in stylistics courses, where students have to learn lots of new analytical approaches and technical terms all at once. Once they have got over this hump they become interested in the material and what we are doing with it analytically, for its own sake.

Another general pedagogical assumption that I have tried to embed in my web-based course, as well as my more traditional teaching, is that students often learn best by doing things, and so getting them to be interactive in class is important.[8] This is why my web-based course often asks students to work out something for themselves, compare it with what I say and then discuss the differences with other students. Because an important aspect of stylistics is being systematic and detailed in analysis, I have also developed the use of checksheets to help students become more systematic in their analyses, in my traditional teaching, my web-based teaching and also in my books (see the ends of chapters in Short (1996a) and also the menu for most of the topics on the web-based course referred to above). The educational principles that I base my teaching on are explored in more detail in Short (1996b), Short and Archer (2003), and Short, Busse and Plummer (2006).

More recently, I have been exploring group-work techniques to help my students learn to do stylistics better. They can learn from one another in this way, as well as from me. The group-work approach is something which has proved very effective and indeed has been copied by colleagues teaching other courses in my department. I don't have the space to describe this approach in detail here, but effectively it involves dividing seminar groups into three or four smaller groups, who work together outside class in between a lecture and its associated seminar. Each group performs a different task each week (lecture summaries, summaries of reading, text analysis, preparing responses to what other groups say, writing up the 'minutes' of seminar discussion) and the tasks are rotated from week to week. The groups have to post the results of their group discussions, and seminar 'minutes', on the course website and they also have to make presentations in class. In this way, they build up together through the year a resource which is available to everyone as they prepare for their assessed work. This approach, which also enhances students' so-called transferable skills, seems to persuade them to work harder and more consistently, which in turn makes them more interested in the work we do together and leads to significant improvements in their ability to perform stylistic analyses and discuss analyses and theories which others have produced.

Since my early career, with the advent of post-structuralism, deconstruction, resisting readings, postmodernism and so on, the concentration on relatively unconstrained response at the expense of a concentration on the text has deepened in literary circles. As I said in the first section, I felt early on in my career that my students were much better at describing their own felt responses than describing texts, and, if anything, this disparity has widened in the United Kingdom over the years. This is not surprising because UK students are now taught little about how to do text description at school (unless they take A-level English Language), let alone how to relate text and response to each other. To my mind this is another argument in favour of the stylistic approach (at school as well as at university). Students need appropriate concepts, terminology and analytical approaches to describe texts accurately and so be in a position to assess more effectively what they, and others, say about the texts we all treasure.

A philosophical beginning of an ending? ('Chapter 3')

After thinking methodologically about my teaching for most of my career, I began to think rather more abstractly about why I teach stylistics, as I responded to a question, or rather a request, from a post-graduate student at the end of a panel discussion at a one-day stylistics workshop in 2006 at the University of Kumamoto, Japan.

I was expecting detailed technical questions about stylistic theory and analysis, but the student asked a much more general question: what advice did I have for him and other students of stylistics? The question was so general that it threw me at first, and then I heard myself saying that although students tended to assume that stylistics was hard for them, yet easy for their teachers, it was important for them to realize that actually it was hard for everyone, including me, and that every day I had to force myself, in spite of my own inherent laziness, to be more and more analytical and precise, and to be more and more systematic in what I did. We stylisticians forced ourselves in this way because we felt it was necessary to get the job of interpreting and valuing texts done well. Listening to myself saying this helped me to see that, although it is easy to perceive stylistics as merely a collection of analytical tools and methodologies, it may be better to think of it also as an attitude of mind, and to consider in a more concentrated way what exactly the advantages were, both for myself and for my students of being (a) analytical, (b) precise/accurate, and (c) systematic.

Perhaps the first thing to notice is that being systematic applies not just to methodology and analysis but also to one's general interpretative approach. It is often assumed by non-stylisticians that we think that texts have one and one only interpretation. However, I am, and always have been, sure that texts can have more than one interpretation and I have never, as far as I am aware, met a stylistician who thinks otherwise.[9] Being systematic interpretatively involves, in part, being open enough to consider any account ('interpretation, reading' or whatever one might want to call it) of a text that has been proffered by others or can be imagined by the analyst, however unlikely it may appear at first sight. The other major aspect of being systematic is probably the thing which has led others to believe that stylisticians think all texts have just one inter- pretation each, as it tends to lead to the rejection of interpretations which do not stand up to analytical scrutiny. To be systematic we also have to examine carefully whether the account suggested can be 'validated' *via* a careful account of the linguistic features of the text itself and the infer- ences that can reasonably be arrived at, based on those textual features in combination with appropriate schematic and other background and contextual knowledge. This is something all stylisticians assume, but I suspect we may not make these general things clear enough to our stu- dents. In my most recent teaching, I have been placing greater emphasis on exploring these generalizations with my students at relevant places in our discussion of particular texts. This helps them to come to terms better with general issues concerning the nature of interpretation and also the 'theory courses' they often take as part of their literary studies.

Although the stylisticians are more aware of this than most critics, another aspect of being systematic which I think we need to teach more explicitly is that we have to try out all the relevant analytical approaches needed for the discussion of a particular text and that we perform these various methods of analysis precisely and in sufficient detail. This is why I have developed the checksheets for students I referred to in the second part of the first section. No text will reveal 'interpretative gold' through every mode of analysis, of course, but it is important not to miss something significant, and an analytical approach which looks unlikely at first sight sometimes yields important insights.

In stressing these aspects of being systematic to my students I am also teaching them important general transferable skills: to be flexible enough to consider seriously any view, however unlikely at first sight, to be careful enough to get the analysis right, to be prepared to challenge views which don't seem to fit the facts, to be prepared to take counter-arguments and counter-evidence to one's own view on board and so always be prepared to change our minds. We and our students need to be constantly aware of some things that the scientists seem to understand much better than the critics: that the devil is in the detail, that 'truth' is always provisional and that we should always be prepared to change our minds.[10] Because stylistics is constantly moving from text to meaning and effect and then back again, and so continually testing out the relation between text and understanding, much in the way that Leo Spitzer (1948) suggested when proposing his 'philological circle' approach.

These transferable skills, which are very important for prospective employers (another argument in favour of the stylistics approach) are also, in my view, important keys not just to accurate understanding and accurate response, but also to the accurate appreciation and evaluation of literary (and non-literary) texts. Textual appreciation, a concept which used to be common in English departments in schools and universities, seems to be a rather rare bird these days. But I see appreciation as an important cultural skill (and consequent pleasure) that stylistics can help students develop. Understanding and appreciating valuable texts usually involves putting in considerable time and effort; but that effort brings special, including aesthetic, pleasures which are difficult (maybe even impossible?) to access without such effort.

Throughout my teaching career, students beginning stylistic analysis have asked me whether knowing how to analyse texts in fine linguistic detail interferes with my ability to read literary texts with enjoyment. The assumption that being analytically precise might spoil one's reading experience is an essentially Romantic notion which opposes science on the one hand with beauty and the imagination on the other. But knowing the science of how rainbows and the colour spectrum are created in no way stops us appreciating 'the rainbow of the salt sand-wave', as Keats calls it in his 'Ode on Melancholy'. Correspondingly, I used to tell my students that I could easily read and enjoy texts without analysing them. But although that is still the case, today I would want to put the case more strongly. In order to appreciate a text in depth one needs to become very familiar with it. This is why studying a text leads to greater appreciation than mere reading, and why learning a poem by heart leads to even greater appreciation. In my view, detailed stylistic analysis can increase felt appreciation even more than learning a text by heart, just as knowing the detail of the science behind the rainbow can increase ones appreciation of the rainbow in the salt sand-wave.

So of late, I have found myself helping my students more and more to make an explicit link between careful analysis, accurate understanding and better appreciation of the texts we explore together. As the pre-dominant culture of the English-speaking world, at least, craves more and more for immediate and obvious pleasures, and for sound-bite edu-cation, these more nuanced and contemplative pleasures become more difficult for our students to access.[11] In the last section of this chapter I will try to develop in a bit more detail how stylistics, because of its attention to detail, can engender appreciation.

Examples of detailed analysis and its relation to appreciation

It is impossible to provide complete stylistic analyses at the end of a general article about pedagogy. Instead, by way of illustration, I will look at a brief excerpt from the beginning of 'Piano' by D. H. Lawrence, a single sentence from *Bleak House* by Charles Dickens and then a brief extract from Alan Bennett's play *The Madness of George III*. These examples are all accessible examples of good writing in a range of text types, the analysis of which I hope will illustrate how they can be used to teach in combination careful stylistic analysis, textual understanding and the appreciation of effective writing. The approach can be usefully applied to texts from any literary or non-literary genre (e.g., political speeches, newspaper journalism, scientific writing, songs), and in my view it is important that we teach our students that there is plenty of good writing to be found, and appreciated, outside the text types stud-ied in university English departments (see, for example, my discussion of point of view in a brief extract from a newspaper magazine article in Short 1994; section 3.8).

The beginning of 'Piano' by D. H. Lawrence

Lawrence's poem is a first-person, present-tense narration which evokes a situation where the persona (probably, but not necessarily, representing the poet himself) remembers an incident from his youth when he sat under the piano while his mother was playing. My more elementary students would be able to tell me that the poem evokes a memory, but, if asked to explain what exactly makes the description so evocative, they would find it difficult to tell me with clarity. Here are the first three lines of the poem:

> Softly, in the dusk, a woman is singing to me;
> Taking me back down the vista of years, till I see
> A child sitting under the piano, in the boom of the tingling strings

Although it is not possible to know for definite the relationship of the woman to the narrator, it is likely that she is not close to him socially and/or spatially. This is because, although the present continuous form in the first line ('is singing') suggests an *in medias res* beginning, 'woman' does not receive the definite article which such a beginning would usually get. This suggests that the woman is new information for the narrator as well as the reader, something which is best accounted for contextually if she is unidentified or unknown to the narrator, and playing the piano, say, in a nearby house or flat.[12] The foregrounded initial manner adverb 'softly' is also consistent with this view. This situation suggests the sort of experience we have all had, where some unbidden external input prompts a particular memory or thought in us. If the contextualization I have inferred from the linguistic detail is accurate, in spite of what is said, the narrator is unlikely to be the intended target for the woman's singing. Rather, 'singing to me' is metaphorical, helping to strengthen the felt evocation of significant memory; and similarly 'taking me' and 'I see' are also metaphorical and so evocative, *via* a MEMORY IS DIRECT PERCEPTION schema, of the kind of memory that would be called a 'flashback' in films.

The clause explicitly evoking the memory process 'taking me back down the vista of years' also contains a significant semantic deviation, 'vista of years', which describes (distant) time in terms of (panoramic) space, and this helps key the reader into another, synaesthetic, metaphor ('boom of the tingling strings') which is part of the strongly realized flashback in the last line of the extract. All of this is viewpoint-related in that the overall flashback effect vividly juxtaposes remembering time and remembered time.

I will now look at the point-of-view factors in more detail before returning to the final synaesthetic metaphor I have referred to above. We have already seen that there are point-of-view contrasts (close first-person narrator vs. distant woman, close narrating time experience vs. distant memory) in the very opening of the poem. But note the tense for the processes related to the child, which are also presented using the present continuous verb form, in spite of the time backshift involved in memory (this reinforces the flashback aspect of the interpretation). And yet the child (who is presumably the narrator when young – typically we remember things that we were personally involved in) is referred to, like the woman, with the indefinite article, thus suggesting emotional and perceptual distance between the adult narrator and his childhood self. But this apparent memory distance is overturned in another set of dramatic flashback effects in 'the boom of the tingling strings'. First, 'boom' is iconic of a long, low-pitched and indistinct sound (long back vowel plus final nasal) but 'tingling strings' in the prepositional phrase which postmodifies 'boom' evokes opposing sounds – short and higher pitched (short high front vowels), if still indistinct (syllable final nasals).[13] This iconic contrast helps us to see that what would be short, relatively high-pitched notes for other listeners will seem longer, louder, lower and more resonant for the child sitting under the piano. Second, this yoking of contradictory descriptions/perceptions also involves synaesthesia, another kind of 'contradiction'. 'Boom' involves the sense of sound but 'tingling' involves touch – though, usefully, it is also very close phonetically to 'tinkling', the participial adjective which would have contradicted 'boom' more straightforwardly, within the auditory domain.

A detailed, systematic and precise analysis of this poem helps my students (and me too) to convert relatively vague initial impressions into a more exact, accurate and integrated characterization of understanding and related effects, and that this more exact understanding, besides being an improvement on less exact interpretation in its own right, in turn increases our ability to appreciate and value the poem more accurately.

This short analysis is by no means exhaustive of the above three relatively straightforward lines, let alone the poem as a whole; yet to achieve it, I have integrated aspects of grammar, phonetics, semantics, given vs. new information in relation to point of view, narratology and schematic assumptions. Analysing texts in this sort of detail can thus help students to understand and appreciate particular literary texts, and so why they are valuable. It also helps them, in what appears to be a virtuous pedagogical circle, to learn more about how language works and how to be more analytical and to use what they have learned again in working to understand and appreciate other texts independently.

A short sentence from *Bleak House* by Charles Dickens

The context for the sentence below is that the young and naïve Richard Carstone, instead of earning money to support his wife and himself, has unadvisedly placed all his hopes in being the beneficiary of a large will which is the subject of a long and very complex law-suit (the Jarndyce suit, which has many claimants) in the Court of Chancery. Richard now comes to see Mr Vholes, the lawyer working on his behalf. The narration in this chapter is in the third-person and the present tense (chapters in this narrative form are interleaved throughout the novel with a series of first-person past-tense narrations on the part of a young woman, a friend of Richard, called Esther Summerson), thus giving it an omniscient, objective feel. As the narrator refers to him by his first name only, we are clearly intended to sympathize with Richard even though we know he is naïve. On the other hand, the narrator refers to Vholes by his last name only, suggesting attitudinal distance and, as it is clear that he is preying on Richard by spinning out the case and so increasing his fees, we are clearly intended to disapprove of him. At the end of an overblown speech where Vholes violates Grice's Quality maxim by declaring duplicitously that he is not after Richard's money and is always open with him, we get the following sentence:

'This,' Vholes gives the desk one hollow blow again, 'is your rock; it pretends to be nothing more.'

If I ask my students to 'act out' this sentence, they will always pause after 'this' or lengthen the pronunciation of the final /s/ of the word (an alternative way of realizing the 'pause' effect) and bang the desk with a fist at the same time. They will pause again between the narrative clause and the rest of the direct speech, and probably again at the semi-colon before the last clause. In effect, they are making clear through their actions that Vholes's statement is insincere and for rhetorical effect.

What is there in the form of the sentence which helps to prompt this performance? The first thing to notice is that what Vholes says is presented in direct speech, making it clear that what is said belongs to him and no-one else, and that he condemns himself out of his own mouth. Secondly, the narrative clause acting as the reporting clause, comes in between 'this' and the rest of the direct speech, rather than after it (which is much more usual). This helps us to infer where the performance of the desk-banging action in the narrative clause has to take place in relation to the words in the direct speech. Next, it is clear, because of the general rhetorical context, that the use of 'rock' is insincere, a point which is reinforced by the fact that when Vholes hits the desk with his fist the resulting sound is described as 'hollow', which thus contradicts the literal meaning of 'rock' and also subverts the final clause too.

Here, we can see considerable writing control in a single sentence in a novel that is more than 900 pages long, helping us to appreciate – in what, after all, is a very simple sentence – the quality of Dickens's writing. In order to be able to characterize the effects accurately and appreciate them fully we have to link together lexis, discourse presentation and speech acts, and appreciate how, in combination, they induce us to make inferences that are not stated overtly.

An excerpt from *The Madness of George III* by Alan Bennett

During the early part of Bennett's play George III has been established as a kind and committed family man and a king who takes his role and the role of the monarchy seriously. Then he starts to become ill and appears to be going mad,[14] which means that he is prey to the ambitions of others, including his son, the Prince of Wales, a wastrel who is heir to the throne. When the king's doctors do not manage to find a cure (they spend most of their time ineffectually examining his urine and bowel movements), Warren, a new and very severe physician, is brought in to deal with the king. In the excerpt below, Warren has decided, with the help of the king's pages, to blister the king's back and legs in the hope of effecting a cure. I have numbered the turns for ease of reference.

1.	WARREN:	Bind him.
2.	FITZROY:	No. This is the King.
3.	WARREN:	Bind him, I say.
4.	FITZROY:	No. Bandage him.
		(*The* KING *struggles with* PAGES, *who take off his dressing-gown and pull him across to the blistering-stool.*)
5.	KING:	No, no. Don't touch me, damn you. I am the King. Go, tell the Queen I am assaulted. The Queen, help!

6.	BRAUN:	Let's have your robe then, sir. Off we come. That's it.	7.	KING:	I was the verb, the noun and the verb. Verb rules; subject: the King. I am not the subject now. Now I am the object, the King governed, the ruler ruled. I am the subordinate clause, the insubordinate George.
8.	PAPANDIEK:	Easy does it, sir.			
9.	FORTNUM:	Come along, sir. Don't make it hard.			

10. PAPANDIEK: Let go, Your Majesty. That's it.
11. BRAUN: Down we go.

(*He is pushed face down on to the stool and pinioned,* PAPANDIEK *holding his arms and* FORTNUM *his legs, while* BRAUN *looks on with evident pleasure. The* KING *begins to pray.*)

George III has clearly moved from being the most powerful person in the land to someone with no effective power at all. In spite of his institutional status, he is being controlled by Warren, whose 'cure' is effectively a kind of torture, which the audience knows will not work. Not surprisingly, we sympathize with George III and are appalled by his treatment at the hands of a member of a profession which has, up until now, been portrayed as little better than a set of comic fools.

Although he only has two short turns, Warren is clearly in control. He speaks first in the extract and commands the pages to tie George III down, so that he can't resist the treatment he is about to receive. So, being acted upon by those whom Warren commands, the king is suddenly at the bottom of the pecking order, not the top. Both of Warren's turns are commands to 'bind' the king, the second of which is more or less a repetition of the first and serves to deny an attempt by Fitzroy in turn 2 to intercede on the King's behalf.

The pages being commanded by Warren to 'do the deadly deed' are all physically assaulting the king. But as we shall see below, although they are subordinate to Warren they all try to soften the blow and so can be seen to be more caring than Warren. Because they are servants they all have to do as they are told but they are clearly unhappy about treating their king in the way that they are being made to.

Of the 25 sentences in the extract, a remarkable ten are imperative commands, showing the strong controlling nature of the struggle going on in action and speech. In addition to Warren's two, directed at the pages (which are also very efficient in producing the desired outcome), the pages have five and the king himself uses three. The king's attempted commands, one to prevent his pages from doing what Warren says and two to get someone to alert the queen, all fail, indicating the extent of the control Warren has over him.

There are also some more commands in the extract which are not imperative in structure, all of which are used by the servants. Braun uses 'Let's have your robe then, sir.' and 'Off we come.' (turn 6) and 'Down we go.' (turn 11), and his use of 'we' suggests that he sees his actions as a cooperative endeavour with the king, not an outright attack. Braun's less prototypical grammatical forms for his commands to the king suggest that, although he is obeying Warren, he is trying to do so in a kind and humane way. The other servants act verbally in a similar way. Papandiek's 'Easy does it, sir' is another of these softer commands, and his use of the address term 'sir', which presupposes that the king is in a higher social position even though he is in the lowest position in terms of the situation he is in, also softens the command's speech act force. Similarly, Fortnum's 'Come along, sir.' in turn 9 mitigates the force of the imperative with the same address term and, as we have seen above, Braun also uses 'sir' in one of his softer commands in turn 6. The one remaining character in the extract, Fitzroy, is an equerry, not a page, and so he does not actually join in the treatment of the king which Warren demands. His turns (2 and 4) show him not just trying (and failing) to countermand Warren's initial order but also trying to soften the character of the proposed attack on the king by using the word 'bandage' (which an examination of the typical contexts for the word in the British National corpus shows has a clearly medical semantic prosody and so caring, associations) for the word 'bind', which has a much wider range of associations, and is clearly related contextually to physical restraint.

So far, we have seen that not all of the king's attackers are the same. The equerry and the pages, who know the king well, of course, are much less forceful than the physician Warren. But apart from noting the ineffectual character of his three attempted commands in turn 5, we have not yet looked at what the king says in any detail.

George III's other turn is turn 7. The first thing to notice about this turn is how it is arranged graphologically. Unlike the others, it does not start at the left-hand margin but is arranged as a separate column to the right, next to Braun's, Papandiek's and Fortnum's turns (6, 8 and 9).

This graphology suggests that in performance turn 7 would not come after turn 6 and before turn 8, but that it would be produced at the same time as turns 6, 8 and 9, which accompany the moment in the passage when the king is physically assaulted by the pages. In other words, Bennett is using graphological alignment to indicate how the turns should be performed in relation to one another, and the fact that he is not allowed to have a turn at speaking when the others remain silent is another indication of his lack of power.

If we now turn to what he says, we can see that turn 7 is a very ineffectual way of preventing what is happening. He no longer tries to command his pages or to address the issue of the assault on him directly. Instead, he merely characterizes his change of status in an extended series of metaphors revolving round a general conceptual metaphor of the form KING IS GRAMMATICAL ELEMENT. He begins by characterizing his earlier status as the verb in a sentence or a combination of subject and verb. This is somewhat ineffectual in that (a) he appears to change his mind about what part of speech he is best seen as (partly because he is havering between a characterization using word class and another using the functional roles of noun and verb phrases in clauses), and (b) the word 'subject' has another meaning ('person who is ruled') and so is unfortunately ambiguous in this context. In another confusion of the conceptual metaphor he is trying to establish, George III then characterizes himself in agent terms as having become an object, not a subject, but again there is a bit of an issue over the ambiguities of the words 'subject' and 'object'. Finally, George III shifts his characterization yet again, from parts of speech and functional roles in clauses to clause type, a subordinate (rather than main) clause. This last characterization is perhaps the most accurate for him in his circumstance (so arguably we can see him in this speech as struggling to find the most appropriate linguistic instantiation of the conceptual metaphor he has invoked), and at the end of his speech he uses parallelism to make a joke about the fact that he can be seen in his present resisting role as being both insubordinate (resisting) and subordinate (low status, both grammatically and situationally) at the same time. What turn 7 adds up to, then, is the speech of a character who is acting very ineffectually (a) linguistically (struggling to control what he is saying), and (b) physically. He does appear to be able to pun well, but that activity is inappropriate to the dreadful circumstances he finds himself in. So he has become a victim both in terms of action and the language he uses to characterize himself.

As with the other examples I have looked at in this section, a detailed analysis of the language involved helps us to see finer discriminations than even a quite careful reading might reveal (for example the linguistic and so attitudinal differences between Warren and the people he controls) and, as a consequence, heightens our appreciation of Bennett's writing in the extract, including the way in which he uses the dialogue to indicate to his actors how to act out the lines. I have only concentrated here on the graphological arrangement of turn 7, but it would also be possible, if more space was available, to show how, more generally in the extract, the language indicates in myriad ways the appropriate range of actions the actors should perform, what kinds of facial expressions and bodily postures would be appropriate and so on (see Short 1988 for more comments on the text-performance relation in plays).

Why I teach stylistics and why I enjoy it

The issues I raised in this chapter have moved us from interpretation and effect to appreciation and value, aspects of literary studies which have been examined less than they should have been (though see Short and Semino 2008 and the volume it appears in; van Peer 2008, more generally). Raising specific issues concerning how to value particular texts, as with interpretation, effects and appreciation, is another way in which we can link the exploration of particular texts to important general theoretical issues in class. Meeting such issues head-on in this way, does not lead to neat answers, of course, but it does helpfully raise important issues in ways which students can come to grips with more easily.

So I teach stylistics not just because I think my students need the analytical skills and methods involved in it (which I certainly do) but also because it can act as a gateway to much more. It engages my students with interesting and enjoyable texts and, at the same time, improves their analytical skills and increases their ability to come to terms with, and enjoy, other, more challenging, texts. It improves their ability to analyse language and understand its complexity and sophistication. It builds and improves a considerable range of transferable skills, ranging from practical and language-analytical skills to the interpersonal and more abstract thinking and argument skills so important in the modern world. And, to my mind most important of all, it can open up a world of careful and rational examination of issues and the reflective pleasures of detailed and careful aesthetic response. Although it is hard work to do stylistics well, it can open up for students the prospect of that special kind of enjoyment found in solving difficult cryptic crossword puzzles, doing a difficult proof, getting an experiment to work well, coming to grips with a sonnet by Donne and so on, which comes from battling through with precision to a job well done. It is not just the devil which is in the detail, but a rather particular pleasure too.

Notes

1. A department of Linguistics and English Language, not an English (Literature) department, I should point out, which makes Lancaster somewhat untypical, even though a goodly proportion of my students are taking combined degrees in English Language and Literature or English Language with Creative Writing, and so spend a fair proportion of their time on literary studies. In the early 1970s I was part of an English department at Lancaster, but in the late 1970s, when the department grew rather large, it was split into constituent parts and now there is a separate department of English Literature and Creative Writing, as well as the department which I teach in.
2. I would be interested to know from colleagues how similar or different their experiences have been to mine. My email address is m.short@lancaster.ac.uk.
3. At that point I was, like most stylisticians today, a member of an English department, which made its students take both literature and language courses, and so stylistics was, theoretically at least, a bridge between the two halves of one discipline. I have always seen myself as both a linguist and a literary critic, not as one or the other.
4. There are many other important things involved in teaching criticism, of course, including helping students to situate works in their socio-historical contexts, describing the development of English literature and attitudes towards it, describing the different genres and sub-genres and how they develop and so on. But all this work depends on an assumption that the texts studied are valuable in themselves, and that we understand them well. So I would argue that helping students to understand and respond to texts accurately is central to English studies.
5. I think that the view that language analysis can largely be ignored was always more common among native-speaking critics than non-native speakers, who understand better the role language plays in understanding, and I was recently pleased to see a rather more open attitude to the interconnections between linguistic and literary study than can usually be witnessed in the United Kingdom, in Freiburg, Germany at the July 2009 conference hosted by the Freiburg Institute of Advanced Studies: *Linguistics & Literary Studies: Interfaces, Encounters. Transfers* <http://www.frias.uni-freiburg.de/lang_and_lit/veranstaltungen/studies-lili?language_sync=1>
6. This situation arguably holds less now, as linguists are better at teaching the more formal linguistic areas in interesting ways and many students have taken English Language at Advanced GCE level at school, and so are not starting the study of English language from scratch at university. That said, I still have plenty of students who have not studied English language at A level.
7. I developed my web-based introductory course to explore whether it was more effective for students to learn stylistic analysis *via* traditional teaching methods, web-based methods or a combination of the two. This research and the thinking behind the course design is reported in Short, Busse and

Plummer (2006) and Short (2006), which are part of a special issue of the journal *Language and Literature* (vol. 15, no. 3), 'The *Language and Style* Pedagogical Investigations'. This special issue is devoted to describing a series of pedagogical investigations in different countries and teaching situations of how students responded to the course.

8. This doesn't mean that I never tell them things, of course. On the contrary, I do plenty of straight lecturing, especially with more advanced students. There are lots of good ways of teaching, and different students learn best in different ways, depending on their personal learning style preferences. So variety is important not just to prevent boredom in the classroom but also to maximize learning opportunities across the student cohort (see Poole 2006).

9. That said, it also seems to me that many texts have a rather small range of genuinely different interpretations (including just one) and that many supposedly different interpretations or 'readings' are actually different instantiations of the same interpretation (see Short 2008).

10. There are many other such transferable skills which stylistics encourages too, for example the ability to read and write more accurately, but here I am concentrating on the more abstract skills.

11. It should be noted that helping students to access such aesthetic pleasures, although not transferable skills in the more narrow business-oriented sense, do have good consequences for employees, helping them to be more balanced and contemplative in the work-place, and so they also have good consequences for business, industry and the state too.

12. She could in theory be in the same room and still unknown to the narrator, but situationally that is less likely, of course. So I think this possible interpretation is not as strong as the one I have suggested.

13. I also comment on these sound symbolic relations in Short (1996a: 118).

14. Although George III was believed during his reign to have become insane, it has been suggested in modern times that he was suffering from porphyria, a condition which induces apparently mad behaviour. There is no conclusive proof, however, of exactly what condition he was suffering from.

References

Leech, G. (2008) *Language in Literature: Style and Foregrounding*. London: Longman.

McIntyre, D. (2003) 'Using foregrounding theory as a teaching methodology in a stylistics course', *Style* 37(1): 1–13.

Poole, J. (2006) 'E-learning and learning styles: Students' reactions to web-based Language and Style at Blackpool and the Fylde College', *Language and Literature* 15(3): 307–22.

Short, M. (1988) 'The dramatic text as a template for dramatic performance', in Verdonk, P., Short, M. and Culpeper, J. (eds), *Exploring the Language of Drama: From Text to Context*, pp. 6–18. London: Routledge.

Short, M. (1994) 'Understanding texts: Point of view', in Brown, G., Malmkjaer, K., Pollitt, A. and Williams, J. (eds) *Language and Understanding*, pp. 170–90. Oxford: Oxford University Press.

Short, M. (1996a) *Exploring the Language of Poems, Plays and Prose*. London: Longman.

Short, M. (1996b) 'Stylistics upside down: Using stylistics in the teaching of language and literature', in Carter, R. and McRae, J. (eds) *Language, Literature and the Learner: Creative Classroom Practice*, pp. 41–64. London: Longman.

Short, M. (2006) 'E-learning and Language and Style in Lancaster', *Language and Literature* 15(3): 234–56.

Short, M. (2008) '"Where are you going to my pretty maid?" "For detailed analysis, sir, she said"', in Watson, G. (ed.) *The State of Stylistics*, pp. 1–29. Amsterdam: Rodopi.

Short, M. and Archer, D. (2003) 'Designing a world-wide web-based stylistics course and investigating its effectiveness', *Style* 37(1): 27–46.

Short, M. and Breen, M. P. (1988) 'Alternative approaches in teaching stylistics to beginners', *Parlance* 1(2): 29–48.

Short, M., Busse, B. and Plummer, P. (2006) 'Preface: The web-based Language and Style course, e-learning and stylistics', *Language and Literature* 15(3): 219–33.

Short, M. and Semino, E. (2008) 'Stylistics and literary evaluation', in Van Peer, W. (ed.) *The Quality of Literature: Studies in Literary Evaluation*, pp. 117–38. Amsterdam: John Benjamins.

Spitzer, L. (1948) *Linguistics and Literary History: Essays in Stylistics*. Princeton, NJ: Princeton University Press.

Van Peer, W. (ed.) (2008) *The Quality of Literature: Studies in Literary Evaluation*, Amsterdam: John Benjamins.

3
Joining the Stylistics Discourse Community: Corpus Evidence for the Learning Processes Involved in Acquiring Skills for Stylistic Analysis

Carol Bellard-Thomson

Editors' preface

Carol Bellard-Thomson's chapter focuses primarily on the processes students go through as they learn the techniques of stylistics. She uses methods from corpus linguistics to investigate the extent to which the analyses produced by students differ from those produced by professional stylisticians. Her aim is to make suggestions about the ways in which we might improve how we introduce stylistic analysis to students in the classroom context. Her study is also in itself an example of pedagogical stylistics, in that she stylistically analyses students' writing to gain insights into how the teaching of stylistics can be improved.

Introduction

This chapter is a report of work in progress as part of a doctoral study entitled: *Joining the Stylistics Discourse Community: An empirical study of student development in learning stylistic analysis*. It addresses questions about how to obtain empirical data from which evidence of some of the processes of learning stylistics can be discovered. Following the lead of Jeffries (2002) in treating responses to what Pope (1995) calls a 'base' text as linguistic data in their own right, the chapter examines some of the data recovered from corpus linguistic analysis of undergraduate assignment work in stylistics produced during the 2008–9 academic year at the University of Huddersfield, and from a comparison corpus of work published by professional practitioners of stylistics. The aim is to throw light on the linguistic performance of learners attempting to demonstrate their acquisition of the skills of stylistic analysis, by searching for describable differences in the way that learners of stylistics use language (and meta-language). The chapter closes with discussion of how the insights resulting from examination of the data might be used to inform the teaching of stylistics.

Although there has been an increasing interest in using stylistic-analytical methods to aid learning in other fields, to date there has been little formal examination of what it is that stylisticians (collectively) teach, and even less examination of what it is that learners of stylistics learn. This chapter addresses questions relating to the latter. With a background in the teaching of (variously) English stylistics, French literature, French language and *la stylistique*, and managing language learning in universities, I have over a number of years been unable to avoid some obvious questions that have no doubt occurred to many other stylisticians:

- what am I teaching when I teach 'stylistics'?
- what are my students learning?
- how do I know what they are learning?
- how is what they are learning affecting the way they use English, if it is?

Twenty years ago, Short (1989: 1) noted that we were in the middle of 'an interesting stage in the development of stylistic analysis and its relations with connected areas of study'. The situation is still interesting, not least because the 'connected areas of study' are many and regularly increase as stylistics appropriates interesting theories that offer new or better ways of analysing and explaining language (Jeffries 2000).

The 'connected areas of study' include such fields as relevance theory, Conversation Analysis and Critical Discourse Analysis, cognitive linguistics, world creation theories, developments in psychological and educational theory, second-language pedagogy, empirical methodologies and so on. I would suggest that one further 'connected area' be added to this list: the study of the learning of stylistics.

In the mid-1980s, at Lancaster University, I was fortunate to be involved, as one of a team of lecturers and teachers, in the redesign of the content and form of delivery of a first-year undergraduate course in stylistics.[1] As a result, I also began to discover how stylistics is taught (and, possibly, learned). Perhaps one of the most interesting aspects of the redesign was what Short (1988) terms its 'problem-raising pedagogy' (1988: 42). However, although the extent of this redesign and the subsequent work on its reception and effects were profound, at that time there was no attempt to examine how students actually learned what they were taught.

Interestingly, it was found over a number of years that one could in fact present the material in a different order, and so Laurillard's claims about the non-sequential nature of learning may be correct:

> There are several aspects of learning that have been investigated in enough detail to admit a general account that can inform teaching. Given [...] the integrative nature of the learning process, the inseparability of knowledge and action, and of process and outcome, there is no logical ordering of parts of the process, as each part is constituted in its relation to the other parts [...] apprehending structure, integrating parts, acting on the world, using feedback, reflecting on goals.
>
> (2002: 42)

The 'Language and Style' course (see Short 2005 for the web-based version) consisted in the 1980s, as now, of (mainly literary-) genre-based materials (prose, poetry and dramatic text). One of the many interesting outcomes of the innovative course redesign was the realization, over a number of years of delivery, that no matter which genre was examined first, neither learners' enthusiasm nor their achievement levels in the course were significantly affected; nor, accordingly, did it seem to matter which genre-specific analytical techniques were presented first.[2] However, certain aspects of the material (e.g., word class identification, sentence-structure grammar, etc.) were seen as basic essentials and were therefore taught early in the course (and reinforced or expanded later), regardless of which genre the examples and practice material were taken from. So although the genre training varied, some of the theoretical and technical content did not.

In second-language teaching, there is the expectation that teachers will undertake a considerable amount of training, usually supported by additional theoretical reading, relating to pedagogical method. Brumfit (2002) provides an overview of the relations between education and linguistics, and there are large numbers of papers on language teaching on the LLAS Subject Centre website, (www.llas.ac.uk/), with research on the teaching of English language on the English HE Academy website (www.english.heacademy.ac.uk/). Despite all this information, however, there is a recognition that language learning is a tremendously complex activity, and that there is no necessary relation between what is taught, how it is taught, even under what circumstances it is taught, and what students actually learn (Allwright 1989). I found myself wondering if this is also true of the teaching and learning of stylistics, which bears some comparison with language learning in that it involves the acquisition of vocabulary, the perception and internalization of new concepts relating to language structures and patterning, and 'training' that enables the production of text using the newly acquired skills.

There is a dearth of materials examining the actual learning processes that students undergo, and for good reason. Although there are notionally a number of useful empirical methods of accessing information about learning, there is of course no means of accessing the process while it is happening.

Laurillard (2002) provides an overview of generalized learning processes ('apprehending structure, integrating parts, acting on the world, using feedback, reflecting on goals'). In the learning of stylistic analysis skills, it may be that even more processes are required, in that learners not only have to understand and be able to operate the analytical skills that they learn, but also to verbalize the process in a clear and precise manner. Laurillard views learning of an active type as involving 'mathemagenic activities' (Rothkop. 1970: 334) of a broad kind, that is, activities which 'give birth to learning', and goes on to discuss what such activities may be.[3] Though Laurillard and Rothkopf are of course not discussing the learning of stylistics, it seems to me that many of the practical activities that learners of stylistics tend to display may be 'mathemagenic', or, rather different, perhaps, that the 'practical' and 'practice' activities they are often prompted to undertake are certainly intended to be so by those who create them. It is also the case that although some mathemagenic activities may be operating when the learning of stylistics takes place, there seems to be a general expectation within stylistics that a great deal of the learning will be undertaken by other means (rote learning, reading theoretical work, reading and re-reading texts or extracts prior to and during analysis, group discussion, lecturer exposition and explanation, course handouts and online information, etc.).

Laurillard claims that the learning process is 'integrative' and without 'logical ordering': however, teaching is not learning, and so teachers inevitably have to find a way of putting the material they wish to convey into some kind of sequential order. Professional teachers of stylistics have of necessity been undertaking such considerations for many years. However, they may not have all been considering the same things, because the range of what is taught tends to vary greatly. It is therefore useful to make a short digression into a consideration of what skills and knowledge are (intended to be) taught.

What professional practitioners of stylistics do

Stylisticians generally agree on the need for analytical rigour and explicit commentary; however, because of the eclectic nature of stylistics in both theoretical and methodological aspects, it is not possible to provide a definitive description of what stylistics involves. The field benefits massively from its openness to new approaches and methods (Jeffries 2000), but this very openness makes it difficult to provide clear and non-restrictive definitions of what stylisticians do. There is, as many readers of this volume will be aware, a large body of academics who perceive a shared interest to the extent that they tend to belong to the same scholarly organizations.[4] There has for decades been much discussion of what it is that 'we' do, but little empirical evidence has arrived to verify or falsify 'our' impressions. Practitioners certainly share an interest in the language used to produce a given text, but there is a wide variation in the published material in the field, ranging from intensive statistical and numerically-based data-driven empirical approaches to more literary and intuitive appreciations. So it is difficult if not impossible to define the content of stylistics courses with any certainty.

There do, however, seem to be some fairly widely accepted elements of pedagogical method, which often include a presentation of the hierarchical, 'layered' nature of language; examination of linguistic patterns and their functions in a given text; consideration of the 'effects' of such patterning, and so on.[5] It might therefore be useful to consider what it is that learners of stylistics are expected to learn in order to become functioning stylistic analysts. The complexity of this task is also considerable, and again there is a lack of hard data, so from experience alone I compiled the following list, which I believe to be broadly representative of some of the kinds of areas that may be covered, variously, under the heading of 'stylistics':

- aspects of phonetics, morphology, syntax, semantics, discourse analysis, pragmatics, areas of linguistic theory (and so on)
- analytical techniques that can be used on each 'language level'
- ideas about how to select those analytical techniques that are the most appropriate for analysing a given text or extract
- suggestions and advice on how to amalgamate findings, in order to describe a text linguistically, stylistically and (sometimes) aesthetically
- an expectation that learners will be able to relate the data produced to their understanding and explanation of the text(s).

This list includes both the analytical processes that learners are expected to be able to use (the first two items), and what I like to term the 'finishing' processes, related to producing an actual written analysis (all the rest). Fabb (2007) provides an alternative list:

- narrative structure
- point of view and focalization
- sound patterning
- syntactic and lexical parallelism and repetition
- metre and rhythm
- genre
- mimetic, representational, realist effects
- metarepresentation, representation of speech and thought, irony
- metaphor and other ways of indirect meaning
- utilization and representation of variation in dialect, accent, and historically specific usages
- group-specific ways of speaking (real or imagined), as in gendered stylistics
- examination of inferential processes which readers engage in to determine communicated meanings.

Note that Fabb's list does not include 'finishing' processes, and is restricted to only the analytical aspects of the activity. Some of his items can of course be mapped on to those I chose to cite, but I shall not attempt this here, the point being only that within stylistics the range of subject-matter and what I call the angle of approach is massive, variable and largely undocumented. It is therefore impossible to provide a full list of such elements, but it seems possible that there may exist a small core of necessary methodological practice that separates stylistics from any other kind of textual analysis, appreciation or critique. If that is the case, we need to define what that involves.

Some theoretical considerations

Overall, however, I would suggest that the best way to understand how learning happens in stylistics is not through a discussion of what we teach, but through an examination of what our students appear to learn, and how they demonstrate that learning. That means there is a need for empirical study to try and determine whether or not there is an identifiable change in students' language-productive skills as a result of doing stylistics.

In my view, acquisition by learners of the appropriate discoursal register (along with the appropriate analytical techniques) can be viewed as processes facilitating entry to the world-wide 'social network' (Marin and Wellman 2010) of stylisticians (which in Marin and Wellman's terms is an 'affiliation network'). Ferenz (2005) links the idea of a social network to the development of academic literacy in L2 learners: here, I link it to the development of stylistic literacy in (mainly) L1 learners, which Short (1989: 1) calls the acquisition of 'a descriptive analytical vocabulary'.

The development of corpus linguistics has provided a means of analysing not only published text, but any and all text produced in electronic form. Jeffries (2002) provides a methodology that is innovative in that it treats actual reader-responses to a 'base'[6] text as themselves worthy of investigation. Hers is one of very few investigations that 'goes farther than looking at the content of readers' responses, and treats them as linguistic data in their own right' (Jeffries 2002: 248; a further example of this approach is found in Chapter 4 in this volume).

Methodology

If reader- or learner-responses of this kind can be constituted as a mini-corpus, then it is no great step to realize that material produced by learners of stylistics may reasonably be treated in the same way. Questions that I wish to address using such corpora are:

- **how** the discourse of learners changes, if it does;
- **when** students begin to demonstrate knowledge and productive skills that approximate a near-professional approach.
- **how** what students produce at various levels differs from what professional stylisticians 'typically' produce when they analyse.[7]

I have therefore collected all the summative assessments produced by undergraduate students learning stylistics at the University of Huddersfield during the 2008–9 academic year, to create three year-based learner corpora (L1, L2 and L3) amounting in all to some 300,000 words (tokens). These will eventually be compared with a comparison corpus (P) created from published professional stylistics work (all articles from 2008–9 issues of *Language and Literature*, and three commonly used stylistics textbooks) which may be taken as illustrating the discourse of the professional stylistics discourse community.[8]

It should be noted at the outset, however, that even the state-of-the-art computational processing that corpus linguistics makes possible will not reveal everything that needs to be revealed about the material under examination. As debates rage (well, simmer) as to whether corpus linguistics is a theory or a methodology, those scholars using the software know only one thing: that 'no useful theoretical model [or methodology] can be as complex as the data that is being described' (Jeffries 2000: 3) (my addition).

Micro-corpora

For the purposes of this chapter, I shall examine some features of two micro-corpora originally created for the PALA 2009 conference.[9] There are some issues of representativeness and balance in relation to the micro-corpora, in that they consist of, respectively, some 30 first-year undergraduate stylistics essays (corpus Micro-L1), and nine professional articles from 2008–9 issues of *Language and Linguistics* (corpus Micro-P).[10] However, for the purposes of this small-scale investigation these issues are not of major concern.

An initial examination of these two micro-corpora using Wordsmith Tools produced information about lexical features as shown in Table. 3.1.

The two corpora are not far off the same size, but there are more types in the Micro- P, that is to say, the professionals are using a wider range of vocabulary than the learners. Micro-L1 has, in fact, only about two-thirds as many lexical items as Micro-P (4170 to 6215) and this is reflected in the type-token ratios (TTR).[11] In this case, the lower TTR in the Micro-L1 (6.22) indicates that there is more repetition of lexical items than in the Micro-P corpus (9.24). In other words, the professionals demonstrate a wider lexical range than the learners.

There are slight differences too in word length and sentence length, where the professionals' usage, again predictably, involves longer words and longer sentences, though in neither case is the difference very marked.

Table 3.1   Statistical data on lexis

	Micro-L1	Micro-P
Tokens in text	67,347	69,000
Types	4,170	6,215
Type/token ratio (TTR)	6.22	9.24
Mean word length (in characters)	4.62	4.91
sentences	2,618	2,230
mean (in words)	25.63	30.18

Table 3.2 Statistical data on word lengths

Word length	Micro-L	Micro-P
1	1,963	3,329
2	13,238	13,071
3	13,956	11,903
4	12,778	9,230
5	7,795	6,341
6	5,094	4,495
7	5,129	4,999
8	3,626	4,457
9	2,559	3,284
10	2,172	2,538
11	1,078	1,707
12	524	837
13	353	505
14	136	402
15	50	128
16	4	33

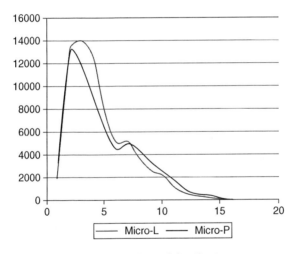

Figure 3.1 Comparison of word lengths and distribution

Mean word length (5) is the same in both corpora, but is differently distributed, as shown in Table 3.2.

The relations between the two are shown in Figure 3.1.

For word length overall, both the L and P corpora follow a characteristic curve (for UK English). There are some slight differences, for example, the number of single-letter words is over 3000 in the L-corpus, but

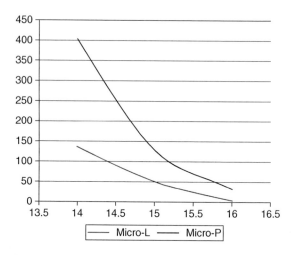

Figure 3.2   Statistical data on longer words

just under 2000 in the P-corpus. This may be due to more first-person usage on the part of the learners. Interestingly, the professionals seem to use slightly more four-letter words than the learners do (I haven't had a look at what they are!). The learners use slightly more 8-letter words, and then consistently use more 9–13 letter ones.

However, as Figure 3.2 shows, for words 14–20 letters long, the professionals consistently use many more. There are in fact about 30 per cent more 'longer' words in Micro-P than in Micro-L1, and the longer the word, the greater the difference in the number of occurrences (e.g., for 14-letter words, the ratio is approximately 3:1 in favour of the professionals, rising to 8:1 for 16-letter words).

The information so far goes to confirm much of what is already known about academic usage, and conversely reveals that the learner usage in Micro-L1 is definitely not of the required register in so far as vocabulary choice and word length are concerned. It may be useful to teachers of stylistics to focus more strongly not only on the acquisition of stylistics terminology, but on general higher-register vocabulary development. Exercises in paraphrase may be useful.

Semantic analysis and keyness

I used Wmatrix2 (Rayson 2003, 2008)[12] to produce lists of those words which are 'key' in each micro-corpus, that is, which occur more frequently or less frequently in the micro-corpora than in the comparison corpus, in this case the British National Corpus (BNC).[13] The key words that appear on the resulting lists are therefore a feature of the language in the study corpora. I then used Watrix2's semantic processing facility to reveal the key semantic domains that are evident in the new keyword lists, that is, to show the areas of meaning that occur more frequently or less frequently in the study corpora than in the comparison corpus.

The first two key semantic domains that my two micro-corpora shared were: COMPARING: DIFFERENT and THOUGHT: BELIEF, and an examination of these shows differences in register between the two micro-corpora.

COMPARING: DIFFERENT

These are all items where the comparison involved is contrastive. Figure 3.3 shows the first 12 concordanced items from the Micro-L1 semantic tagging, in the category COMPARING: DIFFERENT.

Two sets of items are continuations of a single sentence in each case (on lines 3–4 and 11–12). To learners of stylistics at Huddersfield, 'deviation' is of course a new term in its stylistic sense, and it is evident from line 2 (which in the text ends with the word 'foregrounding') that there is doubt in one mind at least about its relation to foregrounding. In two instances the perhaps less forbidding (because perceived as less 'technical') lexical choices, 'contrast' (lines 6 and 7), 'other' (lines 5 and 12), and 'different' (lines 8 and 10) are used, and in one of the two instances of 'different' (line 8) no comparator is given.

Figure 3.4 shows the first 12 items from Micro-P semantic tagging, in the category COMPARING: DIFFERENT.

Lines 10–11 are part of one sentence. Lexical items occuring here that did not occur in the learner usage are: 'disparate', 'incongruity', 'contradistinction/distinction' and 'distinguishes'. There are some shared

```
. The extensive graphological    Deviation    used in the poem is the first
indented once . However this     Deviation    does not cause specific fore
ounding . I believe that this    Deviation    was used so that the deviatio
eviation was used so that the    Deviation    in the final stanza would sta
he further indentation on the    Other        two lines reveals the mentio
s of equipment strike a harsh    Contrast     against the norm of compute
hat the poet has given such a    Contrast     because he believes that pe
but the language used is also    Different     . There are no adjectives use
st of the poem therefore this    Deviation    in the language is highly affe
s to slip off the tongue in a    Different    fashion than the rest of the t
n than the rest of the text .    Deviation    occurs in many other ways t
xt . Deviation occurs in many    Other        ways throughout the poem to
```

Figure 3.3   Concordance of COMPARING: DIFFERENT in Micro-L1

explain who we are , who the	Others	are , how the world works.
bout yourself , when everyone	Else	is insisting upon it . This ar
blending what are essentially	Different	tories , creates the conditi
ing is the means by which the	Disparate	incremental stories within
th a divine spirituality that	Contrasted	sharply with the imagistic
elds an unwelcome ideological	Incongruity	; yet it is a natural concept
ounterpart of that element in	Another	mental space . In contradi
in another mental space. In	Contradistinction	, Hawkes (2001 : 64) ob
esponding with the name being	different	. For instance , while a ma
esponding with the name being	Different	. Aristotle's parenthetical r
istotles parenthetical remark	Distinguishes	between essence and the
Reformer , espouses a similar	distinction	between signs and their di

Figure 3.4   Concordance of COMPARING: DIFFERENT in Micro-P

terms with the Micro-L1 ('other', 'different') but also more high-register choices and a broader range of lexical items.

THOUGHT/BELIEF

Figure 3.5 shows the first 12 items from Micro-L1 in the category THOUGHT/BELIEF.

rikes me . The poet's own	feelings	seem to be reflected in the
estruction is one that , I	believe	, can easily be related to
ose to most of us . We all	wonder	whether our reliance on com
specific foregrounding . I	believe	that this deviation was use
and out more . Therefore I	feel	the meaning of the final st
ore . Therefore I feel the	meaning	of the final stanza is extr
more primitive things . I	believe	that the poet has given suc
such a contrast because he	believes	that people feel that they
se he believes that people	feel	that they would be returned
o reflects the poet 's own	attitude	, in that he may want thing
omputer systems because he	views	them as negative things . I
foregrounds 'the Devil 's	feelings	which show exactly how terr

Figure 3.5   Concordance on semtag THOUGHT/BELIEF in Micro-L1

Lines 6–7 and 8–9 are single sentences. This extract shows a comparatively narrow lexical range, with low-register items that are semantically focused on reactive emotional response. The only exception to this is 'attitude' (line 10), which implies cerebral rather than emotional activity. Use of these emotive terms with the first person is much in evidence ('I believe' occurs three times, 'I wonder' once and 'I feel the meaning' once), making the responses even more personal. In all these cases, the writers are trying to mediate what they believe to be the opinions of the writer of the base text. In lines 8 and 11, there are further attempts to present what the learner sees as the poet's thought / beliefs, and feelings are attributed to the poet, the Devil and 'people'. All of these are very personalized expressions, showing thought processes that are reactive, emotional and 'self-centred' in the psychological sense.

Figure 3.6 shows the first 12 items from the Micro-P in the category THOUGHT/BELIEF.

There is one semantic tagging 'error' made by Wmatrix here: 'assumes' (line 6) here is not to do with THOUGHT/BELIEF but with taking on a role. There are no continued sentences in this list, which might mean that the expression of THOUGHT/BELIEF is not iterated by professionals as it was in the learner discourse. There is evidently a larger lexical range, even in such a limited number of instances. The choices are higher-register, and semantically very focused on cerebral rather than emotional activity. The cerebral activity involved is creative ('conceptualize', 'conceive') and purposeful ('consider'). The only item which might imply a rather passive attitude, 'impression', is something apparently being adjusted by the projection on to it of some other idea that will turn it into a 'theory'. Conscious thought seems to be represented by the various lemmas of 'consider', and 'cognitive' here is to do with consciously adjusting one's understanding of the term 'idolatry'. 'Believe' only occurs once, in contrast to the learner usage, and it appears in a passive structure where it is not the writer of the paper who is believing anything, but a character in the base text that this paper examines. The remaining choices ('iconoclasm', 'logic', 'ontological') are all high-register and clearly academic usage.

It is clear, then, that practitioner usage can be seen to focus on cerebral activity, some of it conscious, rather than on personal and emotional reactions of the kind evident in learner usage. Learners are often told that academic writing is 'less personal' and 'more formal': this focus on lexical choices that express consciously chosen, cool-headed thought

that story , traditionally	Conceived	of as a literary phenomeno
on to their salient role in	Conceptualizing	experience , stories can be
usible , particularly when	Considered	as emanating from or struc
) proposes that the way we	conceive	of experience , the manner
rmine which stories will be	Believed	. Othello is both a figure i
ast as a lascivious Moor he	Assumes	the role of the erring barba
reconciled. Idolatry vs	Iconoclasm	: the story of Reformed reli
sult . Idolatry, then , in	Cognitive	terms , can be understood t
of the soul , Aristotelian	Logic	(1938 : 13) proposes a the
projected onto a conceptual	Impression	, a theory that finds modern
eir divine referents in his	Consideration	of the visible sacraments :
o imbue the sign with false	ontological	value , which was for Refo

Figure 3.6 Concordance of THOUGHT/BELIEF in Micro-P

may be part of what that is intended to mean. Again, for learners, practice in paraphrase could be useful, or we might even consider providing our students with lists of 'more' or 'less' formal expressions that they can use in expressing their stylistic opinions.

Other aspects of learner writing

There are additional considerations that need to be addressed. Some of the 'problems' in stylistics-learner discourse are related to their ideas about what is required of them. Those who have not 'done' English language, and especially those whose experience is limited to the writing of literary essays, may simply be trying to do the wrong thing. Yet merely giving information about what to do is clearly insufficient to bring about acquisition of the necessary elements. It seems to me that there must be some conceptual difficulties interfering with what would otherwise be a fairly simple process, and, as I shall explain later, that these conceptual difficulties are closely related to what I termed the expression of 'personal and emotional reactions'.

A few examples show the kinds of problems that were evident.

(a)   ...further indentation on the other two lines reveals the mention of 'runic rods' and 'notched bones'. Both 'runic rods' and 'notched bones' are things which are indeed primitive...

(b)   ...when the 'software Armageddon' arrives nobody will be 'lifted' to heaven.

(c)   The line is stating a prediction that 'will' come and that it was 'written'.

(d)   They are hidden in the computer system as 'numbers', 'numbers' which 'dance' and are part of the system crisis.

Examples (a)–(d) show the kind of iteration typical of many of the first-year essays and may well be part of the 'vocabulary choices' that bring about the lower type-token ratios discussed above. The writers persistently use the words of the base text instead of describing the linguistic features and stylistic effects of the words chosen.

In Micro-L1 there was in evidence a great deal of inconsistent and often idiosyncratic use of quotation, including great variability in layout. All contributing learners of stylistics are given some instruction in how to set out quotations, and yet many seem not to be able to put those instructions into operation. This seems to make little sense: after all, if instructions are provided, why is it apparently so difficult for learners to follow them?

It seems to me that the failure to apply instructions about how and when to quote is close kin to the failure, noted in relation to the comparison of the THOUGHT: BELIEF semantic domains in the two micro-corpora, to disconnect personal and emotive reaction from cerebral consideration. Both processes involve distancing processes that learners have not yet acquired.[14] In some sense, learners write from a viewpoint that appropriates a stance intrinsic to the base text (i.e., they try primarily to empathize with the author), whereas academics examine texts from a more extrinsic stance. That may be one reason why learners find it difficult to avoid citing base texts: they *want* to feel that the author's words are the best that can be chosen to convey meaning.

I suggest that a useful way to approach explaining this need for 'distancing' to learners might be to characterize it in relation to the long-established 'show/tell distinction' (Booth 1983, *passim*). In creative writing, learners are told that they should 'show' what is happening rather than 'tell' their reader about it (the distinction seems often to be taken to equate to dialogue/narrative, though that is over-simplifying). In stylistics, learners intuitively begin with a kind of deictic process, by 'showing', that is, quoting or otherwise indicating large sections or numerous small sections of the base text. They can even be said to be 'showing' their reactions, in their personalized, emotive language choices, rather than 'telling' what those reactions are in a more neutral academic register. In fact, what they have to learn to do is to 'tell' what they are seeing and understanding, using an appropriate 'descriptive analytical vocabulary' (Short 1989).

Conclusion and prospect

Sinclair (2005: 81) makes the sound and consoling point that 'it is important to avoid perfectionism in corpus building'. That is even more true when the corpora in question are intended to show developmental features, which, by definition, will be partially or totally absent at the beginning of the process. There is also an art in selecting items from and interpreting the data produced by corpus-linguistic processing, and so reducing the massive quantities of information that such analysis provides. In this chapter I chose to examine elements that were common to the two micro-corpora, but it may be that there is much of significance to be gained from examining, for example, the differences between the two lists of key semantic domains. I have, however, shown that data so obtained can be used as a basis for alerting learners to important characteristics of their own writing and thinking processes, so that they can begin to seize on those skills that will enable them successfully to operate stylistic analysis.

Notes

1. More recently, the course has been developed into a web-based module, and e-learning issues in relation to it are addressed in a 'special issue' of *Language and Literature* (15(3), August 2006). The focus of that volume is more on issues to do with e-learning and reactions to it than on issues of learner development. Nevertheless, it constitutes one of the very few sources of hard data on the teaching and learning of stylistics. Short's paper 'E-learning and Language and Style in Lancaster' (234–530) provides hard (statistical) data on student achievement in both coursework assessments and examinations over a three-year period, and on student attitudes to their experience of taking the course.
2. Certain types of analysis lend themselves to some genres better than others, for example, discourse analysis relates easily to the analysis of dramatic text; phonetic analysis often relates well to the analysis of poetry. However, there is no possibility of saying that any given technique belongs exclusively to a certain genre. One of the more interesting processes that professional stylisticians operate is that of selecting which types of analysis will be most productive for analysing a given text or extract.
3. Rothkopf (1970) defines 'mathemagenic' as referring to 'attending phenomena', and 'derived from the Greek root *mathemain* – that which is learned and *gignesthai* – to be born'. Thus he intends to include 'the student's actions that are relevant to the achievement of specified instructional objectives' (p. 325).
4. For example, the Poetics and Linguistics Association (PALA), the annual Corpus Linguistics Conference (CLC), the British Association for Applied Linguistics (BAAL), etc.
5. The following material was presented at the 2008 PALA conference at Sheffield University and included in Bellard-Thomson 2010.
6. Pope 1995.
7. This element of the PhD study therefore involves the examination of a corpus of published academic work in stylistics, with the aim of trying to identify some of the linguistic and stylistic features common to professional discourse, without which it is not possible to decide whether or not the developing discourse of learners is approaching that of professional stylisticians.
8. A 'discourse community' (Swales 1990) is situated in a *locus*. In this case I would argue that the locus of formal professional stylistics discourse is found in published form in *Language and Literature* (Sage), probably the community's foremost stylistics journal.
9. The material appeared in my presentation 'Words on words: Corpus analysis and the language of learners of stylistics'. 2009 Poetics and Linguistics Association (PALA) Conference at the Roosevelt Academy, Middelburg, Netherlands.
10. The software used is Wmatrix2 (Rayson 2003, 2008a) and Oxford Wordsmith Tools 4.0 (Scott 2004). Prior to using these packages, text was marked up (using XML tags) and processed using the Multi-Lingual Corpus Toolkit

(Piao, Wilson and McEnery 2002), in order to leave main corpora which consist as far as possible of only learner or practitioner discourse.

11. The total number of words in a corpus constitute its number of 'tokens', and the type count gives the number of 'original' words in the corpus, so the ratio between the two shows how much repetition occurs in a given corpus. Lower TTRs indicate more repetition and higher TTRs , less repetition, i.e., a more varied use of lexis.

12. Wmatrix2 automatically processes plain text files using the CLAWS part-of-speech tagger (http://ucrel.lancs.ac.uk/claws/) and the UCREL Semantic Tagset (http://ucrel.lancs.ac.uk/usas/). Full details are at http://juilland.comp.lancs.ac.uk/wmatrix2/

13. The BNC website (www.natcorp.ox.ac.uk/) describes the BNC as 'a 100 million-word collection of samples of written and spoken language from a wide range of sources, designed to represent a wide cross-section of current British English, both spoken and written'.

14. I do not use the term 'distancing' in its linguistic-stylistic sense here.

References

Bellard-Thomson, C. (2010) 'How students learn stylistics; constructing an empirical study', *Language and Literature* 19(1): 35–57.

Booth, W. C. (1983) *The Rhetoric of Fiction*. Chicago: University of Chicago Press.

Breen, M. P. and Short, M. (1988) 'Alternative approaches in teaching stylistics to beginners', *Parlance* 1(2): 29–48.

Brumfit, C. (2002) 'Education and linguistics', in *Guide to Good Practice*, Subject Centre for Languages, Linguistics and Area Studies, at www.llas.ac.uk/resources/gpg/90 (accessed 27 April 2010).

Dahlman, I. (2007) 'Extraction methods – description', on project website for *Second-language fluency (SLSF) and the role of pauses in automatically extracted mult-word units*, at https://www.nottingham.ac.uk/english/research/cral/doku.php?id=projects:slsf/ (accessed 27 April 2010).

Fabb, N. (2007) 'The teaching of stylistics', in *Guide to Good Practice*, Subject Centre for Languages, Linguistics and Area Studies, at www.llas.ac.uk/resources/gpg/2755 (accessed 27 April 2010).

Ferenz, O. (2005) 'EFL writers' social networks: Impact on advanced academic literacy development', *Journal of English for Academic Purposes* 4: 339–51.

Jeffries, L. (2000) 'Don't throw the baby out with the bathwater: In defence of theoretical eclecticism in Stylistics', *PALA Occasional Papers* 12.

Jeffries, L. (2002) 'Meaning negotiated: An investigation into reader and author meaning', in Csàbi, S. and Zerkowitz, J. (eds), *Textual Secrets: The Message of the Medium*, pp. 247–61. Budapest: Eötvös Loránd University.

Marin, A. and Wellman, B. (2010) 'Social network analysis: An introduction', in Carrington, P. and Scott, J. (eds), *Handbook of Social Network Analysis*. London: Sage.

Piao, S., Wilson, A. and McEnery, T. (2002) 'A multilingual corpus toolkit', AAACL 2002, Indianapolis, Indiana, USA (Poster). [MLCT is available at https://sites.google.com/site/scottpiaosite/software/mlct (accessed 27 April 2010).]

Pope, R. (1995) *Textual Intervention: Critical and Creative Strategies for Literary Studies*. London: Routledge.

Rayson, P. (2003) *Matrix: A Statistical Method and Software Tool for Linguistic Analysis through Corpus Comparison.* Unpublished PhD thesis, Lancaster University.

Rayson, P. (2008) *Wmatrix: A Web-based Corpus Processing Environment.* Computing Department, Lancaster University. Available at: http://ucrel.lancs.ac.uk/wmatrix/

Rothkopf, E. Z. (1970) 'The concept of mathemagenic activities', *Review of Educational Research* 40: 325–36.

Scott, M. (2004) *WordSmith Tools* 4.0. Oxford: Oxford University Press.

Scott, M. (2009) 'In Search of a Bad Reference Corpus', in Archer, D. (ed.), *What's in a Word-List? Investigating Word Frequency and Keyword Extraction*, pp. 79–91. London: Ashgate.

Short, M. (ed.) (1989) *Reading, Analysing and Teaching Literature.* London: Longman.

Short, M. (2005) 'Ling 131 Language and Style', at http://www.lancs.ac.uk/fass/projects/stylistics/index.htm

Sinclair, J. (2005) 'Corpus and text: Basic principles', in Wynne, M. (ed.), *Developing Linguistic Corpora: A Guide to Good Practice*, pp. 30–46. Oxford: Oxbow Books.

Swales, J. (1990) *Genre Analysis: English in Academic and Research Settings.* Cambridge: Cambridge University Press

Bibliography of articles used in Micro-P

Allwright, D. (1989) 'Why don't learners learn what teachers teach? The interaction hypothesis', in Singleton, D. M. and Little, D. G. (eds), *Language and Learning in Formal and Informal Contexts.* Dublin: IRAAL.

Blakemore, D. (2009) 'Parentheticals and point of view in free indirect style', *Language and Literature* 18(2): 129–53.

Bowles, H. (2009) 'Storytelling as interaction in *The Homecoming*', *Language and Literature* 18(1): 45–60.

Canning, P. (2008) '"The bodie and the letters both": "Blending" the rules of early modern religion', *Language and Literature* 17(3): 187–203.

Clark, B. (2009) 'Salient inferences: Pragmatics and *The Inheritors*', *Language and Literature* 18(2): 173–12.

Corduas, M., Attardo, S. and Eggleston, A. (2008) 'The distribution of humour in literary texts is not random: A statistical analysis', *Language and Literature* 17(3): 253–70.

Ji, M. (2009) 'Corpus stylistics in translation studies: Two modern Chinese translations of *Don Quijote*', *Language and Literature* 18(1): 61–73.

McIntyre, D. (2008) 'Integrating multimodal analysis and the stylistics of drama: A multimodal perspective on Ian McKellen's *Richard III*', *Language and Literature* 17(4): 309–34.

Seargeant, P. (2009) 'Ideologies of English in Shakespeare's *Henry V*', *Language and Literature* 18(1): 25–44.

Sinclair, J. (2005) 'Appendix: How to build a corpus', in Wynne, M. (ed.), *Developing Linguistic Corpora: A Guide to Good Practice*, pp. 79–83. Oxford: Oxbow Books.

Winn, M. B. and Idsardi, W. J. (2008) 'Musical evidence regarding trochaic inversion', *Language and Literature* 17(4): 335–49.

4
Processes of Interpretation: Using Meta-Analysis to Inform Pedagogic Practice

Mick Short, Dan McIntyre, Lesley Jeffries and Derek Bousfield

Editors' preface

Like Carol Bellard-Thomson's chapter, this chapter by Mick Short, Dan McIntyre, Lesley Jeffries and Derek Bousfield treats the writing produced by readers as data in its own right. Short and colleagues subject this data to corpus stylistic analysis in order to demonstrate that there is a level of interpretation at which readers agree despite individual differences in their experience of reading a literary work.

A common practice in stylistics is to use stylistic analysis to support or challenge a general interpretation of the text in question. However, while much classroom time is spent teaching analytical techniques, not nearly as much time is given over to explaining processes of interpretation or, indeed, what we mean when we talk about interpreting texts. This chapter reports on a small-scale investigation designed to explore the nature of interpretation – what it is and how it differs from simple description. The reason for the experiment was to generate insights into good practice for teaching this aspect of stylistics. In this chapter we discuss the investigation and reflect on what the results suggest for stylistics teaching.

A workshop on interpretation

At the 2006 Poetics and Linguistics Association conference in Joensuu, Finland, we advertised a workshop on interpretation and invited interested participants to read two poems in preparation. These were 'Of Mere Being' by Wallace Stevens and 'Mittens' by Peter Sansom. For reasons of space, we concentrate on the latter, which is reproduced at the end of this chapter. In setting up the workshop, the questions we wanted to consider were:

- Can a reader 'get it wrong' and what do we mean by this?
- Are some valid interpretations more general than others?
- What is the relationship between personal response and textual interpretation?
- Can we distinguish between topic and theme in texts, and if so, how?
- Can we distinguish between readings and interpretations of texts, and if so, how?

In the workshop we asked participants to read the poems again and then to write down their interpretations of the texts. The instructions we gave were as follows:

> Please read the two poems, 'Mittens' and 'Of Mere Being', and write down your interpretations of the poems in the relevant spaces below. At this stage we do not want you to do any detailed stylistic analysis. Rather, we are interested only in your general impressions of the poems – for example, what you think each poem is 'about', what effect (if any) it has on you, etc. Try to avoid simply describing what happens in the poem.

Having written their individual responses, we then asked participants to work in groups and share their ideas. We were particularly interested in any commonalities or major differences in interpretation that the participants came up with. Below are the responses (in their original unedited form) that participants generated in their groups:

Group 1

(i)   Clearly about a 30 or 35 year old man going home to visit his mother. Stanza 2 is the here and now and stanza 1 is the memory. Not sure if he was male or female till the last line (mittens is female! – think kittens!) So the revelation at the end was his gender! Since, still, then etc – deixis. Deviant line bows my face to her (reminded me of me Mum!).

(ii) Memory in stanza 1, present in stanza 2. Not sure of stubble. Warm memory of the mother, nostalgia, triggered by the word 'red' and 'hand-knitted'.

(iii) Mother's relationship, though she is not identified as such, so it stands for the female caring role in general. Individual and

society – the difference between how you may behave at home and how you have to behave in society.
(iv) Mother-son relationship, memory and nostalgia.

Group 2

(i) Speaker a young man (13 or 14) Shift in roles in the family from male to female? From more protective role to sexual. Seeing women differently as you grow up.

(ii) Time shift – three different phases of life. Infant in past (toilets) child in past (mother relationship) and adult in present (stubble). Sends me back to the beginning and makes me see things in a slightly different way.

(iii) Complete 'reading' – my Nana has been in a home – personally upsetting. My background (rural) relevant but not the main reaction. I 'mother' my nana and this was how I read the poem – as a mother-child relationship, but related it to my relationship with Nana.

(iv) Relationship, male-female, roles, timeshift

Group 3

(v) Old man – perhaps in childhood home – the door indicates familiarity. Senility? Vivid memories (pegs, stink) – quite concrete memories.

(vi) Reminded me of home-coming of grown up person and reminiscences. His mother wants to take care of him again. Reminded me of my childhood! Element of passivity and impairment not noticed to start with. Mismatch of adult versus childish clothes etc.

(vii) Grown up person who positions himself as a child. He doesn't fit his identity as a child. Mittens – he has forgotten how to grip. The other person (wife? Mother?) he gives authority to her. He is not comfortable in this role, but he doesn't try to change the situation. It is metaphorical. He's not an old man.

(viii) Agreement – the more abstract level he is an adult in the position of a child, but his own positioning was disagreed.

Group 4

(ix) Realistic – son coming home to mother who puts on new mittens and he remembers the past. He's about 20 years old. Didn't 'get' stubble – he might be 30s.

(x) He's an old man in a home. Wearing mittens and triggering memory.

(xi) Not sure – a marriage that infantilizes the husband.
(xii) [As a group] we're agreed it's a dream or memory. Some sadness. Can't agree on age.

For the remainder of the workshop we discussed in a fairly subjective manner the nature of interpretation and what participants thought they were doing when they interpreted texts. However, as we were primarily interested in investigating these questions in a more rigorous manner, we took the participants' responses away and, after the conference, subjected them to corpus linguistic analysis. The results of this are reported in the remainder of this chapter, along with a discussion of how all this might affect the ways in which we help students frame interpretations in their written work.

A corpus linguistic approach to reader response

Our approach to investigating readers' responses has been to focus on the 'shadow' of the text (cf. Jeffries 2002), treating the responses of participants themselves as our data. The responses that participants wrote during the workshop were typed up to form a small electronic corpus. We then used WordSmith Tools (Scott 2004) and Wmatrix (Rayson 2003, 2008), two software packages for corpus processing, to analyse the data.

Using Wmatrix, we compared the participants' responses against the BNC (British National Corpus) written sampler – 968,267 words of contemporary written British English. This generated the list of key semantic domains in Table 4.1. The term 'key semantic domains' is used by Wmatrix to refer to semantic fields which are over-represented in the data when compared against a 'reference corpus', which in our case was the BNC data. Note that the LL score refers to the 'log-likelihood' which is a test to determine statistical significance; LL figures above 15.13 indicate 99.99 per cent ($p<0.0001$) confidence of significance. The standard social science significance threshold of 95 per cent ($p<0.05$) is a log-likelihood score of 3.84, so the significance hurdle we are using here is high, partly to take account of the fact that the data set is small in corpus linguistic terms.

Domain 1 (LANGUAGE, SPEECH AND GRAMMAR) in Table 4.1 contains meta-language related to the task in hand (e.g., 'poem', 'words', 'language', 'first person', 'reading', etc.). Given the nature of the task, we would expect to see this kind of lexis in the data, so there is little that can be gleaned from participants' use of such language. The other

Table 4.1 Key semantic domains in the 'Mittens response' corpus

No.	LL	Domain
1	95.94	LANGUAGE, SPEECH AND GRAMMAR
2	51.58	MENTAL ACTIONS AND PROCESSES
3	29.24	KIN
4	27.95	TIME: OLD; GROWN-UP
5	24.03	EMOTIONAL ACTIONS, STATES AND PROCESSES GENERAL
6	19.95	ALIVE
7	18.60	PEOPLE
8	17.97	CLOTHES AND PERSONAL BELONGINGS
9	17.88	UNMATCHED
10	15.08	MENTAL OBJECT: CONCEPTUAL OBJECT

domains, however, offer more insight into what participants focused on in their efforts to interpret the poem.

The domain MENTAL ACTIONS AND PROCESSES is composed of three words: 'memory', 'memories' and 'dreams'. Each of the seven usages of these words refers to what the participants think the poem is about – that is, a dream or memory on the part of the narrator. Domain 3, KIN, specifies the participants' responses further by making it clear that most participants interpret the relationship between the narrator and the female character as a familial one, with most respondents suggesting a mother-son relationship (cf. the power relationship implicated). Words in this domain are 'mother', 'relative', 'nanna', 'motherly', 'mothers', 'family', 'son', 'siblings' and 'marriage'.

Domain 4, TIME: OLD; GROWN-UP, includes 'growing up', 'grown up', 'adult', 'old' and 'mature'. The context in which these words/phrases occur all involve speculations about the narrator of the poem being an adult male. It is significant that participants feel the need to use the words associated with being an adult. This might be implicit in other contexts, but because the poem is confusing about the child/adult nature of the narrator, the groups were not explicit about their final interpretation.

Domain 5, EMOTIONAL ACTIONS, STATES AND PROCESSES GENERAL, relates not to the fictional world that respondents perceived in the poem, but rather to their emotional responses to reading it. Words in this domain include 'nostalgia' (which participants claim is evoked by the poem), 'emotionally' (related to how the poem affects readers; for example,, 'the mother involves me emotionally in the poem'), 'emotional' and 'mood' (which respondents use in relation to the general mood that the poem evokes). Domain 6, ALIVE, comprises four uses of 'life', though like domain 5, these four instances seem related more to participants' general responses to the poem than their efforts to interpret the events in the narrative. Here it seems that participants are attempting to draw a general interpretation from their specific responses. Here are the concordance lines from this domain:

```
tendency of people to arrange their  life  the way it used to be at some early
      to be at some early stage of their  life  : the narrator 's life resembles his
    age of their life : the narrator 's  life  resembles his childhood but he is an
    many countries , not to lose them .  Life  was hard after the WW11 and later on
```

Domain 7, PEOPLE, provides further indication of the respondents' understanding of the characters in the poem and shows a particular focus on the narrator as either a child or childlike. Nine of the 15 words in this domain are 'child' or 'children'. This links to the point made earlier about the adult nature of the narrator. They clearly see this person as *actually* adult, but *like* a child.

Little can be drawn from domain 8, CLOTHES AND PERSONAL BELONGINGS, since this is composed primarily of references to the narrator's mittens, and discussion of the role of the mittens in the text. Domain 9, UNMATCHED, is something of a miscellaneous category, containing all those words that Wmatrix was unable to assign to a particular semantic domain. Of these, 36 of the 55 items are quotations from the poem and are unassigned to a specific semantic domain because of the quotation marks that Wmatrix has not been able to deal with. Of the remaining words in this category, some are unmatched because of participants' spelling errors while some are two words separated by a forward slash. Below are the remaining concordance lines once quotations have been removed and spelling errors corrected.

```
nded by the last line . The      present/past           distinction is quite strong
     age = "30s"> This poem is    subtextually           , about growing up , adolesc
 g on and letting go and the     insecurity/fear         that goes along with it . 'M
    and females ( 'She' ) from    protection/dependence   to sexuality ( ? the missing
   e shift in perspective onto    her/him                 ) . The effect it has on me
  ow in a home suffering from     Alzheimers              and Dementia . It is hard to
    be the first person i talk    to/care                 for in a motherly way and th
   r and person suffering from    Alzheimers              or a disability or stroke et
      within the lines , and the  nostalgic               atmosphere ( senses ) that c
    ) that contribute to this .   Clothing/clothes         are being used as a main met
      stubble , 2 meters 'still'. positions/positioned    as child 'she' treats him as
     oilets and cloakroom pegs -  childhood.              The image of this adult thru
    s something like senility ,   Alzheimers              , a condition that allows hi
     m . Life was hard after the  WW11                    and later on . The image of
      a long absence . His mother knitted                 a pairof mittens for him wit
     nce . His mother kniitted a  pair of                 mittens for him with bright
        to have his mother wipe his face.                 reminds me of 1960s . <"unkn
```

Some of these lines indicate specific personal responses to the poem. For example, the references to 'alzheimers' are all from the same respondent, who was reminded of a family member's experiences by the poem. Other items indicate uncertainty on the part of the respondent (e.g., 'insecurity/fear', 'protection/dependence', 'her/him'), while one respondent makes it clear that the poem has a meaning beyond its surface narrative ('This poem is *subtextually* about growing up').

Finally, domain 10, MENTAL OBJECT: CONCEPTUAL OBJECT, refers to the mental processes of the respondents. What is interesting here is the extent to which participants draw on their own life experiences and/or schematic knowledge in order to interpret the poem (e.g., 'It *reminded* me', 'It *reminds* me'). Also interesting is the degree to which participants see interpreting the poem as akin to solving a puzzle (note the references to 'clues'). This suggests that, in spite of the commonly held critical view that interpretations vary considerably from one person to another, these respondents were subconsciously assuming that textual meaning is waiting to be uncovered. Here is the full concordance of this domain:

```
ic discourse or the text , but i   thought        i 'd share it with you anyway - t
alf , and instead , the shift in   perspective    onto her/him ) . The effect it ha
r sure with respect to people 's   thoughts       ) . <sex = "F"  nat = "British"
ion of the mittens 'with string'   remind         me greatly of my own ( rural , wo
"unknown"> We agree - grown up .   Clues          stubble , 2 meters 'still'. posit
 a child because of the temporal   clues          in the first stanza and the stubb
s relations with his mother . It   reminded       me of my childhood , going to kin
ce what is happening : different   ideas          may converge . May come up with a
e . May come up with a different   view           , if agreed , and for different v
have his mother wipe his face.It   reminds        me of 1960s . <"unknown"> Quite f
pleasant clinging , even in this   dream          . : 'you ca n't go out like that'
```

Following this analysis of key semantic domains, we then turned to the keywords in the participants' responses. Keywords are individual words that are 'over-represented' in the data when compared against a reference corpus. Using WordSmith Tools, we compared the Mittens corpus against a reference corpus of 1,000,000 words of written British English (the Lancaster-Oslo-Bergen corpus, or LOB[1]). This produced the list of keywords in Table 4.2 – that is, those words which are statistically 'over-represented' in the 'Mittens response' corpus in comparison to the LOB corpus.

What we can notice from the list in Table 4.2 is that some of the keywords are key because they turn up in the poem (e.g., 'mittens', 'stubble') while some reflect what readers appear to consider as key themes (e.g., 'childhood', 'memory', 'nostalgia', 'relationship', 'past'). (Some of these key themes are reflected in the list of key semantic

Table 4.2   Keywords in the 'Mittens response' corpus

No.	Keyword	No.	Keyword
1	Mittens	12	Narrator
2	Poem	13	Is
3	Childhood	14	Nostalgia
4	Mother	15	Relationship
5	Stanza	16	Past
6	Memory	17	Child
7	Shift	18	I
8	Stubble	19	Me
9	Alzheimers	19	My
10	Nanna	20	The
11	Adult		

domains gained from the Wmatrix analysis, as we explain below.) Some keywords are metalinguistic terms ('poem', 'stanza', 'narrator'). What we found particularly interesting are the words that do not fit neatly into these categories – for example, the grammatical words ('is', 'I', 'me') and the lexical words that are not part of the poem but which are not necessarily 'theme'-related (e.g., 'mother', 'shift'). These words are clearly statistically significant in our corpus and if we look at the concordances of these words, they begin to explain why the words are interpretatively significant.

Unsurprisingly, 'I' turns up as a keyword because we asked people to write first-person accounts. More interesting is the fact that 'me' is a keyword. Figure 4.1 is a concordance of 'me' and shows that there is a focus on what the poem – or, more specifically, the experience of reading the poem – *does* to the respondent; that is, a focus on how the poem affects them (e.g., concordance lines 1, 4, 5, 7, 9, 10, 11). So, there is a sense of the poem as an agent that acts on readers. One of the indications of this in the concordance for 'me' is the collocation of the node word with the lemma[2] 'remind' (three instances of 11 collocations for 'me') and a further four are rough affect equivalents ('brings home', 'makes…think', 'give' 'involves'; for discussions of the concept of affect, see Graesser and Klettke 2001; and Steen 2006). The other interesting point to come out of this concordance is the emphasis that respondents put on their interpretations being personal – for example, 'for me personally' (2), 'to me personally' (3), 'for me' (6), 'the key words for me' (8). It seems that respondents are very conscious of the subjectivity of their interpretations – perhaps partly because they are conscious that the goal of stylistic analysis is a more dispassionate account and partly because of a tendency to hedge the public declaration of their initial responses. This may also suggest a lack of confidence on the part of the participants about their interpretations, and were we to carry out the experiment again, we would ask participants to rate this.

The fact that 'mother' is a keyword in our data is interesting because it is a lexical word that does not actually occur in the poem (see Figure 4.2). There appears to be a strong sense that the 'she' in the poem is the speaker's mother or is acting in an analogous role. This is indicated by the existential presuppositions generated by the definite noun phrases ('the mother') and genitive noun phrases ('her mother'). What is striking is the lack of hedging and modality here. It would seem that once respondents have decided on an interpretation, they don't consider other potential interpretations.

Figure 4.3 shows the concordance for 'shift'. What is noticeable about the way participants use this word is that the shift is described impersonally; that is, the shift just occurs: it is an apparently agentless process because it is presented as a noun. None of the respondents made themselves the subject of 'shift' as a verb. Despite what happens in cognitive terms during the reading process (see, for example, Emmott 1997), our readers still described texts as having particular properties and as being active in some way.

Figure 4.4 shows the concordance for 'is', the most frequently used verb in the corpus. In 30 of the 35 concordance lines (1–3, 5–6, 9–15, 17–27 and 29–35) 'is' occurs in an epistemic (non-modal) declarative structure, suggesting a clear conviction about the statement being made. Only twice, in lines 10 and 21 are the statements prefaced with 'I think'; in line 32, the force of conviction is increased further with 'Of course'. Only four instances of 'is' occur in an interrogative structure (lines 4, 7, 16 and 28), and one as an imperative (line 8). There is a strong degree of confidence in the way that readers talk about how the poem *affects* them (e.g., lines 9, 22, 24), but also in the way they talk about what happens in the poem and what they think the poem is *about*. What we can also note here is that there are some clear commonalities of interpretation amongst the responses produced by participants. This belies a common critical view that interpretations are personal responses to texts and that there are as many possible ways to interpret texts as there are readers.

'Interpretation' and related terms in our data set

In addition to carrying out the bottom-up corpus analysis described above, we also searched for particular words in our 'Mittens response'

01 ut home-coming of a grown up person, his relations with his mother. It reminded **me** of my childhood, going to kindergarten

02 This is not an easy poem to read for **me** personally (emotionally) and i think the

03 i talk to/care for in a motherly way and the second stanza brings this home to **me** personally. This is not an easy poem to read

04 n to 'childhood' and the poem's description of the mittens 'with string' remind **me** greatly of my own (rural, working class??) up - bringing

05 it makes **me** think of my Nanna who is now in a home suffering

06 For **me** this poem brings a tear to my eye

07 half, and instead, the shift in perspective onto her/him). The effect it has on **me** may be described in terms of sympathy

08 -is it sad? happy? other? It is about a marriage -that (?) The key words for **me** are = 'it still sticks' - meaning that

09 . Quite frankly, i do not understand this poem and that gives **me** an insecure feeling about the main mood of the poem

10 is much taller now and has to bow to have his mother wipe his face. It reminds **me** of 1960s. Quite frankly, i do not understand this poem

11 ach stanza is interesting - from 'I' to 'she'. The shift to the mother involves **me** emotionally in the poem - particularly the clause 'and

Figure 4.1 Concordance of *me*

01 hink the poem is about home - coming of a grown up person, his relations with his **mother** . It reminded me of my childhood
02 wore mittens last is long ago. The language the 'she' uses is typical of how a **mother** speaks to a child, but we know the 'I' is not
03   when the person is not your child to ' **mother** '. relationship - uncomfortable -physical
04 lend from past to present (stubble) Personal experience caring for relative. ' **mother** ' when the person is not
05 towards a shift past and present merge demonstrated in the last line. Female = **mother** . the blend from past to present (stubble)
06   Culturally specific = describes an English western setting. **mother** at end could be the nurse in an old people's home.
07 writer has to wear mittens, which reminds him of his time at school, and of his **mother** . culturally specific = describes an English
08 m to wipe a stain on his face. He is much taller now and has to bow to have his **mother** wipe his face. It reminds me of 1960s. Quite
09   helped him dress properly. When he is a mature adult man going out, his **mother** stops him to wipe a stain on his face. He is much
10 ol. He might have hated to go to school or had a fight with older siblings. His **mother** helped him dress properly. when he is a mature
11   A son has come home after a long absence. His **mother** knitted a pair of mittens for him with bright red
12   different interpretations or not. Mood: dream or memory of childhood and **mother** Is he old or young? - can't agree Sad (?)
13 this is close to the (physical and emotional) relationship i have with my own **mother** . Of course, such a reading would not appear in any
14 ading (i'm a bit slow!). of course the narrator is now male and taller than the **mother** - this is close to the (physical and emotional)
15 first line of each stanza is interesting - from 'I' to 'she'. The shift to the **mother** involves me emotionally in the poem - particularly
16   childhood memory. She - **mother**. I assumed at the very beginning that the

Figure 4.2   Concordance of *mother*

```
01 the last line with the word 'stubble'. This is further enhanced in the temporal shift , evident in the change in tenses (past, present
02 od moment/instance/experience is evoked through references to senses. The major shift (turning point is final) occurs in the last line
03 ence to sexuality (? the missing 'mittens' in the second half, and instead, the shift in perspective onto her/him). The effect it has on
04     uncomfortable - physical (body contact), clothes -as protection. 'Roles Time shift control. This poem is sub
05     Nostalgia - a moment in childhood (sensation = senses) slow moment towards a shift past and present merge demonstrated in the last
06 ronoun in the first line of each stanza is interesting - from 'I' to 'she'. The shift to the mother involves me emotionally in the poem
```

Figure 4.3 Concordance of *shift*

```
01  Beginnning and end: set in present, frame the remainder of the poem which   is   in the past = mittens a trigger of memory.
02  oing out on stage to be seen and so the (?) must pretend that the surface    is   reality. Topic/theme It's ab
03  ure feeling about the main mood of the poem -                                is   about a marriage - that (?) The key words for me are = 'it
04  m and that gives me an insecure feeling about the main mood of the poem -     is   it sad? happy? other? It is about a marriage - that (?) The
05  adult man going out, his mother stops him to wipe a stain on his face. He     is   much taller now and has to bow to have his mother wipe his
06  ight with older siblings. His mother helped him dress properly. when he       is   a mature adult man going out, his mother stops him to wipe
07  ent interpretations or not. Mood: dream or memory of childhood and mother     is   he old or young? - can't agree sad (?)
08  er on. The image of threaded mittens is very vivid. Notice what               is   happening: different ideas may converge. May come up with a
09  Life was hard after the WW11 and later on. The image of threaded mittens      is   very vivid. Notice what is happening: different ideas
10  nguage losses? I think the poem                                              is   about home - coming of a grown up person, his relations with
11  e' uses is typical of how a mother speaks to a child, but we know the 'I'     is   not a child because of the temporal clues in the first
12  , when the 'I' wore mittens last is long ago. The language the 'she' uses     is   typical of how a mother speaks to a child, but we know the
13  se words seem to imply that the childhood, when the 'I' wore mittens last     is   long ago. The language the 'she' uses is typical of how a
14  else take decisions, instead of him, does not suit him. The message then,     is   that one cannot - should not - return to the position of a
15  y stage of their life: the narrator's life resembles his childhood but he     is   an adult and his position of a person, who lets somebody
16  2 meters 'still'. positions/positioned as child 'she' treats him as child     is   place a childhood home or setting? He has to bend now ( and
17  us e of the continuous and perfect). In the initial (first stanza) there      is   a flowing rhythm to the poem with the length of the
18  ing point is final) occurs in the last line with the word 'stubble'. This     is   further enhanced in the temporal shift, evident in the
19  ce is evoked through references to senses. The major shift (turning point     is   final) occurs in the last line with the word 'stubble'.
20  ce, which seems to be nostalgic. A childhood moment/instance/experience       is   evoked through references to sens es. The major shift (
21  easy poem to read for me personally (emotionally) and i think the author      is   writing about this relationship - carer and person suffering
22  therly way and the second stanza brings this home to me personally. This      is   not an easy poem to read for me personally (emotionally) and the poem's
23  my Nanna who is now in a home suffering from Alzeimers and Dementia. It       is   now in a home suffering from Alzeimers and Dementia. It is
24  poem brings a tear to my eye because it makes me think of my Nanna who        is   also characterised by a changing relationship between males
25  ith it. 'Mittens' serves as a symbol for this transitional period, which      is   subtextually, about growing up, adolescence, the tension
26  Time shift } control. This poem                                              is   not your child to 'mother'. relationship - uncomfortable -
27  ubble) Personal experience caring for relative. 'Mother' when the person      is   teh poem about? Males - Females Changing relationship throug
28  way! A slip of memory is the narrator male or female? What                   is   the narrator male or female? what is teh poem about? Males -
29  n line 3. I like the poem a lot by the way! A slip of memory                 is   interesting too - hyperbole or surrealism?And the omission
30  t, but i thought i'd share it with you anyway -the 'a couple of metres'       is   close to the (physical and emotional) relationship i have
31  wl). of course the narrator is now male and taller than the mother-this       is   now male and taller than the mother - thisis close to the (
32  il the second or third reading (i'm a bit slow!). of course the narrator      is   interesting -from 'I' to 'she'. The shift to the mother
33  wing up. The change in personal pronoun in the first line of each stanza      is   'about' memory, nostalgia, growing up. The change in
34  tinction is quite strong in the poem ("since", "still" etc) and the poem      is   quite strong in the poem ("since", "still" etc) and the poem
35  assumption was confounded by the last line. The present/past distinction     is   quite strong in the poem ("since", "still" etc) and the poem
```

Figure 4.4 Concordance of *is*

corpus and in the group response data. Perhaps the first thing to notice is that, in spite of our instruction to write down their *interpretations*, none of the respondents used the term 'interpret' or 'interpretation' in (a) their initial comments, or (b) their summaries after the respondents had worked together in groups. They just concentrated on the job, rather than naming it. However, the terms 'reading' and 'read' in the roughly synonymous senses to 'interpretation and 'interpret' do occur three times across (a) and (b). This usage probably connects to the fact that the more relaxed term 'reading' has effectively replaced 'interpretation' in much modern criticism.

'Reading' and 'read'

If we examine the instances below, we can begin to see some of the typical characteristics of readings. The instance below is the seventh item in our list of post-discussion workshop comments from the beginning of the chapter:

> Complete '<u>reading</u>' – my Nana has been in a home – personally upsetting. My background (rural) relevant but not the main reaction. I 'mother' my nana and this was how I <u>read</u> the poem – as a mother-child relationship, but related it to my relationship with Nana.

This is not an interpretation in the normal sense of the term (we will discuss what is normally meant by 'interpretation' below), but an individual reaction based on a perceived connection between the content of the poem and individual experience, as the scare quotes are presumably meant to indicate. Readings are often personal, in this sort of sense. The instance of 'read' above, however, does relate better to the traditional understanding of interpretation in that, at the very least, it spells out a thematic preoccupation of the poem and suggests, although not very clearly, an attitude towards it (something which we will return to below).

One of the other two instances, which both appear in respondents' initial comments, also assumes the personal view of 'reading' which we saw in the use of 'reading' above, and interestingly suggests that, because the response is very personal, it does not really belong in the world of academic (more dispassionate?) discussion:

> Of course the narrator is now male and taller than the mother- this is close to the (physical and emotional) relationship i have with my

own mother. Of course, such a reading would not appear in any academic discourse or the text, but i thought i'd share it with you anyway...

The final instance (of 'read') also suggests the individuality of personal response, but it is difficult to see whether it connects to perceived parallels with personal experience or what might be characterized as ideological differences between the participants concerning how to characterize their understandings:

> ... we all agree on some sort of poor fit between this adult who shaves himself but can't put on his own scarf – we disagree in how we 'read' this inconsistency ....

From the above we can see some characteristics of 'reading' which distinguish it from 'interpretation'. Readings are more personal (and so allow different views more easily) and can often be ideological (e.g., a feminist or a Marxist reading), suggesting that the understandings relate as much to an already held predisposition or viewpoint as to the text itself.

'Interpretation'

How, then, are interpretations different from readings? In our view, interpretations claim to be more dispassionate than readings, and although everyone takes knowledge about the world to texts in order to understand them, the text is given greater sway in the 'understanding equation' than personal or ideological predispositions. Interpretations can more easily be challenged by contrary evidence from the text than readings can, which in part may explain the modern critical popularity of the latter term. Readings, because they involve 'slants' of some kind, are essentially less disprovable (i.e., they are unfalsifiable).

What, then, is an interpretation? Besides being more dispassionate than readings, in our view interpretations need to be overt or explicit, so that they can be clearly understood and challenged by others. They also need to have some sort of *structure* (as we will see below when we compare them with topics and themes), and effectively count as hypotheses or theories about texts to be tested against the text concerned in the light of common assumptions about reading processes (i.e., how readers interact with texts). In theory terms, then, interpretations are in principle *stronger* than readings in that, by being more explicit and structured and less personal and slanted, they lay themselves more open to attack and disproof than readings. This is probably why stylisticians tend to refer to interpretations more than other critics. Interpretations go with the stylisticians' practice of 'putting everything clearly on the table' in order that their subsequent analyses should be replicable and falsifiable.

Topic

Interpretations and readings can be said in general terms to refer to what a particular text is 'about' and so can the notion of topic. So we also searched for that term in our data. The word 'topic' only occurs once in the data set, where it is part of a heading *Topic/theme* which suggests that topic and theme are the same thing. But we do not think this is the case.

If we consider what the topic of the poem 'Mittens' is, the most obvious answer is mittens, but this seems a most unlikely candidate for one of the themes of the poem (we will examine themes below). 'Mittens' is the title of the poem, the same word occurs four times in the first stanza of the poem and there are also two pronominal references to mittens (one to the persona's remembered childhood mittens and one to his current adult ones). This makes a total of seven instances in the 69 words comprising the title and first stanza (a startling 10 per cent of the total). So mittens is the most obvious candidate for what the poem (or at least the first half of it – see below) is 'about'. This textual meaning for 'topic' corresponds well with its use in traditional sentence grammars, where the subject of a simple sentence is said to be its topic and the predicate is 'what the sentence says about the topic'. This kind of grammatical description corresponds well with the sentence in line 7 of the first stanza, 'The mittens are red, hand-knitted.' (though the other instances of the word appear in a variety of sentential positions). The 'topic' of a text is thus arguably the most transparent thing the text is about, with the titles and the subjects of sentences, and word repetition, being the most obvious places to look for poem topics. As Semino (1991) puts it: 'Topic titles straightforwardly indicate what is being talked about or described in the poem. [... T]he main feature of Topic titles is that they contribute to the readability of the poem by activating relevant portions of background knowledge in the mind of the reader.' (Semino 1991: 96).

All that said, the second stanza of the poem does not include the lemma <mitten>, and so it is less easy to characterize this stanza as being on the topic of mittens. Effectively, stanza 2 describes the more general activity of which putting one's mittens on is a part, namely 'getting ready to go out in cold weather'.[3] That concept is not referred to explicitly in the poem, but it is clear schematically that putting on mittens is one part of preparing to go out in cold weather, as are the wearing of a scarf and a coat with toggles, which are referred to in stanza 2; and the other activities involved are parts of the more generic 'getting ready to go out' schema (in any weather) for children: hair-brushing, and being made to look presentable. So the topic of stanza 2 is effectively a schematic widening of the established topic for stanza 1, which explains how it is still possible to see the topic for the whole poem as being mittens, which now also represent the wider preparing to go out topic.

'Theme' and interpretation

The word 'theme' only occurs once in the data, in the 'topic/theme' heading referred to above. But the specification of themes is what seems to dominate the data. In the participants' concluding remarks, quoted at the beginning of this chapter and also in the initial workshop response data, most of what is said arguably refers explicitly or less explicitly to themes, specifying the perceived thematic preoccupations at a more specific or more abstract level. The idea of the stereotypical mother-child relationship being 'repeated' through a relationship between a grown (perhaps old) man and a woman (mother?, wife?, other carer?) who looks after him is what seems to dominate the discussion. Below we have 'stripped down' the summaries quoted at the beginning of the chapter so that only theme-related material is left. It is difficult to do this with absolute objectivity, but 259 words (55 per cent) remain below of the 473 words of original quotation, showing the prevalence of thematic specification and related material in the group summaries:

- Mother's relationship, though she is not identified as such, so it stands for the female caring role in general.
- Mother-son relationship, memory and nostalgia.
- Shift in roles in the family from male to female?
- Time shift – three different phases of life. Infant in past (toilets) child in past (mother relationship) and adult in present (stubble).
- ...this was how I read the poem – as a mother-child relationship, but related it to my relationship with Nana.
- Relationship, male-female, roles, timeshift
- Old man – perhaps in childhood home – the door indicates familiarity. Senility? Vivid memories (pegs, stink) – quite concrete memories.
- Reminded me of home-coming of grown up person and reminiscences. His mother wants to take care of him again. [...] Element of passivity and impairment not noticed to start with.

- Grown up person who positions himself as a child. [...] The other person (wife? Mother?) he gives authority to her. He is not comfortable in this role, but he doesn't try to change the situation. It is metaphorical. He's not an old man.
- ...he is an adult in the position of a child ...
- ...son coming home to mother who puts on new mittens and he remembers the past. He's about 20 years old.
- He's an old man in a home. Wearing mittens and triggering memory.
- Not sure – a marriage that infantilizes the husband.
- ...it's a dream or memory. Some sadness.

Given that the instructions for the workshop highlighted the need for participants to write down their interpretations, it appears that a specification of theme must be an important part of what is involved in interpretation. However, we would argue that most of what we see above does not really constitute interpretation because it does not say what the writer does with the themes referred to more or less abstractly and more or less accurately. An example of an interpretation of the sort we might suggest would be:

> 'Mittens' explores, from the viewpoint of the person being cared for, the awkwardness involved in caring for other adults in situations where they have to be treated as if they were children.

If we compare our attempted interpretative statement with the quotations above, some interesting features emerge. First of all, there is a tendency for themes to be referred to by nouns or noun phrases, as, for example, in the theme of isolation in Conrad's *The Secret Agent*, 'the theme of war in contemporary German fiction',[4] 'Mother-son relationship, memory and nostalgia' above and so on. Interpretations, on the other hand, necessarily need one or more propositional structures in order for them to be able to spell out exactly what they are claiming about a text (and so be 'tested against' the text concerned). Effectively, then, interpretations involve the construction of (sequences of) propositions concerning the themes of texts.

That said, although themes are prototypically represented by noun phrases, those noun phrases referring to themes may be complex NPs and so, in effect, contain propositions somewhere in their surface or underlying structure (cf. 'a marriage that infantilizes the husband' and 'shift in roles in the family from male to female?' above), and it is certainly possible to represent themes with clauses. Graesser et alia (2002), for example, claim a 'haste makes waste' theme for 'How Leisure Came' by Ambrose Beirce and refer to Bransford and Johnson's (1972) experiment which demonstrated the increase in informants' recall abilities produced by giving a text the thematic title 'washing clothes' (a non-finite clause), compared with those given the same text without a title.[5] In other words, although themes are prototypically represented by noun phrases and interpretations by one or more propositions, there is clearly some overlap at the boundaries of the two concepts, in addition to the 'structural interaction' between them described at the end of the last paragraph. This overlap helps to explain the fact that our informants tended not to spell out fully-fledged and considered interpretations, but to refer mainly to themes. We will come back to this below.

Our original research questions

We have, as have others before us, distinguished topic and theme (and indeed theme, reading and interpretation) in our discussion of the data, so the answer to 'Can we distinguish between topic and theme in texts, and if so, how?' is yes, although more work clearly needs to be done in explicating their relationship.

We would argue that readers can indeed 'get it wrong' and that some interpretations are more valid than others. In their initial response, one of our informants said that the text was about 'growing up, adolescence' and another said that it deals with 'the desire/tendency of people to arrange their life the way it used to be at some early stage of their life'. It is difficult to map these stated preoccupations on to the text because it is clear that the male figure being prepared to go out is not able to take control of this process himself, whereas both the above thematic descriptions presuppose competent adults. Part of the issue here is that the lack of competence of the narrator/persona which most sensitive readers would see in this poem is not stated, but a matter of subtle implicature and inference. This is bound to mean that some readers will struggle to get successfully to the inferences needed to understand the text fully, and it is interesting to note in this respect that both of the informants referred to above were non-native speakers of English.

Another way in which readers can 'get it wrong' is to arrive at an inappropriate level of interpretative abstraction. The interpretative specification for the poem we produced above is relatively abstract (even though it is propositionally structured) compared with 'He's an old man in a home', or 'mother-son relationship', in the above end-of-workshop responses for example. The issue here is that it is perfectly possible to imagine that the persona is an old man (perhaps with dementia), but then any mother-son relation must be metaphorical (perhaps involving a daughter or institutional carer in the 'mothering' role). Similarly, it is possible to impose a literal mother-son relationship on the poem, but then the son cannot easily be an old man, and the likelihood of a younger man with early-onset dementia, Down's syndrome or some other mental disadvantage becomes stronger. In other words, the mother-adult son relationship and the carer-old man relationship can both be seen in the text, precisely because the poem does not state that one is the case but leaves the reader to infer what is happening; but these two interpretations are logically or schematically inconsistent with one another, even though both are possible on their own. This effectively means that we need to move up a level of abstraction in our interpretation, so that both of these readings can be accommodated, as we did in our interpretative statement above.[6] Note also how the term 'reading' seems appropriate for the two interpretations at the lower level of abstraction, but considerably less so for the more general statement. Hence it may be that some readings may be related to interpretations in a subordinate-superordinate relation (though this claim would need careful research to verify or disprove it). Although much more research needs to be done on what constitutes more and less valid interpretations and the appropriate level of abstraction/generality, we would suggest that our analysis of our informants' responses does mean that we need to distinguish degrees of validity and levels of subtraction carefully when we discuss literary texts.

We can also begin to see more clearly some of the relationships between personal response and interpretation, and in ways which we wish to connect to issues of pedagogy. Arguably, none of our informants made clear and exact statements of interpretation. They began, not surprisingly, with personal response and appeared to be struggling towards readings and interpretation, but not quite getting there in the duration of the workshop. It is interesting to consider why this was. First of all, the workshops were online-processing events where individuals interacted with one another in real time over what was clearly too short a period to come to agreed conclusions of the heavily post-processed sort they would want to be committed to if going into print. In other words, the time, spoken medium and social-interactive constraints mitigated against our informants achieving what we were hoping for. This means that we have to rethink how we investigate the process of interpretation in particular. Fully-fledged interpretations are clearly the product of extended and careful thought and need to be written down and revisited in order to be sensibly arrived at. They don't sit well with first-time understanding 'on the fly'.

Moreover, the situation involved in class discussion in schools and universities looks rather like the workshop situation we devised for our informants. So it looks as if (a) it is unreasonable to expect students (who in theory at least are less competent interpretatively and analytically than us) to arrive at fully-fledged interpretations during class discussion, and (b) the class discussions which do take place are unlikely to be effective ways of preparing students to write essays which spell out well-formulated interpretations and support them with good stylistic analysis. In other words, as teachers we have to think much harder about (a) how we help students to interpret texts, and (b) the demands we make of them, both in class and in contexts of assessment.

Implications for teaching interpretation

In this section we reflect on what the above corpus analysis suggests about the ways in which we might improve students' capacity for interpreting poems prior to analysing them stylistically. One of the common ways to approach the teaching of stylistic analysis, particularly in relation to poetry, is to ask students to make an initial interpretation of the text, noting the points where something interesting seems to be happening, but also trying to articulate what they feel the poem is saying. These first impressions are then followed up more systematically using stylistic methods of description.

What the research reported here shows is that even readers who are professional stylisticians tend to use a range of types of reaction to a poem as they strive for understanding. As teachers, one of the things we can do is to use students' own initial (written) responses as a starting point for discussing a text. They can be encouraged to distinguish those areas where they are hedging and therefore seem to be acknowledging the possibility that their interpretation is personal, from those areas of interpretation where they seem to be using categorical statements, which may seem to be more central to the consensual meaning of the text. Working with students' written interpretations of a text prior to beginning to do stylistic analysis also allows students to compare their interpretations with those of other students in a more detailed way than through simple discussion. This is important because it allows students to determine more accurately the points on which they agree or disagree with other students. The value of this is that their initial interpretations can then be used to generate research questions to focus their stylistic analyses. For example, with regard to the poem discussed in this chapter, the following questions (moving from the particular to the more general) could be given to students, along with the poem, for them to write down answers to before they come to class. Alternatively, they could be used as the basis for group discussion in class, after the students have prepared the poem, without prompts, before coming to class. The questions below are merely indicative of the kinds of questions that need to be asked and they may need to be adapted to relate better to the knowledge-base of different groups of students:

- How old do you think the narrator persona is in the poem and what is his cognitive state? What linguistic and non-linguistic evidence is there for your views?
- What do you think the relationship is between the narrator/persona and the female figure and how old is she? What linguistic and non-linguistic evidence is there for your views?
- How do the two stanzas differ from one another? What linguistic and non-linguistic evidence is there for your views?
- How much does personal knowledge and schema-based knowledge theory explain your initial reaction to the poem?
- Underline the parts of the poem which evoked most strongly/clearly your emotional responses. What linguistic and non-linguistic triggers for your responses are there in these parts?
- What are the main themes in the poem? What linguistic and non-linguistic evidence is there for your views?
- What is your interpretation of the poem and how do your answers to the above questions affect this overall interpretation, including the level of abstraction that you feel is most appropriate for the poem?
- What does your consideration of the above questions tell you about the relationship between personal response and interpretation?

Our corpus-informed research suggests that teachers do not always distinguish clearly the complex relationships among topic, theme, reading interpretation and personal response. So we need to help our students to understand these concepts, and their interrelations, more explicitly if they are to use them with confidence and precision. These conceptual relationships could, of course, be discussed in purely theoretical terms, but our own teaching experience suggests that such abstract discussion is best undertaken after consideration of the issues in relation to a number of specific texts which students have analysed and discussed.

In relation to 'Mittens', we suggest that the following questions might be helpful:

- What is the topic of 'Mittens' and what evidence can you give for your view?
- What is the topic of the first stanza and what evidence can you give for your view?
- What is the topic of the second stanza and what evidence can you give for your view?
- What are the main themes of 'Mittens' and what evidence can you give for your view?
- How do the topic(s) and the theme(s) of the poem differ and how are they the same/similar?
- What do you have to do to turn your theme statement(s) into a fully-fledged interpretation of the poem?
- Do you have a reading for the poem which is different from your interpretation and, if so, how do they differ?
- What is the relationship between a reading and an interpretation in general terms? Are they different? If so, how? Do they overlap? If so, how?

Conclusion

There are a number of implications arising from our work, including:

- It would be possible to conduct the style of corpus analysis described here on students' written responses to other texts, as a way of comparing what students do with what our informants did.
- Teachers could use this technique with students to enable them to investigate the extent of their own interpretative overlap.
- The results of such an exercise can also be used pedagogically to help students to distinguish between (i) topic and theme, and (ii) reading and interpretation on the basis of their own responses.

Training students to see how their own use of language (for example, the use of 'shift' as a noun rather than a verb) betrays their attitude to textual meaning has a clear value in relation to understanding how we arrive at the interpretation of texts. This kind of work can usefully be done in addition to examining the language of the text itself (in 'Mittens', see, for example, the unidentified reference to the 'she' in the poem, the heavy repetition of 'mittens' in the first stanza but not in the second and the tense changes and other deictic signals of memory).

By using metadata – written reactions to a text – as another primary material for stylistic analysis in addition to the target text, we can introduce students to new ways of thinking about their relationship with the texts they read and, at the same time, provide more practice in stylistic analysis too.

Acknowledgement

We are grateful to our original workshop participants for their permission to reproduce their responses in this chapter.

Mittens

I am wearing mittens.	[1]
I've not worn mittens since Infants,	
can still smell the stink of the toilets,	
still feel the grey thick-painted cloakroom pegs.	
I don't know if there was string to them then	[5]
but there's string to these,	
a couple of metres threaded through the sleeves.	
The coat is bright blue.	
The mittens are red, hand-knitted.	
I'd forgotten how hard it is to grip in mittens.	[10]

She tucks my scarf in and fastens	
the last toggle, 'Stand up straight.	
Don't pull faces, you'll stop like it.'	
She brushes my hair. 'There.'	
We are by the back door now. It is smaller,	[15]
almost so that I have to bend.	
It still sticks. 'Wait,' she says, and	
bows my face to hers, 'you can't go out like that.'	
She licks her hankie, and rubs	
at the stubble on my cheek I must have missed.	[20]

(Peter Sansom)

Notes

1. While we used the BNC as a reference corpus for our Wmatrix analyses, we used LOB with WordSmith because it is more compatible with this particular software package. This does not appear to be a major methodological issue,

since Scott (2009) has demonstrated that choice of reference corpus has little statistical impact on the identification of those keywords that distinguish the target corpus. That said, our corpus is very small and comparing it with a large corpus may well produce some skewed results.

2. The term *lemma* is used in corpus linguistics to refer to the root form of a word. A corpus search for the lemma <remind> will include 'remind', 'reminds', 'reminded', 'reminding', 'reminder' and 'reminders'.

3. Mittens are most commonly worn by young children, and sometimes by women. They are rarely worn by men which makes this use in the poem foregrounded schematically as well as through word repetition.

4. This is actually the title of an article by Horst Daemmrich in Louwerse and van Peer (2002: 321–52), a collection devoted to the interdisciplinary study of themes.

5. Semino (1991) examines the differences between theme titles and topic titles in a small corpus of poems.

6. Short (2002 and 2006) makes similar suggestions concerning different levels of abstraction for interpretations in relation to a two-line poem by Robert Frost called 'The Secret Sits'. See also Short (2008).

References

Bransford, J. D. and Johnson, M. K. (1972) 'Contextual prerequisites for understanding: Some investigations of comprehension and recall', *Journal of Verbal Learning and Verbal Behavior* 11: 717–26.

Daemmrich, H. (2002) 'The theme of war in contemporary German prose fiction', in Louwerse, M. M. and Van Peer, W. (eds), *Thematics in Psychology and Literary Studies*, pp. 321–40. Amsterdam: John Benjamins.

Emmott, C. (1997) *Narrative Comprehension*. Oxford: Oxford University Press.

Graesser, A. C. and Klettke, B. (2001) 'Agency, plot, and a structural affect theory of literary story comprehension', in Schram, D. and Steen, G. J. (eds), *The Psychology and Sociology of Literature*, pp. 57–67. Amsterdam: John Benjamins.

Graesser, A. C., Pomeroy, V. and Craig, S. (2002) 'Psychological and computational research on theme comprehension', in Louwerse, M. M. and Van Peer, W. (eds), *Thematics in Psychology and Literary Studies*, pp. 19–34. Amsterdam: John Benjamins.

Jeffries, L. (2002) 'Meaning negotiated: An investigation into reader and author meaning', in Csábi, S. and Zerkowitz, J. (eds), *Textual Secrets: The Message of the Medium*, pp. 247–61. Budapest: Eötvös Loránd University.

Rayson, P. (2008) *Wmatrix: A Web-based Corpus Processing Environment*. Computing Department, Lancaster University. Available at: http://ucrel.lancs.ac.uk/wmatrix/

Rayson, P. (2003) *Matrix: A Statistical Method and Software Tool for Linguistic Analysis through Corpus Comparison*. Unpublished PhD thesis, Lancaster University.

Scott, M. (2004) *WordSmith Tools 4.0*. Oxford: Oxford University Press.

Scott, M. (2009) 'In search of a bad reference corpus', in Archer, D. (ed.), *What's in a Word List? Investigating Word Frequency and Keyword Extraction*, pp. 79–91. Farnham: Ashgate.

Semino, E. (1991) 'Towards a theory of topic titles', *Parlance* 3(2): 90–122.

Short, M. (2002) 'Who is stylistics and what use is she to students of English language and literature?', *Poetica* 58: 33–54.

Short, M. (2006) 'Designing and piloting a world-wide web-based stylistics course', in Gerbig, A. and Müller-Wood, A. (eds), *Rethinking English: Reconciling Literature, Linguistics and Cultural Studies*, pp. 131–66. Lampeter: Edwin Mellen.

Short, M. (2008) '"Where are you going to my pretty maid?" "For detailed analysis", sir, she said', in Watson, G. (ed.), *The State of Stylistics*, pp. 1–29. Amsterdam: Rodopi.

Simpson, P. (1993) *Language, Ideology and Point of View*. London: Routledge.

Steen, G. J. (2006) 'Discourse functions of metaphor: An experiment in affect', in Benczes, R. and Csábi, S. (eds), *The Metaphors of Sixty: Papers Presented on the Occasion of the 60th Birthday of Zoltán Kövecses*, pp. 236–44. Budapest: Eötvös Loránd University.

5
Using Stylistics to Teach Literature to Non-Native Speakers

Anna Chesnokova and Valentina Yakuba

Editors' preface

The ongoing globalization of English means that, increasingly, stylistics is being taught to students for whom English is not a first language. However, the false distinction between language and literature which is often in evidence in monolingual educational settings is not as readily apparent in second- and foreign-language classrooms. There is, therefore, much that we can learn from the experiences of teachers in non-UK contexts about the benefits of using stylistics to bridge the language and literature divide. This chapter by Anna Chesnokova and Valentina Yakuba discusses this issue particularly in relation to teaching stylistics in Ukraine.

This chapter discusses the benefits of using stylistics to teach literature and language to non-native speakers of English. It argues that the analytical precision offered by stylistics is useful for learners of English who often have a better grasp of structural elements of language than native English speakers. Consequently, stylistics can be a useful methodology to use in the interpretation of otherwise difficult literary texts.

Introduction

Teaching English stylistics to learners in Ukraine has always been part of a language/foreign language course. Surprisingly, even now teaching literature in the country is formally separated from teaching linguistics, so to study stylistics students need to enrol for a full four-year language study BA programme. In the course, students have no freedom in choosing which subjects to take up, as the pre-defined curriculum remains the same for all students with the same major. Thus a course of stylistics is a compulsory element of a BA university programme in foreign linguistics. In virtually all language schools (in the Ukrainian cities of Kyiv, Kharkiv, Zhytomyr, Nizhyn, Sumy, Chernihiv to name just a few), by lecturers (and fairly often by the students as well), stylistics is regarded as the most important subject among all linguistic courses taught. It is twice as long as others, is based on prerequisite competence in grammar and lexicology and incorporates knowledge of English together with vast reading experience.

Even outside stylistics classes, students are expected to demonstrate their literary competence as they are exposed to excerpts from literary works while mastering the English language. Their books normally include pieces from English textual sources serving as models of authentic language use. This methodology provides non-native learners with historical and cultural knowledge alongside the development of language skills. In addition, universities in Ukraine rely upon the students' literary competence, acquired on the basis of their secondary school courses of home and foreign literature.

Methodological background

Both authors of this chapter are, or were at some point, affiliated to Kyiv National Linguistic University (henceforth KNLU), which is one of the oldest Ukrainian schools specializing in foreign language instruction. Studying stylistics here starts at undergraduate level and is usually based on local manuals (Galperin 1977; Мороховский et al. 1991; Кухаренко 2003; Арнольд 2004; Єфімов 2004) with rare exceptions[1] (Simpson 2004).

Other schools (e.g., Kyiv National Taras Shevchenko University) alternatively offer a course in Comparative stylistics of English and Ukrainian (Дубенко 2005), which has both advantages and disadvantages. On the one hand, students are well trained in contrastive skills; on the other hand, learning *English* stylistics often suffers as excessive focus is put on mastering *Ukrainian* stylistics. The course books are written in any of three languages – Ukrainian, Russian or English – with no real preference. The background of local textbook authors is mostly Ukrainian or Russian. The reason for this dates back to the Soviet school of stylistics, which, before the collapse of the Soviet Union in 1991, made no national distinction, and Ukraine at the time was part of the Union of Soviet Socialist Republics (the USSR).

The methods of contemporary stylistics in Ukraine originate from a particular field of academic inquiry, from the early twentieth century, that has had a direct and long-lasting impact. This field straddles two interrelated movements in linguistics: Russian Formalism

(Viktor Shklovsky and Boris Tomashevsky) and the Prague School of Structuralism (Jan Mukařovský and Vilém Mathesius). The scholar literally linking both movements, Roman Jakobson, moved from the Moscow circle to the Prague group in 1920. Many of the central ideas of these two schools, including the concept of foregrounding and the notion of the poetic function of language, are incorporated in contemporary Ukrainian stylistics.

Both the Formalist and Prague School movements have had a significant bearing on the way stylistics has developed in ex-Soviet countries. As a result, in Ukraine nowadays there are four main approaches to teaching stylistics, exemplified by the following groups: the French school (typified by the work of Dolinin, Bally and Riffaterre); the British school (Turner, Crystal, Leech, Short, Simpson); the Russian school (Arnold, Galperin, Screbnev), and the Ukrainian local school (Morokhovsky, Kukharenko and Vorobyova).

Speculating on the importance of teaching the subject to non-native speakers of the English language, the main author of the most authoritative Ukrainian book on stylistics (Мороховский et al. 1991) as well as the founder of the national school, Professor Oleksander Morokhovsky (1911–1994) argues that:

> learning stylistics as a theoretical subject should, in the first place, follow practical aims. First, learning stylistics should serve a means to cultivate in students skills to help them to deeply penetrate into the text's meaning, to 'extract' from it not only the external plot, but also the deep conceptual and aesthetic meaning that the text contains. Second, learning stylistics should stimulate students to consciously select stylistic resources of Modern English so that they can be later used in speech and teaching other students.
>
> (Мороховский et al. 1991: 5)

Professor Irina Arnold (1908–2010) is the author of the highly respected book on the stylistics of the Moscow school (Арнольд 2004), which is widely used to teach the subject in many linguistic universities of the ex-Soviet republics, including Ukraine. In her turn, Arnold claims that stylistics 'not only develops skills of close reading, but also creates the foundation for the development of artistic taste; it encourages language normalization and helps students to speak and write clearly and expressively' (Арнольд 2004: 8), which is crucial for non-native speakers of the language.

The above-mentioned scholars, as well as others who contributed to the development of English stylistics, to a great extent depended upon Vladimir Vinogradov's (Виноградов 1963) approach to textual studies, with his 'text as a monologue' doctrine. It was the most widely spread approach and the only one officially approved of in the USSR. Vinogradov's basic focus was on the author and his/her message to the reader, on the choice of appropriate language means to convey the message, and on the mechanics of writing and editing. Consequently, text interpretation was seen by Vinogradov as the reader's ability to follow the process of creation backwards, step by step.

Vinogradov's theoretical opponent Mikhail Bakhtin claimed that a text is a polylogue with the potential reader incorporated into its texture. Bakhtin holds that it is important to focus on the reader's, but not on the creator's work while interpreting a text (Бахтин 1979). The latter approach was unfamiliar to the Soviet reader until the late 1980s.

All approaches to teaching stylistics in Ukraine tend to emphasize the unity of the systemic and pragmatic scope of studies, the interrelations of different language levels and the power of analysis to explicate messages, the authors' meanings[2] and implications. So, in modern Ukrainian academia stylistics is regarded as a branch of linguistics, which studies the principles and effects of choice and the combination of different language elements in rendering thought and emotion under different conditions of communication. Consequently, it is based on the following principal notions: language, speech and speech behaviour, the spoken and written varieties of language, variant/invariant, expressive means and stylistic devices.

Due to the abundance of theoretical approaches and the substantial contributions of Ukrainian, Russian and European scholars that affected the development of stylistics, the subject is mainly taught in a descriptive way; consequently, the classical approach to teaching stylistics is based on assumptions and personal interpretations rather than empirical data. The main notions of stylistics are defined in different ways, and textbooks normally include a historical description of how ideas developed, opposed each other, merged or became estranged. Thus, students learn about the different research projects of many scholars and are rarely taught to do their own.[3]

Course structure

At KNLU, students in their fourth year (usually aged 20) attend a class of two academic hours (90 minutes) of stylistics per week. The structural parts of the course are: theoretical foundations of stylistics, stylistic phonology and graphics, stylistic morphology, stylistic lexicology, stylistic syntax, stylistic semasiology (i.e., semantics) and text stylistics. The course lasts for two semesters, 17 weeks each, which gives a total of 54 in-class hours. The classes are organized either as lectures for a group of about 100 students (the so-called 'stream') or as seminars where small groups of not more than 15 students come to discuss practical issues. The choice of attending either a lecture or a seminar is never made by students themselves as the structure, including lecture/seminar alternation, is fixed.

The lectures are rarely interactive, and the lecturer only presents certain issues, narrating them to the students with the latter either taking notes or just following the information in the PowerPoint presentation. Normally, with such a large audience, the lecturer only occasionally asks a question or addresses a student at random. In their turn, if students come up with a query, it is answered briefly, to be addressed in detail at seminars. This form of in-class work permits all students to become familiar with basic theoretical issues. This is very important for EFL practice: it prepares the students for reading similar information from original linguistic pieces in textbooks, which often abound in complex syntax, terminology and details.

The biggest drawback in such a mode of teaching is the monotonous speaking-listening procedure, with few challenging tasks or active involvement for the students. Much depends upon the personality of a lecturer, who is free, within the limits of the course structure, to use his/her own examples, illustrations and text samples during the lecture, and interactive teaching techniques. The task is quite a challenge for the lecturer. On the whole, the practical value of lectures is to introduce students to the functional style and terminology of stylistics alongside clear, precise and simple explanations of the issues under discussion.

However, the practical classes in stylistics, the seminars, differ dramatically from lectures. As the assignments are known to the students well in advance, learners can prepare their questions and feedback upon the issue. The assignment usually comprises theoretical issues for the students to speak upon and a set of exercises to practise recognizing and differentiating language items in their stylistic functions. The exercises may include short or long extracts from original pieces, and sometimes even full texts. The activities are mainly focused on picking out specific devices and sorting out different stylistic means in given texts.

Very often such classes do not provide enough context for practise in defining or recognizing certain stylistic phenomena, and this is where general knowledge and literary competence (Виноградов 1963; Culler 1977) play an important role. The issue of personal experience of reading original texts then becomes crucial. It is taken for granted that students are familiar with most well-known works of British and American literature and are capable of recognizing them in the exercises. Consequently, teaching stylistics in Ukraine (as well as in most post-Soviet countries) depends upon a profound high-school education and vast personal reading experience – something the Soviet school was very proud of, boasting of being the home of 'the most reading nation.'

The texts on which the stylistics course is based are usually of two types: fiction and media articles. The range of authors representing the former is vast: it is traditional in Ukrainian universities to discuss tropes against the examples of renowned writers, ranging from W. S. Maugham to J. D. Salinger. The authors usually represent the United Kingdom, the United States and, rarely, Canada or Australia, while colonial literature has never been included in the curricula. Drama and poetry are equally rarely taught, and verses are only quoted to exemplify how individual authors use tropes in creative ways.

The stylistics course *per se* is usually supported by a course of Analytical Reading, which is run simultaneously and gives learners two more academic hours of small-group work per week. Being part of the EFL course, it helps students to practise their language skills, interpreting literary texts by way of linguo-stylistic analysis (henceforth LSA). The focus is both on the vocabulary and grammar of the texts as well as on the stylistic devices and expressive means used by the authors, which is helpful in improving language and cultivating close-reading skills.

The choice of writers whose texts are analysed is usually fairly diverse, though the list remains stable for all the students of the course and rarely changes over the years. As an example, for decades the students of the English department at KNLU worked on six texts during the academic year. The passages are quite short (usually not longer than a couple of pages) but stylistically rich pieces from Harper Lee's *To Kill a Mockingbird*, Edgar Lawrence Doctorow's *Ragtime*, Richard Gordon's *Doctor in the House*, Hector Hugh Munro's *Lumber Room*, P. G. Aldrich's 'Growing Up with the Media' and Christopher Morley's *Thursday Evening.*

Both courses, on analytical reading and stylistics, are followed by an oral one-to-one examination by the lecturer. In the interview, a student takes a card at random and is then required to talk on two theoretical issues and to support his or her arguments practically by analysing a piece of text – usually fiction, and only rarely a media article or a poem.[4]

The course exam in stylistics is not the last time students revise this subject in their academic experience. The examination procedure of their BA state exam, which directly follows the stylistics course, is largely based on the subject: 50 per cent of the exam questions are from the stylistics curriculum, and LSA is an integral part of the examination card. The MA course includes Text Interpretation, which some time ago used to be a sub-part of the stylistics course, later evolving into a separate subject. At the MA oral exam, text interpretation is one of the main skills checked, as it is considered to be a key component not only of a language teachers' training, but also that of translators and interpreters.

Teaching stylistics through research

Teaching stylistics in Ukraine is, in its ideal form, tightly linked to independent research done by students. All of them have to hand in their course papers once a year, and while the choice of topics is quite varied, many of them prefer to work on stylistic rather than grammatical, phonological or historical issues. Such topics as metaphor (conceptual metaphor in particular) in various texts or stylistic peculiarities of an author's language are preferred by learners because they are very familiar with the issues due to regular training at stylistics lectures and seminars as well as in analytical reading classes.

Lately in their course papers, KNLU students have combined traditional hermeneutic literary interpretation with empirical approaches to research, and this has also helped them to acquire additional skills in stylistics and to check the effects produced by language patterns on readers. This fortunate tendency gives birth to a number of projects not only submitted to supervisors for grading as course work, but also presented at international conferences (Viana et al. 2007; Paliichuk 2007; Sergeyeva and Chesnokova 2008).

To stimulate research activity amongst students, apart from the compulsory subjects, including stylistics, universities offer optional (elective) courses. Undergraduates are free to choose one such course per semester and later carry on their independent project. The list includes a variety of possibilities: Text Interpretation, Cognitive Stylistics and Poetics, Discourse and Grammar, Non-Fiction Writing, Situation-Bound Lexicon, Language and Gender, Emotiveness in Communication, Phonostylistics and many more.

Literary Awareness (Zyngier 1994) is one such option. Teaching stylistics is successful only if students possess extensive knowledge of literature and are experienced readers of native, foreign, classical and modern authors. Evidently, reading experience has to be taken into consideration at the early stages of language learning and must be regarded as an important requirement for linguists' professional training. Commendably, many non-native speakers of English demonstrate deep knowledge of English literature and profound penetration in the texts they study. For them, language learning and reading literature are the two facets of one process that brings useful results for developing both communication skills and linguistic background. At the same time, the content of linguistic subjects, including stylistics, has to be carefully selected by instructors to fit the needs of professional training and to achieve academic aims as well as to allow students to enjoy the process of linguistic inquiry and literary criticism.

From this perspective, literary awareness (henceforth LitAw) as a theoretically grounded methodology (Zyngier 1994, 2002), which aims at sensitizing students to verbal art by having them respond to a number of stylistic patterns in different text types, is a highly productive means of teaching stylistics to non-native speakers. The linguistic perspective of the method sees language in context and the way it works to produce effects on readers. When the context in consideration is the classroom, it is understood that the strategies developed should be learner-focused and that the teacher is only a mediator of the process of learning.

LitAw focuses on such key notions of modern stylistics as transitivity and personification, suspension by subordination, vagueness by modality, iconicity, register mismatch, time/tense contrast, point of view, the function of the mediator, and the like (Zyngier 2002), which are usually not included in the scope of stylistics courses taught in Ukraine. The LitAw course is scheduled a year before the students start learning stylistics. As a result, it helps them to achieve the goals of the subject as the teacher introduces both terminology and theoretical background in manageable amounts in each class, giving detailed explanations and demonstrating the practical value of basic notions of stylistics to be pursued the following year.

The basic principle of the LitAw methodology is the creative work of students. This means that learners do not just practise identifying stylistic techniques and devices, but analyse the way that particular stylistic tools produce a certain impact and then try to achieve the same effect in their own pieces of writing.

The results of a combination of the traditional approaches to teaching stylistics and the latest innovations in the academic process exhibit many advantages to EFL learners; they master the foreign language while at the same time learning *about* it. Preliminary elective courses introduce the basic notions, terms and phenomena, which are immediately illustrated, identified and practised with the teacher's careful monitoring. Such supervision serves as a clear guideline for individual research and provides the basics of theoretical analysis and its practical implementations. The traditional stylistics course gives a substantial background in approaches and methods of research, giving a chance to practise standard stylistic analyses of well-known texts. Finally, performing their independent study, students benefit from access to the author's message,[5] implications and ambiguity that arise from the use of different linguistic techniques, which they recognize and adequately interpret.

Teaching stylistics empirically

Apart from more traditional research, independent empirical projects by students, which eventually enhance their language awareness and skills in interpreting texts, are now becoming popular. A lot of similar activities are carried out within the framework of the International REDES project (Viana et al. 2007, 2009) that helps students in the Humanities, especially in the early academic stages, to actively participate in intercultural cooperative research activities. This, apart from other obvious benefits, develops the language and stylistic awareness that is crucial to EFL learners. Below we describe a case of teaching students stylistics by way of empirically testing their sensitivity to one of the LitAw components – lexical repetition.

The project was conducted in 2007 at the Translators' Department of Kyiv National Linguistic University. In it, undergraduate learners were asked to read Poem 809 by Emily Dickinson:

> Unable are the Loved to die
> For Love is Immortality,
> Nay, it is Deity –
>
> Unable they that Love – to die
> For Love reforms Vitality
> Into Divinity
>
>   (Johnson 1961: 394).

The verse is clearly rich in reiteration at different levels. Lexical repetition is most conspicuous in the poem: the lemma 'love' is used by Dickinson six times in just six lines of the verse, which is noteworthy even for a romantic author. Additionally, the author anaphorically reiterates 'Unable' and 'For Love' and epiphorically, 'to die.' Syntactically, the parallel structures 'Unable ... to die' and 'For Love + verb in Present Simple' create the clear rhythm of the poem and iconically (by their repetition) signify the author's belief in immortality produced by love. Dickinson's broken asymmetrical punctuation at first sight violates the rhythm of the poem as the first dash finishes the first stanza while the second one suggests an emphatic pause before the final element in the first line of the second stanza. Yet even this punctuation pattern seems not to lessen the impact of the otherwise clear repetitive structure of the verse where hidden semantic ('Deity' and 'Divinity') and phonetic (dominance of [l] and [n]) repetitions only add soft lyrical sound to the poem, liquid and nasal sounds having a less harsh impact than those sounds (plosive and fricative) which constrict the airflow more severely.

The experiment was aimed at checking non-native readers' aware-ness of the repetitive patterns in the poem and testing the possible influence of these structures on the poem's perception. To this end, randomly chosen students were asked to read the poem and anony-mously fill in the specially designed one-page questionnaire. First, the respondents had to describe the emotions they felt while reading the poem and contribute five adjectives they would associate with the read-ing. Second, the students were asked to state if the verse evoked any feelings in them (a simple 'yes' or 'no') and to justify their answer in an open way. Finally, they were asked to underline what in their opinion were the most striking elements in the text and to number them from the most to the least striking.

The setting of the experiment was a regular class in the Text Interpreta-tion optional course, so the academic atmosphere stimulated students to actively cooperate with the teacher and thus helped to get valid results. The context of the experiment (Fowler 1981: 2) was taken into account as it assisted in building logical and reasonable interpretation when the readers 'felt' the text and then justified their impressions from a linguistic perspective. In our case, the context included the setting (a traditional university room), the experiment duration (about 20 minutes) and com-prehension intensity (cursory or close reading).

The results of the experiment lent support to the idea that repetitive structures indeed influence learners' perceptions of poetry. From the prac-tical point of view, both the teacher and the students later acknowledged that the experimental way of dealing with stylistic issues largely contributed to acquisition of patterns by non-native speakers and stimulated them to further deepen their knowledge and enhance their skills of text interpretation.

Ninety-two per cent of the experiment's participants mentioned that the poem evoked feelings in them. The adjectives that best described their reactions were the following (listed from the most to the least popular): 'optimistic', 'inspiring', 'lovely', 'romantic', 'cheerful', 'eternal', 'happy', 'interesting', 'lofty', 'sad' and 'thought-provoking'. Interestingly, only one adjective in the list ('sad') has a negative connotation, so obviously the poem got positive feedback from most readers.

Answering the question about the most striking elements in the verse, the respondents focused both on lexical elements ('love', 'deity', 'vitality', 'immortality' and 'to die') and on patterns. Fifty-four per cent of the participants underlined the full pattern 'Unable are the Loved to die / Unable they that Love – to die'; 46 per cent chose 'Love is Immortality'; 69 per cent marked 'Vitality', while 'Divinity' and 'Nay, it is Deity' was the choice of 46 and 15 per cent of respondents respectively. These results clearly demonstrate that non-native speakers of the language are equally sensitive to both form and meaning.

Additionally, in the answers to the open question about justifying their reaction to the poem, students mentioned that 'the rhythm and stress can change our comprehension of poetry', that ''for' is tricky, that's why some phrases cross' and that 'the text is parallel'.

On the whole, the experiment is an example of how stylistics can be empirically taught to non-native speakers who, without having an innate natural feeling for the language, are nevertheless able to increase their sensitivity to the verbal artistry of an author by way of carefully organized classes where an experiment can serve as a useful tool.

Outcomes and current challenges

Teaching stylistics to non-native speakers of the English language leads both to benefits and problems to be solved. On the one hand, learners from non-English speaking cultures might have natural troubles acquiring not only stylistic skills, but also, and prior to this, language awareness. On the other hand, they are sometimes more motivated to do so than English students as they understand the incredible practical advantages that learning stylistics brings: from simply being more educated in their country to getting a better-paid job as a result of being a more qualified applicant.

The obvious fact about teaching stylistics to EFL learners is that the course has a two-faceted aim, serving both as an important component of professional training and at the same time contributing to the language competence of the students. Due to this, instruction in stylistics permits the development of the critical appreciation of literary works and improves the language perception skills of learners. Original texts, especially if familiar from previous reading experience, provide an authentic cultural background, thus allowing the students to penetrate into the layers of implications and hidden messages of the author.

Learning a foreign language, students not only develop their lexical competence and grammar skills, but also evaluate and rethink various phenomena of life and civilization, as they are reflected in different language items. Being foreign to the English-speaking cultures, the students need to find out about many stereotypes and practices thus giving them a fresh look upon the reality of the two worlds (the native and that of the text) they are inevitably comparing. The potential of language tools to express different ideas varies in their own and foreign languages, thus the explication of what may be obvious to native speakers can lead to acquisition of historical and cultural knowledge for non-native speakers. For example, reading Harper Lee's *To Kill A Mockingbird* the reader has to know about the Ku Klux Clan, consequently a foreign (in our case, Ukrainian) reader will have to refer to American history to understand what threats the protagonist and his family encountered and why. Evidently, the language competence of English learners expands and develops due to extensive reading of literary works.

However, in addition to the benefits, teaching stylistics to non-native speakers, especially in the ex-Soviet world, also has noticeable drawbacks. The financial and technical challenges of the Ukrainian educational system in general result in slow or even lack of access to modern literature in universities. Consequently, teaching stylistics to students of English often suffers from the inability of teachers, students and even universities in general to handle information. Despite so many current trends and new approaches in linguistics, academic programmes and curricula remain traditional and outdated. Adding innovative elements takes so long in administrative terms that they have already become old before they are introduced into the Ukrainian education system. Due to this, stylistics has transformed into an accumulative subject, which compiles different historical information about approaches and trends, but gives few instruments for analysis and develops few professional skills of potential linguists.

Nowadays Ukraine is striving to mend old lapses in education. The country is speedily, though not always successfully, harmonizing its university system with general global standards. To be competitive in the international market of higher education, the curricula of linguistic subjects are updated according to the rapidly evolving modern trends. The content of the curriculum is adapted, and the issue of quality becomes more and more important as the aims and tasks of modern stylistics change. We in Ukraine fully realize that academic subjects with the old formats do not catch up with the new methods of calculating data or handling on-line resources.

No matter how uncertain the picture might seem, teaching stylistics remains crucial in EFL instruction. Reading for the sake of learning becomes a new challenge for students with linguistic majors because, apart from checking their level of language acquisition, reading literary works provides a good opportunity for students to improve their cultural competence and aesthetic perception. While dealing with a text in a foreign language and interpreting it, students shift their priority from entertainment to educational reading. Insight and precision become students' main instruments while working on the text, which permits them to develop a sharper perception of the author's ideas and messages and a quicker grasp of implications, layers of meanings, and semantic differentiation of lexical items. Thus teaching stylistics as part of EFL curricula definitely has its future, though it needs to address problematic issues.

Notes

1. This is for both financial reasons (foreign textbooks are costly) and cultural reasons as well, since it is traditional to use the work of 'home' authors where possible.
2. Note that researchers, such as the authors of this article, are more inclined to take reader meaning into account than the stylistics curriculum in Ukraine, which at this point still privileges the author's meaning.
3. This forms an interesting distinction to the situation in the United Kingdom, since stylistics has a more established sense of itself as a discipline in Ukraine, which has led to this quasi-canonical approach to the subject matter of the discipline.
4. It is not clear why fiction is the preferred genre for this exercise. The authors have seen poetry used only very occasionally.
5. The so-called 'author's message' is not considered by the authors to be the ultimate authority on textual meaning, but it remains a central part of the intellectual tradition of Ukrainian stylistics and is referred to here amongst other more reader-oriented notions, such as ambiguity.

References

Арнольд, И. В. (2004) *Стилистика. Современный английский язык.* Москва: Флинта: Наука.

Бахтин, М. М. (1979) *Эстетика словесного творчества*. Москва: Искусство.
Виноградов, В. В. (1963) *Стилистика. Теория поэтической речи. Поэтика*. Москва: Издательство АН СССР.
Дубенко, О. Ю. (2005) *Порівняльна стилистика англійської та української мов*. Вінниця: Нова книга.
Єфімов, Л. П. (2004) *Стилістика англійської мови*. Вінниця: Нова книга.
Кухаренко, В. А. (2003) *Практикум зі стилістики англійської мови*. Вінниця: Нова книга.
Мороховский, А. Н., Лихошерст, Н. И., Воробьёва, О.П. and Тимошенко, З. В. (1991 [1984]) *Стилистика английского языка*. Киев: Высшая школа.
Culler, J. (1977) 'Structuralism and literature', in Schiff, H. (ed.), *Contemporary Approaches to English Studies*, pp. 59–76. Totowa, NJ: Barnes & Noble.
Fowler, R. (1981) *Literature as Social Discourse: The Practice of Linguistic Criticism*. London: Batsford Academic and Educational.
Galperin, I. R. (1977) *Stylistics*. Москва: Высшая школа.
Johnson, Th. H. (ed.) (1961) *The Complete Poems by Emily Dickinson*. Boston, New York and London: Little, Brown.
Paliichuk, E. (2007) 'Human trafficking and media: Is language that powerful?', in Zyngier, S., Chesnokova, A. and Viana, V. (eds), *Acting & Connecting: Empirical Approaches to Language and Literature*, pp. 171–83. Munster: LIT Verlag.
Sergeyeva, M. and Chesnokova, A. (2008) 'Language allergy: Myth or reality?', in Zyngier, S., Bortolussi, M., Chesnokova, A. and Auracher, J. (eds), *Directions in Empirical Literary Studies: In honor of Willie van Peer*, pp. 283–395. Amsterdam and Philadelphia, PA: John Benjamins.
Simpson, P. (2004) *Stylistics: A Resource Book for Students*. London: Routledge.
Viana, V., Fialho, O., Sopčák, P., Sergeyeva, M. and Rumbesht, A. (2007) '(In)visible networks in action: Four perspectives', in Zyngier, S., Chesnokova, A. and Viana, V. (eds), *Acting & Connecting: Empirical Approaches to Language and Literature*, pp. 23–49. Munster: LIT Verlag.
Viana, V., Chesnokova, A., Zyngier, S. and van Peer, W. (2009) 'Budding researchers in the Humanities: An intercultural online project', in Gearhart, D. (ed.), *Cases on Distance Delivery and Learning Outcomes: Emerging Trends and Programs*, pp. 231–44. Hershey, PA: IGI Global.
Zyngier, S. (1994) *At the Crossroads of Language and Literature: Literary Awareness, Stylistics, and the Teaching of EFLit*. Unpublished PhD thesis, University of Birmingham.
Zyngier, S. (2002) *Developing Awareness in Literature*. Rio de Janeiro: Faculdade de Letras/UFRJ.

6
Learning Without Teaching: Literature and the REDES Project

Willie van Peer, Sonia Zyngier and Anna Chesnokova

Editors' preface

Wille van Peer, Sonia Zyngier and Anna Chesnokova's chapter deals with a problem that is particularly apparent in the university systems these authors are familiar with; namely that research skills tend not to be taught explicitly at undergraduate level. While this is less of an issue in the United Kingdom, their solution is an intriguing and innovative blend of empirical research methods and international collaboration which is aimed at empowering students. The enthusiasm with which students involved in the REDES project take up the challenges set for them provides an example of how stylistics can engage them in the practice of research.

Let there be light

In Dostoyevsky's *The Brothers Karamazov*, Smerdyakov, the young man, asks the following question: 'God created light on the first day, and the sun, moon, and stars on the fourth day. Where did the light come from on the first day?' (Dostoevsky 1976: 112). This young man (or rather Dostoyevsky) saw through what nobody seemed to have noticed for the last 3000 or so years. For us, light comes from the sun. But before there was the sun, where did it originate? The biblical story seems to have got the events in the wrong order, Smerdyakov implies. Something of this happens, we believe, in literature teaching a good deal of the time: first light is created (or so many think) and then the bodies from which this light emanates eventually get their due. We read and discuss poetry, fiction or plays with our students in seminars at length, believing they are being enlightened. But that light is *ignis fatuus*.[1] So that we create real light, conditions for the source should first be made available, namely an awareness of the ways in which one may find one's own light in the first place.

In this chapter we describe how the international REDES project has introduced young people to autonomous critical thinking in literary studies and stylistics. The first step is to provide an environment where light may be ignited: learning how to carry out research. Many literature teachers, however, have tended to turn their backs on this fruitful road due to a tradition which emanates from reading and interpreting the Scriptures, a practice which is not subject to research methodology. Their tendency has been to find explanations, but not to experiment. We are convinced, however, that it is possible and necessary to change the way texts are studied, and that includes stylistic analyses (Clark and Zyngier 2003; Watson and Zyngier 2006; Zyngier 2006). We understand that the time has come to immerse students in active and autonomous research, albeit under supervision. We will ground our conviction in a brief account of what we see as the major flaw in literature teaching at university level and will then describe the nature of the project we have engaged in, together with a report of its results. We believe that such projects as the one described here are vital if literature is to survive as a discipline. But we also remain sceptical as to the readiness of some practitioners to give up their entrenched ideas that literature in the classroom must necessarily and exclusively involve textual discussion. That is not to say that there is no value in such discussion. For some purposes analysing and discussing a text in group may well be enlightening. We question, however, whether this is to be taken as the best, or even the main, pedagogical model. Our experience with the REDES project in different cultures and settings has shown us that there are more efficient methods to promote students' cognitive and emotional abilities with respect to literature, both in terms of their intellectual development and their motivation.

A flawed model: school versus university

Here is what we often ask students taking their first seminar: we ask whether they can explain the difference between a university and a school. Most often they cannot. How could they, since most Humanities disciplines are structured along the lines of a school curriculum? Maybe you might say that it is simply much more than youngsters can assimilate at school, or that the content is more abstract or more advanced. While all of these things are true, they do not really catch the real difference between the social functions of schools and universities. Or you may think that what is taught at university is processed by students in a more critical way, which often does not happen at school. But that says a lot about the level of school teaching. Maybe you think that students entering university are not ready for autonomous critical analysis (let alone for carrying out research) and so we must do remedial work, at least in the initial phases of their study. The problem with this argument, however, is that it perpetuates the problem. Instead of confronting the school system with its own deficiencies, we turn our universities into schools. For indeed this is what we can observe: the 'remedial' teaching is perpetuated until graduation. Most people believe that what students learn at school is to be digested, memorized and then delivered in an exam. Where is the critical thinking? Well, this is not our idea of how schools should prepare young people for life or for further studies. But even if schools may teach uncritically in most countries, that aspect is not the ultimate difference between a university and a school. The central issue is that schools disseminate *existing* information while universities produce *new* information by means of research. However, this is something university students engaged in literary studies only rarely encounter. As a rule, they are almost never involved in research themselves. In stylistics, the situation is somewhat brighter because there are exceptions to this rule, as the 2009 PALA[2] conference panel specifically for undergraduate work can attest. In addition the extent to which practitioners focus on 'pedagogical stylistics' is a testimony to the awareness of the problem. Still, independent research by undergraduate students in literary studies needs to be stimulated.

In literary studies, the model is that of the scholar who does bibliographical research and creates grand narratives (or denies the possibility thereof), based on a claim and a few quotes. There have been countercurrents, no doubt, such as those by the New Critics and the Russian Formalists. But in most departments, students graduate without having been involved in methodological investigations. Their production is based and evaluated on essay writing. We have witnessed the debacle of the idea of the unity of teaching and research which the German philosopher von Humboldt propagated in the nineteenth century and which has been taken over only in name by most literature teachers.

As a consequence, research *methodology* is hardly ever taught in literature departments. It looks as if studying literature does not require much methodological reflection, entailing that students never really learn how to evaluate the merits of contributions to the field. Why is that so? For some unknown reason, many scholars in the area are convinced that literature must not be subjected to unnecessary experiments.

Others see teaching literature as just trying to explain the contents of texts. There is little awareness here of any methodological problems that the field would pose (see, for instance, <http://www.english.heacademy. ac.uk/explore/publications/newenglish.php.>). In fact, specialists in the area resist getting acquainted with the basics of hypothesis formation and testing, with sampling and data analysis, with alternative interpretations and intervening variables. Nor do they train their students in logical thinking, or in argumentative analysis or historical critique. All that is basically the bedrock of research remains a mystery for them. But precisely that ignorance is then invoked to explain why students are not believed to be able to carry out research themselves. As argued elsewhere, 'Humanities departments are involved in a self-fulfilling prophecy: first we do not teach research methodology, and then we declare that students are unable to engage in research, because they lack the necessary knowledge and skills in methodology!' (van Peer 2007: 18–19).

In a nutshell, the state of the art in literary studies is particularly precarious: students are hardly confronted with research, staff are hardly aware of methodological issues, and graduation occurs without students ever having taken part in original investigations. Any reference of exceptions to this should be remembered, indeed, as what they are: exceptions. These conclusions could be somewhat mitigated if they were inevitable or if they could not in any way be overcome. Neither of these objections, however, holds. Over the past years, the REDES coordinators, also called here senior researchers, have prepared students, called junior researchers, to carry out autonomous research, not just in a vacuum, but 'in the flesh', leading to the volume by Zyngier, Chesnokova and Viana (2007), which belies the reasoning given for the absence of methodology and research in literary studies: the volume (which may be unique in this sense) contains 17 reports of innovative research carried out independently by students (including undergraduates). It results from several years of cooperation between the three authors of this chapter[3] in a project we founded (together with Dr Frank Hakemulder of Utrecht University, The Netherlands) in 2002. The project originated from our dissatisfaction with the present situation in literary departments as described above. Actively changing that situation, by opening up possibilities for research within an academic curriculum, was the major aim. But it was joined to other aims, laid down in the philosophy of the REDES project (further information may be found at www.letras.ufrj.br/redes). We believe it is informative to quote the philosophical charter of the project in full.

The REDES project

REDES, an acronym meaning **RE**search and **D**evelopment in **E**mpirical **S**tudies, is a new way of doing literature and related areas, namely by coaching students into research so as to make them carry out independent, creative and autonomous studies. (For further information on the project, see also Viana et al. 2009.)

REDES was born out of the need to offer students a more intense and involved journey towards knowledge. It implies commitment, self-discipline, academic generosity, mutual respect and, in many cases, volunteer work. Credits for the research are not necessarily linked to grades or to the institutional setting. In REDES we want to prepare qualified thinkers by developing and promoting exchange of knowledge and ideas, and thus to collaborate for a better world.

More than a research project, REDES works and functions as a source of cultural education and international exchange, where friendships develop and where differences are recognized. We understand we are part of a scientific community as individual beings and thus help each other on several different levels. [...] Joining REDES means one becomes part of a cooperative effort, a long-term commitment to working together and supporting others' efforts in both their research and lives. [...] In REDES, we try to do away with typical academic niches, with individualism, with self-promotion, and with the academic industry of hoarding titles. In REDES, we share experience and knowledge, doing as much teamwork as possible, and using the Internet as a meeting ground.' (From <http://www.redes.lmu.de/philosophy.htm>)

Hence a whole new way of getting engaged with literary studies was conceived: instead of sitting in seminar rooms, students went outside and discussed topics for research. They would set up projects, formulate hypotheses, collect independent data and analyse them so as to gain crucial information needed to test their hypotheses. Moreover, they would do this jointly beyond cultural, geographic and institutional boundaries as the project managed to link in virtual space students of three countries on two different continents.

From philosophy to practising research

Dreaming up a philosophy is one thing; putting it into practice is another. As outlined above, one serious impediment to students carrying out research was their lack of methodological training. This ambition was further thwarted by the scarcity of introductory books on methodology for literature students. This is why the founders of the project produced such a handbook (van Peer et al. 2007) to cover basic insights in the philosophy of science, types of research design, planning an investigation, methods of data collection, developing questionnaires, setting up experiments, methods for data analysis, including descriptive and inferential statistics and how to communicate research results to the academic community.

When we introduced the project to our students, the pattern of involvement differed radically in the countries where the project developed. In Ukraine, due to rigorous prescription of the university curriculum by the Ministry (see Chapter 5 in this volume), where research by students is off-limits, there simply was no room (nor the needed ministerial permission) to integrate such a project in the learning programme prescribed by the government. So all REDES activities occurred outside the university programme as a form of idealistic involvement on the part of the highly motivated students who strongly believed in what they were doing. In Brazil, some forms of activities could be incorporated in the university curriculum, most notably studies carried out within the framework of an MA or PhD project, but most students also joined the project as an extra-curricular activity on a voluntary basis. In Germany, the activities initially also started voluntarily, but soon requests were made by students to provide opportunities to acquire study credits for REDES activities, which – due to the highly flexible and free curriculum in Humanities departments at German universities – was easy enough to grant. But in all three countries students' involvement with the project went far beyond the usual time and effort invested in seminars (see Zyngier et al. 2007).

When the materials that were later to become part of the handbook began to be created and used, the practice changed overnight. Students went out for themselves to look for ideas and possibilities to carry them out. They started their own links with other students in the REDES project in the different countries where it operated. Lecturers were no longer expected to set readings of particular texts. Instead, students started to read the texts they needed for their research – of course, making use of the teachers' experience and expertise where it could be used meaningfully. A more correct description of what happened is to say that teaching, in the traditional sense, stopped altogether. The seminar room became transformed overnight into some kind of laboratory, where students tried out ideas, supporting each other, getting involved sometimes in two or three projects at a time – all independently and autonomously, marking the difference between school and university.

Reading lists disappeared, and no topics for discussion were necessary: students provided all this themselves, collaborating, asking for information from their peers. And instead of being text-oriented, seminars became problem-oriented: text analyses were needed to answer research questions, not because they had been demanded by the lecturer.

We also made a point of not providing topics for work – making it abundantly clear that finding or developing such topics is an integral part of research. In the beginning they often found this a rather frightening experience. Especially with the very first groups, we had to engage in some emotional comforting, mainly through encouraging students to acknowledge these feelings and try to come to terms with them, emphasizing at all stages that these were 'natural' emotions that researchers always experience. As time went by, however, and more advanced students could help less experienced ones, the problems rapidly disappeared.

Another side-effect of having students come up with topics for research themselves was that they contributed with topics that sometimes deviated substantially from the immediate concerns of a stylistics or literary studies programme. In these cases one had to apply wisdom to see whether the proposed topic was exciting enough in itself to allow it to go through. In general, we favoured students' own choices even when they were not immediately related to course work in the field – but one could, of course, be less lenient, depending on the case. Another feature to be noticed in this respect is that often the proposed topics were not directly amenable to research, either because they were too ambitious or too vague. We saw this as an advantage of the approach: in talking over their proposals we were now able to show the principles of solid research, namely that one should concentrate on a concrete question that could be investigated in some straightforward way.

The result of such discussions was not only a heightened consciousness of methodological principles underlying research, but also an emotional relief, to see that they could actually sit down and start doing the research which sprang from their genuine interest. In general, we spent proportionally much more time discussing research topics with students – an activity that for the student was more constructive than just getting a paper marked so as to pass a course. Now the responsibility shifted to the students' side: it was *they* who had to run the seminars, and 'passing' was no longer on their radar screen: all research activities followed naturally, and curiosity was the main engine of their activities.

We also encouraged cooperation where small groups would collect or develop materials that could then be used by another group. For instance, division of labour and team work meant that some students would hunt for text materials to be used in a reading experiment, others would draft a questionnaire, yet others would collect data in different countries, and so on. In all cases generosity and mutual help were the norm. Also, the fact that students discovered their own research topics allowed for a far greater identification with their learning than had hitherto been the case: now it was 'their' research, something unique produced by them, something they could be proud of. And these were presented at international conferences, which many of the students had previously believed were the privilege of professors only.[4]

Apart from preparing their research for presentations, students demonstrated the ability to organize international conferences themselves. Ten ECEL[5] conferences in Rio de Janeiro, six REDES conferences in Kyiv, and five REDES meetings in Munich were organized largely by the efforts of junior researchers (the term used by REDES members to mark reassessment of roles in the project) when area coordinators helped them with advice and ideas, but never did the job for them. In several cases, books were published, edited by junior researchers together with one of the coordinators (Zyngier, Viana and Jandre 2007; Zyngier, Viana and Jandre 2009; Zyngier, Viana and Silveira 2008; Zyngier, Viana and Spallanzani 2006, among others) and even by themselves (Fedorova et al. 2006).

A word of caution is necessary at this stage. It is all very well seeing that students learn how to do research, but there are simply not enough positions for all of them to become researchers at universities or specialized institutes after they graduate. The fear that we were preparing them for university careers for which they would not find a job later, however, vanished when we realized that those students who had been involved in the REDES project were also much more successful in acquiring interesting (and well-paid) professions on the job market far beyond academia. Many became course coordinators; others took MBA's or went into management, politics, international business or industry, and one even changed areas and took an MA at the School of Computer Science at the Federal University of Rio de Janeiro, looking at the way language and computing could integrate.[6] (One could discuss whether we should prepare people to go into business or take up jobs in industry. One can certainly frame arguments against, but we are of the opinion that it is beneficial to have former students of literature taking part in important economic decisions – at least better than leaving these decisions to be made by economists only.)

Let us add some examples here on how learning was promoted. One of them was a course on identification and literature taught in 2004/5 in Munich, Utrecht and Rio de Janeiro. Here is the course description:

> Identification in reading a story, or in watching a movie, comes almost spontaneously to most of us. We see through the eyes of the characters, we experience (we think) what they experience, we feel (we believe) what they feel – in short, we identify ourselves with them. This often happens even in the case of characters we would normally find immoral, unjust or even repulsive.
>
> Ubiquitous as this phenomenon may seem at first sight, it soon becomes highly problematic once one starts thinking about it at a deeper level. To begin with, what exactly is the nature of these identificatory processes? What happens to us when we identify with characters? Obviously we cannot literally experience the experiences of the characters in a novel or a play – so what exactly is it that takes place in our mental apparatus when we identify with someone else? Moreover, are these processes different when we identify with fictional characters compared to when we identify with real people (for instance the victims of a catastrophe or crime)? Such questions need a finer-grained analysis than the mere label of 'identification' can offer.
>
> Secondly, why do we do this? Why do we have these (often powerful) emotions when identifying with a character? And how are they caused? Precisely what mechanisms trigger the psychological processes that make us identify when reading or watching a soap opera? Are these processes innate or have we learned them (and if so, when, where, and from whom)? Are there situations or factors that may hinder or even make it impossible for us to identify with characters?
>
> Finally, what are the (short- and long-term) effects of identification? Or to begin at the beginning: ARE there any effects to be expected? If no, then what function does the identification fulfil? If yes, what kind of effects are these? Do they operate mainly in the cognitive domain, in the affective domain, on our attitudes or behaviour? Are there different effects to be expected through different media or different genres?
>
> During the seminar we will ask ourselves all such questions. We start off by critically reading the relevant literature on the subject, after which participants will carry out research projects, in which one aspect of the problem will be investigated. Participants have

the possibility of cooperating with students from other participating universities (Munich, Rio de Janeiro, Utrecht). Students hand in a written report of their research, containing the theoretical background, hypotheses investigated, materials used, data collected, analysis and discussion.

As a result of this course, several projects were set up jointly by junior researchers across the Atlantic, all in virtual space, resulting in papers and in dissertations, as, for example, Teles's (2006) study, which looked at the influence of dubbing and subtitling on viewers' involvement, identification and empathy with films.

Part of the students' work also consisted in learning the skills of writing abstracts. Here is one by Haua (2007), a student who investigated the way elementary public school students from Rio de Janeiro reacted to the textual manipulations of fairy tales:

> Following Bakhtin's social view of language (1929/1997), which considers that it is impossible to understand language apart from its ideological content, Machado (1993: 37) states that no work is ideologically naïve, since every literary work reflects a set of beliefs, values, opinions and archetypes in accordance with the historical and cultural moment of its creation. Based on these premises, the present study aims at verifying the influence of two versions of a fairy tale text on the description of the protagonists and on the endings created by participants after reading those texts. It also focuses on whether participants' linguistic choices are gender-marked.

In what follows, we will briefly outline some of the other projects that were successfully conceived and carried out by junior researchers. One piece of research (Boechat 2008) dealt with the reading of original literary texts compared to that of abridged readers. Readers' reactions were compared on items measuring cognitive, emotive and attitudinal impact. Another study (Paliichuk 2009) looked at priming effects in modern media discourse on human trafficking and responses to media differences in treatment of human trafficking, showing that readers were very sensitive in their emotional perception of media text saturated with literary devices. Junior researchers from two different universities (Munich and Rio de Janeiro) together investigated the representation of gender-related disease in German and Brazilian literature (Mäkinen and Lemos 2008). Another study, in which a junior researcher from Brazil worked in collaboration with another from Germany (Coachman 2009), looked at taboo breaking and obscenity in postmodern literature and culture-specific settings (Irish vs. German, and vs. Brazilian; German vs. Japanese) and gender-specific reactions to them. Two juniors (Menezes and Mendes 2003) replicated a study carried out by a German student on the influence of authorial prestige on the reception of poetic texts by doing a similar study in Brazil, coming up with interesting differences. More work was conducted on metaphors of restricted space in postmodern literature (Rumbesht 2009). One piece of research (Chychkova 2009) entailed an effort at defining the characteristics of English limericks. Yet another one aimed at finding out how real readers from Ukraine respond to a literary text containing artistic details that present a national symbol-archetype with the aim of checking whether the inherent vision of the symbol-archetype is strong enough to withstand the influence of a literary piece (Shurma and Chesnokova 2010). Issues of gender differences in reading were also investigated, especially how readers of different cultures respond to love poems (Chesnokova and Mendes 2006).

These are only some of the dozens of research projects that were successfully conceived and carried out by junior members of the project, which gives some idea of the richness of possibilities and approaches.

In addition to publications, meetings, conferences and courses which were arranged between coordinators so that junior members on both sides of the Atlantic would have access to the same course and bibliographical materials, some junior groups (especially those in Brazil) got together on a voluntary basis and organized a Special Interest Group for undergraduates on empirical philosophy and methods. Such groups would meet without the presence of the coordinator and produced materials for future groups. Another example of the idealism generated through the project was the extra-curricular courses conducted by junior researchers themselves, who introduced research methodology to beginners at the Federal University of Rio de Janeiro.

Challenges and problems

The previous description has sketched some of the effects on all participants, both junior and senior. Certainly a lot of the problems of traditional teaching evaporated: suddenly there were no difficulties in finding a topic for BA or MA theses, or indeed for seminar essays. Intrinsic motivation and effort to study rose exponentially. Also, members actually presenting papers in international conferences not only boosted their own self-image, but also had a significant effect on the other participants in the group. Our contribution to classes also took on another form: instead of 'teaching' we turned into advisors, whose technical skill and professional knowledge were sought out by junior members – and appreciated for what they were.

This is not to say that there were no problems. One of the major obstacles was the fact that university calendars in different countries do not run synchronically, so planning joint courses was not always easy. Another problem consisted in differences in academic traditions and mentalities, especially with regard to the way in which criticism was formulated and dealt with in the cultures concerned. In some cultures open and direct criticism is not part of academic politeness, and this sometimes created misunderstandings, sometimes also unexpected emotions. Though one may see the emergence of such differences as another positive part of the project, in practice it was not always easy to deal with. One of the most promising ways we encountered was when students themselves engaged with each other about their preoccupations.

When starting out on the REDES project we hoped that others would join in and that literary studies would thus become reinvigorated. We talked to colleagues and presented the project at a considerable number of local and international conferences, such as the PALA and IGEL conferences. The chapter on how such projects could help shape budding researchers in the Humanities is described in Viana and colleagues (2009). So far the signs of university classes in such departments qualifying students to become actively involved in problem solving and research are not particularly encouraging. Will it work in future? The answer will depend on what we want: do we wish to continue on the traditional road? Or do we decide resolutely for constructive innovation and turn the 'university-as-school' into a real university?

Back to the beginning

In another scene in *The Brothers Karamazov*, the two children, Nastya and Kolya, are discussing where babies come from. It is an example of the way even young children can build hypotheses and test these, the embryonic kernel of scientific thinking:

'I shall never, never believe,' Nastya prattled, 'that the old women find babies among the cabbages in the kitchen garden. It's winter now and there are no cabbages in the kitchen garden, and so the old woman couldn't have taken Katerina a daughter.'

'Whew!' Kolya whistled to himself.

'Or perhaps they do bring babies from somewhere, but only to those who are married.'

Kostya stared at Nastya and listened, pondering profoundly.

'Nastya, how silly you are,' he said at last, firmly and calmly. 'How can Katerina have a baby when she isn't married?'

Nastya was exasperated.

'You know nothing about it,' she snapped irritably. 'Perhaps she has a husband, only he is in prison, so now she's got a baby.'

'But is her husband in prison?' the matter-of-fact Kostya inquired gravely.

'Or, I tell you what,' Nastya interrupted impulsively, completely rejecting and forgetting her first hypothesis. 'She has no husband, you are right there, but she wants to be married, and so she's been thinking of getting married, and thinking and thinking of it till now she's got it, that is, not a husband but a baby.'

'Well, perhaps so,' Kostya agreed, entirely vanquished. 'But you didn't say so before. So how could I tell?'

(Dostoevsky 1976: 492–3)

The question we wish to ask ourselves at this point is: why do we see so little of scientific thinking in literary studies seminar rooms, when even small children can do it?

Notes

1. *Ignis fatuus* refers to a phosphorescent light that hovers or flits over swampy ground at night, possibly caused by spontaneous combustion of gases emitted by rotting organic matter. Can also be called *will-o'-the-wisp, wisp*. The Latin name is used metaphorically to indicate an illusion or misleading information.
2. PALA is the international association for stylistics, the Poetics and Linguistics Association. At its annual conference in 2009, there was a session dedicated to research carried out by undergraduates.
3. Nominally the University of Alberta in Canada is also involved in the project, but it never really got off the ground there, in spite of several efforts by some of the students there, namely Paul Sopčák and Olivia Fialho.
4. In http://www.arts.ualberta.ca/igel/Newsletter11.htm#PALA
5. ECEL stands for Encontro de Ciência Empírica em Letras (Meeting of Empirical Studies in Letters).
6. Natalia Silveira is currently a PhD student at Stanford University, USA.

References

Boechat, R. (2008) *Original ou adaptado? Estudo empírico sobre a recepção de textos literários*. Unpublished MA dissertation. Rio de Janeiro: Universidade Federal do Rio de Janeiro, Faculdade de Letras. Available at http://www.letras.ufrj.br/linguisticaaplicada/teses.php (accessed 2 May 2010)

Chesnokova, A. and Mendes, M. P. (2006) 'Reading Dickinson: Identification and cultural stereotypes', *KNLU UNESCO Messenger* 12: 150–4.

Chychkova, O. (2009) 'English limericks as a literary genre', in *Abstracts of The 5th Annual Conference 'Cultural Research: Challenges for the 3rd Millennium'*, pp. 6–7. Kyiv: REDES.

Clark, U. and Zyngier, S. (2003) 'Towards a pedagogical stylistics', *Language and Literature* 12: 339–51.

Coachman, E. (2009) *Linguagem vulgar: uma questão cultural?* Unpublished MA dissertation. Rio de Janeiro: Universidade Federal do Rio de Janeiro, Faculdade de Letras. Available at http://www.letras.ufrj.br/linguisticaaplicada/teses.php

Dostoevsky, F. (1976 [1880]) *The Brothers Karamazov*. New York and London: W. W. Norton.

Fedorova, Y., Ivanyuk, L., Korolchuk, V. and Yemets, N. (2006) *The Catchers in the Rhyme*. Kyiv: Lenvit.

Haua, R. (2007) *'E viveram felizes para sempre?' Versões de contos de fadas, gênero e leitores: uma perspectiva empírica*. Unpublished MA dissertation. Faculdade de Letras, Rio de Janeiro: Universidade Federal do Rio de Janeiro. Available at http://www.letras.ufrj.br/linguisticaaplicada/teses.php

Mäkinen, T. and Lemos, J. P. (2008) *Disease and Gender in Brazilian and German Contemporary Fiction: An Empirical Study on the Representation of Disease and Gender in Literature*. Munich: Ludwig Maximillian University.

Menezes, D. A. and Mendes, M. P. (2003) 'Authorial prestige and reader's response: An empirical study'. Paper presented at the 23rd PALA International Conference *Challenging the Boundaries*, 2003, Istanbul.

Paliichuk, E. (2009) 'Priming effects in media discourse on human trafficking', in *Abstracts of The 5th Annual Conference 'Cultural Research: Challenges for the 3rd Millennium'*, pp. 28–30. Kyiv: REDES.

Rumbesht, A. (2009) 'Metaphor of restricted space in postmodern fiction', in *Abstracts of The 5th Annual Conference 'Cultural Research: Challenges for the 3rd Millennium*, pp. 19–20. Kyiv: REDES.

Shurma, S. and Chesnokova, A. (2010) 'Raging sea in Ukrainian poetry: Can stereotypes be broken?', in *Abstracts of The 6th Annual Conference 'Cultural Research: Challenges for the 3rd Millennium'*, p. 4. Kyiv: REDES.

Teles, C. X. M. (2006) *Identificação, Envolvimento e Afeto: a influência das técnicas de tradução na apreciação de filmes estrangeiros*. Unpublished MA dissertation. Rio de Janeiro: Universidade Federal do Rio de Janeiro. Available at http://www.letras.ufrj.br/linguisticaaplicada/teses.php

Van Peer, W. (2007) 'Preface', in Zyngier, S., Chesnokova, A., and Viana, V. (eds), *Acting and Connecting: Cultural Approaches to Language and Literature*, pp. 17–20. Münster: LIT.

Van Peer, W. (2008) 'The inhumanity of the Humanities', in Auracher, J. and van Peer, W. (eds), *New Beginnings in Literary Studies*, pp. 1–22. Newcastle: Cambridge Scholars.

Van Peer, W., Hakemulder, J. and Zyngier, S. (2007) *Muses and Measures: Empirical Research Methods for the Humanities*. Newcastle: Cambridge Scholars.

Viana, V., Chesnokova, A., Zyngier, S. and van Peer, W. (2009) 'Budding researchers in the Humanities: An intercultural online project', in Gearhart, D. (ed.), *Cases on Distance Delivery and Learning Outcomes: Emerging Trends and Programs*, pp. 231–44. Hershey, PA: IGI Global.

Watson, G. and Zyngier, S. (2006) *Literature and Stylistics for Language Learners: Theory and Practice.* Basingstoke: Palgrave Macmillan.

Zyngier, S. (2006) 'Stylistics: Pedagogical applications', in *Encyclopedia of Language and Linguistics,* , Volume 12, pp. 226–32. Oxford: Elsevier.

Zyngier, S., Chesnokova, A. and Viana, V. (eds) (2007) *Acting & Connecting: Empirical Approaches to Language and Literature.* Munster: LIT Verlag.

Zyngier, S., Viana, V. and Jandre, J. (eds) (2007) *Textos e Leituras: Estudos Empíricos de Língua e Literatura.* Rio de Janeiro: Publit Soluções Editoriais.

Zyngier, S., Viana, V. and Jandre, J. (eds) (2009) *Linguagem, Criatividade & Ensino: Abordagens Empíricas e Interdisciplinares.* Rio de Janeiro: Publit Soluções Editoriais.

Zyngier, S.,Viana, V. and Silveira, N. (eds) (2008) *Ver & Visualizar: Letras sob o Prisma Empírico.* Rio de Janeiro: Publit Soluções Editoriais.

Zyngier, S., Viana, V. and Spallanzani, A. M. (eds) (2006) *Linguagens e Tecnologias: estudos empíricos.* Rio de Janeiro : Publit Soluções Editoriais.

Part 2
Pedagogy in Practice

7
Teaching the Stylistics of Poetry

Lesley Jeffries

Editors' preface

Lesley Jeffries's chapter demonstrates how stylistics can be used in the teaching of poetry. Using a model of language that separates out the structural levels, she provides a systematic account of the stylistic features in a single poem and suggests ways in which this technique could be used with students in the classroom.

Introduction

In this chapter I will introduce the stylistic analysis of poetry, explain why it can be useful in a wide range of HE classrooms and demonstrate both the analysis and how it can be taught by reference to a single poem, 'Summer Evening', by Peter Sansom (2001: 17).

Why poetry shouldn't be avoided

I have the impression, from my children, their teachers, my students and others, such as the members of my book group, that poetry is on the whole to be avoided. These are people who in other ways are big readers and who would extol the virtues of 'literature' if asked. Why, then, is poetry avoided by the otherwise highly literate, and could stylistics be one of the ways to help reinstate it at the centre of the textual arts?

If this ambition is a step beyond the scope of this book, perhaps I should add a lower level aim, which is to demonstrate here how and why the stylistics of poetry is perfect for teaching about any or all of the following things:

- How to read and understand poems
- How language works

- How stylistics approaches text analysis
- How poems – and their readers – make meaning

It may occur to the reader at this point to ask who can be taught this kind of approach to poetry and when it is appropriate. I would argue that those who can benefit from learning how to do this kind of analysis include students of Language, Literature, Linguistics and others who may read poems either for recreation or as a supplementary source of information for other studies (such as History, Sociology and so on). What I am saying, then, is that a stylistic approach to poems enhances the aesthetic appreciation of the poems themselves and yet it also takes away the fear of reading difficult texts in general, so that anyone who wishes to read and understand poetry, or indeed any text, would benefit from the tools that stylistics makes available.

This scope for taking the fear out of reading poems is, of course, a supplementary strength of stylistics and not its main purpose. The point of stylistics is to understand how texts make meaning (in conjunction with their readers) and stylistics has traditionally focused more on literary than other texts, though this is no longer the only type of data it is concerned with. So, stylistic analysis helps the student to see how literary and other effects are achieved by the combination of the words and structures in texts and the reading process. In doing so, the student learns how language in general works. This is not only because it is necessary to understand some basic linguistics in order to succeed in stylistic analysis. It is also because poetry, though often inclined to break the rules of text structure and of language in general, nevertheless is different from other texts, mainly in the *extent* to which the rules are broken or stretched. I would argue that it seems far-fetched to hypothesize that when a reader begins to read a poem, rather than, say, an advertisement or a news article, s/he is carrying out a qualitatively different kind of cognitive process. The consequence of such a view would be to suggest that we develop a very large number of deeply different skills in relation to different genres and text-types. Whilst there may be some differences of expectation and approach in reading different text types or genres, stylistics takes the other view: that reading a poem is fundamentally the same as reading any other type of text, though the purpose and outcome may differ. Thus, the tendency for poetry to stretch language to its limit of understanding is no more than a (more extreme) version of what is seen in some kinds of advertising, some prose literature, some comic language and so on.

The question of why poems are particularly useful for teaching stylistics, and by extension for teaching linguistic analysis, is relatively straightforward to answer. Although prose might be easier to read for the average student, poetry has at least four advantages. First, it is shorter than prose generally. This makes a complete analysis of a lyric poem possible within the framework of a class, an essay (or a book chapter!). Second, though poems are generally short, they can be very difficult to read. This makes the task of stylistic analysis both more challenging and also more satisfying as a result, giving the student a sense of the value of stylistic analysis at the same time as providing a sense of achievement when the analysis is successful. Third, poems, as I have already said, tend to experiment more with linguistic structure and form than other texts. This very playfulness with the language is a way of allowing us to reflect on the 'norms' of language which are being stretched or broken. Poetry can thus be very useful as a way of teaching some of the fundamentals of linguistic structure. Finally, the superficial textual meaning of a poem and its deeper interpretation are usually closer together than in a novel or play, where the reader is able to respond to the text at many different levels separately, and not always in the same reading event. Poems, by contrast, often *require* us to access the interpretative core of the text in order to be able to process it at all. This means that they are ideal for illustrating the complex relations between text, context and reader that make up textual meaning.

   In order to illustrate the advantages of analysing a complete poem, I will use just one poem as my example in the whole of this chapter. This poem is 'Summer Evening' by Peter Sansom. Here is the whole poem:

Summer Evening
after Stanley Cook

Every summer comes an opaque evening
before the beach is photos and the leaves
let go to relight autumn. It's brisk in Wickes
and the garden centre's scented colours
are loaded in the backs of estates. In parks
that saw offices undress for lunch
lads career in the wake of the World Cup
and wood after deliberate wood finds
a path in its own curve to the jack.
Everywhere is couples, and pushchairs
that make sense of last year or last but one,
till pubs overflow round continental tables
on main roads, laughing like it might last.

> Sooner or later, swans on a river
> disprove the moon they paddle through,
> cameod by willows. The rowing boat
> moored there is a temptation you decline,
> though all the time you walk, taking
> the long cut to the car park, you imagine
> being out on that water, the drag
> and viscous ripples as you pull,
> then shipping oars and just letting it drift.

What a stylistic analysis of this kind tries to do is to evidence literary insights and interpretations by reference to the workings of the language. Most often, stylistics of poetry will draw upon the long-standing notions of foregrounding through deviation and parallelism to identify those features of style which are significant in a particular text. Once identified, these features need to be described accurately in linguistic terms and the literary effect linked to the particular linguistic choices that have been made by the text/s producer. Of course, not all stylistic features can be found in a single poem, though this one is rich in different types of feature. Nevertheless, it makes better sense to use a single poem, so that the reader can see how such a process would impact on the students. If poetry is relatively difficult to read, it is even harder to read only small fragments of poems to illustrate stylistic features. Where I have done so (e.g., in Jeffries 1993 and 2010b) I have tried to give enough context to make sense, and also to repeatedly use the same poems, so that the reader becomes familiar with a body of poetry in stages.

The rest of this chapter will aim to exemplify the range of what can be taught in a stylistics of poetry classroom, and will also try to give some suggestions as to the best ways to teach this subject. I take a slightly different approach from Mick Short (this volume and elsewhere) who tends to start from the assumption that he is teaching students of literature who know little about language, and may be slightly afraid of facing linguistic learning. It may be because I come from a linguistics and not a literature background, or it may be that I have been influenced by teaching the increasing numbers of students in the United Kingdom who are studying English Language up to A Level at school. So, I do tend to assume that students will first learn the basics of English Language description (such as might be found, for example, in Jeffries 2006) and that this can then be applied to poems. Of course, the reverse is also true and poetic language can help to show students how the 'normal' language works.

Where relevant, I will comment on this aspect of stylistics below, as I analyse the poem. The final part of the chapter will summarize the significance of poetry for stylistics and stylistics for poetry.

What to teach about poems

General principles of stylistics

There are many approaches taken to the study of literature, and stylistics is among the most rigorous and objective in its aims (see van Peer 1986). I will not rehearse here the history and scope of the subject (though see Chapter 1 of Jeffries and McIntyre 2010 for this). It is important, however, to note that what makes stylistics so attractive to students is the sense that they are being given some tools of analysis which, whilst difficult to acquire, allow them to explain their reactions to literary works in an explicit way. There remain aspects of interpretation of poems, and other literary texts, which are less directly attributable to textual features, though even these are traceable to aspects of the text, otherwise how could they be identified by readers? An example here would be the possibility of interpreting Sansom's poem as something other than a simple description of a summer's evening, given the tinge of melancholy that has been recognized in some of the individual features and the culturally-based tendency to link seasons with lifespan. Even such metaphorical interpretations, however, have empirical and rigorous stylistic aspects (see, for example, Steen 1994, 2007).

The main concepts that stylistics brings in addition to the linguistic tools it uses are those of foregrounding, deviation and parallelism. Foregrounding has a long history of recognition as being of literary significance, from the Russian formalists (see Erlich 1965) to recent stylistic approaches (van Peer 2007). Leech (2008) collects together his work from the last 40 years, and much of this concerns aspects of foregrounding in literary work. What the concept of foregrounding recognizes is that language, though in a constant state of flux, nevertheless has some stability, at least within speech communities, and that this stable 'system', the 'langue' in Saussure's (1959 [1916]) terms is the norm against which creative language use stands out, like foregrounded features in a landscape.

Stylistics spent many of its early years working out the very many different ways in which texts can foreground features. The two general means by which foregrounding happens are deviation and parallelism. The former identifies ways in which the language of a poem or other text deviates from the norm, and the latter identifies patterning through repetition (of either structure or exact wording). Deviation can challenge the perceived norm of the language (whether that is a standard language or a dialect) and this is labelled external deviation. An example would be where standard syntax is not used or where a new word has been invented. On the other hand, deviation might be against a norm that has been set up within the text itself and this is known as internal deviation. A lack of rhyme in an otherwise rhyming poem would be one example.

Micro-stylistic analysis

One way to approach the stylistic analysis of a poem is to take the 'levels of language' model as the structuring device for the analysis, and to look in turn at phonology, morphology, lexical relations, syntax and higher-level structures in turn. The practical way to do this once you are adept at it is to make several copies of the poem and label each one with the appropriate level, noting all the foregrounded aspects of the language at this level on the page. Once this is complete, of course, it may be more practical, and more relevant to interpretation, to combine the discussion of the different levels where they seem to work together in the poem. However, for students (and researchers), it is often useful to separate these stages out. Here, then, is a systematic analysis of these aspects of 'Summer Evening'.

Phonology

The first thing to notice about the poem is that it has a relatively regular metrical structure of between 8 and 11 syllables per line, with the majority being 10 syllables, some of them even having a repeated metrical foot. The first line, for example, is made up of five trochaic feet (i.e., stressed + unstressed syllable) which lends it a regular rhythm, though this pattern is soon broken and is not dominant. Whether the students wish to make anything of this establishing and then breaking of a pattern in relation to the meaning of the poem is for the teacher to discuss with them. What is important at this stage is their appreciation of the potential importance of poetic form and its relation to the musicality of the poem, and to the syntax, where there can be tensions or synergies, depending on the occurrence of enjambment, and end-stopping and so on.

Apart from the form, the poem also foregrounds certain words and phrases by the patterning of their phonology. Whilst the traditional labels of 'alliteration' and 'assonance' can be helpful here, their use can also be restrictive, because it may lead students to look only at the most obvious cases, dictated by spelling rather than sound, and in the case of alliteration, only at the beginnings of words. I prefer to introduce students, even those focusing on literature, to the basics of articulatory phonetics (see Jeffries 2006), so that they start to recognize the more intricate patterning that is commonly found in good poetry. Being systematic about analysis helps to uncover some of the effects which will otherwise remain vague impressions.

So, a complete phonological transcription is one possible way of proceeding, but that is usually quite difficult for students. Another way to proceed is to get them to read the poem aloud and note those sections where they feel that there is something phonological going on. This will, of course, raise issues about accent, the poet's own accent and so on, but will also allow students to see that there is often consensus about the *musical* parts of a poem. To what extent this musicality is also *meaningful* (i.e., sound-symbolic) is often a cause of debate, though the minimum requirement to support a claim of meaningfulness in phonology is that it can be justified in terms of the articulatory or physical aspects of the sounds concerned. We will see what this implies below.

The opening few lines of this poem demonstrate a number of fore-grounded phonological features. Line 1 has an almost complete internal rhyme ('summer', 'comes'), where the vowel will be assonantal in most accents of English (either /ʌ/ or /ʊ/ in the United Kingdom) and is anyway a half-open back or central vowel which combines with the /m/ to produce a pattern of sound that is noticeable and could be said to produce a rounded, humming sound. This is followed in lines 2 and 3 with a concentration of /l/ sounds ('leaves', 'let', 'light') which are mainly significant because of their proximity to each other and their contrast to the /ʌm/ or /ʊm/ in line 1. The lateral /l/ sound is known in phonetics as a 'liquid' because of its lack of any plosive, fricative or nasal effect; in other words, it puts less pressure on the escaping air than the other consonantal manners of production and as a result the air flows fairly freely from the lowered sides of the tongue. We therefore have the /m/ of summer, at the front of the mouth (bilabial) contrasting with the /l/ of autumn, slightly further back in the mouth and softer and smoother in sound. This, it could be argued, coincides with the poem's representation of summer as being full of hectic activity, though as we shall see, there are other options imagined at the end of the poem.

The end of line 3 produces another contrast when the frantic busy-ness of the DIY store (Wickes) is reflected in the repeated short vowel /ɪ/ ('It's', 'brisk', 'Wickes') combined with the fricative /s/ and plosive /t/ and /k/. These consonants are all voiceless and thus contrast with the earlier nasal /m/ and lateral (liquid) /l/ which are voiced, and have the potential in their articulation to last longer than the plosives (/t/ and /d/). The fact that we can hum on nasal sounds means that they can last as long as we have air to expel from our lungs. This is despite the fact that nasal sounds ultimately finish with a small plosive burst of air when the articulators are released. In the case of /l/, we may also extend the pre-release phase of the sound, whilst the vocal chords are producing voicing. This is not possible with plosives, where the closure phase is so complete that it produces no sound and where the build-up of air behind the closure in the mouth forces the articulators apart when the pressure has built up.

The next line includes another internal rhyme ('centre's scented') which forms part of a four-word phrase with a trochaic (dum-de) rhythm ('garden centre's scented colours') and thus provides a small section of regular rhythm within an otherwise changing rhythmical context. I will make no more than a musical point here, though other readers may wish to draw some kind of interpretative point from this. In a way, the joy of stylistics is that, rather than closing down the interpretative possibilities to a single 'meaning' (as some believe), it legitimizes a range of possible responses, whilst also acknowledging that there are text-imposed limits to them.

In lines 3– 6 there are generally a large number of fricative sounds (/s/, /f/, /ʧ/) which, because of their noisy articulation (air escaping through a small gap or slit between articulators), may evoke the bustling that is referred to here. This effect comes to a halt in line 7, 'lads career in the wake of the World Cup', where the gentler sound of the bilabial approximant /w/ is combined with long vowels and diphthongs which produce an altogether more relaxed effect. This is a result of the resonance of vowels (particularly long ones) and voiced approximants like /w/, where there is no closure putting pressure on the exhaled air. What we might make of this relaxing of tension in the poem is perhaps more individual, though one might note that this is not 'real' football being played, so nothing is at stake and it is simply a relaxing knock about. My own reaction to the sounds of the poem at this point is that it seems to be a more distant view of the football players that is evoked by the softer sounds. The viewing perspective of the poem, panning like a film camera across the sights and sounds of the park, is more distant from some than others.

Line 8 takes in the sight of the players on the bowling green, where the knock of the bowling balls is echoed directly in the short vowel and plosive ending of their name, 'wood', and reinforced by the four-syllable word 'deliberate' which also includes a number of plosives and two full vowels (/dɪlɪbərət/) and as a result cannot be reduced or shortened. Although the third and fourth syllables, then, are unstressed, they are nevertheless given their full value in timing, and this is symbolic of deliberateness.

Line 9 allows us to discuss the effect of accent on poetry. I want to argue that the plethora of long vowels in this line iconically represent the woods rolling across the bowling green, but I am aware that this argument works better with my (Southern British) accent than with the poet's – or indeed with Stanley Cook's (the former from Nottinghamshire and the latter a Yorkshireman to whom the poem was dedicated). I would have three long vowels (or diphthongs) in this line ('path' /pɑːθ/, 'own' /əʊn/ and 'curve' /kɜːv/, whereas a northern speaker might have a short vowel in 'path' (/æ/) or possibly a longer version of it (/æː/). The vowel in 'own' might also be a pure vowel in some northern accents (/ɜːn/) though this does not change the point being made as it remains long.

In the first stanza, the only other clearly foregrounded sound effect is in the final line, 'laughing like it might last'. Here, there is a neat pattern of sounds, with the two outer words containing the same open front /æ/ (northern) or open back /ɑː/ (southern) vowel following the lateral /l/. This pattern is often called reverse rhyme, as it involves the same initial consonant and vowel instead of the same vowel and final consonant as in traditional rhyme. Between these two, we have alternating /ɪ/ ('ing', 'it') and /aɪ/ ('like', 'might') sounds, so the vowel pattern in total (assuming northern accent) is /æ – ɪ – aɪ – ɪ – aɪ – æ/. In addition, there is another initial /l/ in 'like', which adds to the liquid alliterative effect. As in many cases of poetic music, this little pattern of sounds may do no more than attract the attention of the reader, in other words, a concentration of particular sounds or sound groups may simply foreground words and phrases whose effects might be other than phonological. Here, the implicature that 'it' won't last seems strong to this reader, and the phonological foregrounding seems to me to provide the superficial jollity that belies the underlying knowledge of summer's end.

The second stanza has fewer really salient foregrounded sound effects, though there are some musical uses of assonance, for example in line 15: 'disprove the moon', where the long close back vowel /uː/ is previewed by 'sooner' on the previous line and echoed in the last word of the line 'through'. It is possibly pushing the notion of sound-symbolism too far to suggest that there is any reflection of the reflection(!) of the swans in this usage, since most human language is based upon arbitrary use of sounds, so I will leave it as a claim for the musicality of repeated sounds, which is found again in line 16 in 'cameod by willows' where the diphthong /əʊ/ is the final vowel in both main words.

The final lines of the poem revert to the music of consonants, with line 19 (and line 18 to some extent) being dominated by the sharp sound of plosives ('cut to the car park') whereas the more dreamy final two lines of the poem are dominated by fricatives, with the potential for some iconic representation of the movement over water and the accompanying sounds. The following representation of where these fricative sounds occur is not as accurate as a phonetic transcription, but it does provide a sense of their concentration here:

> and **v**i**s**cou**s** ripple**s** a**s** you pull,
> **th**en **sh**ipping oar**s** and **j**u**s**t letting it dri**ft**.

By contrast, the earlier lines mentioned have a relative concentration of plosives:

> though all the **t**ime you walk, **t**a**k**ing
> the long **c**u**t t**o the **c**ar **p**ar**k**,

This technique of comparing the consonantal and vocalic content of parts of poems is open to debate in relation to whether there are indeed foregrounded effects, and still more as to their potential for meaning. However, the tools of phonetics do at least allow us to discuss something more subtle and closer to the musicality of poetry than the blunt tools of (spelling-related) alliteration and assonance.

Lexis

There are different ways that you can (for the sake of convenience) split up the levels of language. For students, I find that dealing with everything that concerns the word at an early stage is helpful as you are starting from their point of departure. Word-level analysis can then be split further into issues of form (morphology), issues of combination such as collocation and issues of semantics, including sense relations such as opposition and synonymy.

As with many contemporary poems, this one does not exploit the word-formation system of English to create many neologisms (invented words). However, the relatively subtle process of 'zero derivation' is used to create a verb from a noun in 'cameod'. This process is one where a word class change is brought about by the position in the syntax with no additional morphemes. However, the new word class may, as in this case, require the addition of regular inflectional morphemes. Thus, the noun 'cameo' would normally only be subject to the addition of a plural morpheme, as in 'cameos', but here it has had the past participial morpheme {–ed} added, producing an adjectival version of the verb form. This is such a familiar process to English speakers that rather than alienating the reader, it allows her/him to engage with the idea of a cameo (a still shot picture of something) as a process rather than a product.

By far the most common exploitation of lexis in contemporary poetry is the use of collocation to produce new ideas and interesting images. This poem is no exception to this general rule. We can use the term collocation to describe a range of different kinds of combination of lexical items, which have been discussed in different linguistic contexts, but which fundamentally amount to the tendency for words to regularly occur in the near context of other words. I will introduce these types of collocational tendency in order for the reader to recognize them in other work.

The restrictions that some lexemes have on them as to the semantic categories of words that they can co-occur with have been called 'selectional restriction' in some linguistic theories. So, for example, the verb 'eat' requires its subject to be an animate being capable of eating and its object to be a concrete item which is edible. Thus, 'the girl ate the biscuit' is fine, and 'the idea ate the cupboard' is not. This, of course, ignores the fact that much everyday creative language defies these restrictions (see Carter 2004) and we all understand sentences like 'the sofa has eaten my remote control'. Poetry is quick to exploit our understanding of such restrictions, and there are many examples where metaphors and other images are produced by the breaking of selectional restrictions.

Collocation is normally seen as a tendency, which is not necessarily semantically explained, for words to occur in proximity to each other. Thus, the expectation on hearing the word 'stark' that it will be followed by 'naked' but not 'nude' is one of the more extreme examples of restricted collocation, which cannot be explained by semantics. It is simply an accidental or historical association which has grown up in the English-speaking community. What is significant, for creative use of the language, is that these very restricted collocational tendencies are evoked by only one of the words. Thus, my favourite and much-quoted example from Samuel Beckett's play, *Footfalls*, where the protagonist (who has been pacing up and down in an odd manner) is described as 'standing stark still' and the reader is inclined to see her as both mad ('stark staring mad' is another common collocation) and possibly also naked, though neither of these adjectives is used.

A final case of collocation is what is known as 'semantic prosody', where the general collocational habits of a word are seen as colouring the meaning of that word, usually in an evaluative way. This is not quite the semantic restriction on co-occurrence of selectional restrictions, nor the very focused restricted (but apparently random) collocations we saw in the last paragraph. Rather, it is an almost unnoticeable habit of words to collocate in certain ways which add something to their 'flavour'. The actual semantic prosody of a word can only really be traced by searches of its collocates in large corpora, and the advent of corpus linguistics with searchable corpora has made it easier to support claims of semantic prosody.

The poem under scrutiny here exploits all three of these lexical combination types. As with many contemporary poems, selectional restrictions have been broken a number of times.

In line 2, for example, we see the memorable clause 'before the beach is photos' where the syntax is perfectly acceptable, if a little odd because the number of the subject is singular whereas the number of the complement is plural. This syntactic oddity also foregrounds a semantic strangeness that is likely to strike the reader as peculiar, but which may remain mysterious unless the reader considers *why* this is an unusual collocation. A search of the British National Corpus (BNC) brings up 51 cases of the string[1] 'the beach is' which are followed by a very restricted set of possibilities. These include the adjectival complements, such as 'shallow and safe' or 'narrow and sandy' as well as nominal complements which are almost always a reference to distance or size as in 'a short walk away' or 'three miles long'. What we don't tend to see is the kind of equivalence being presented here, where the beach, as it were, *becomes* photos. This apparent transubstantiation, of course, refers to the way in which summer holidays become mere memories recorded in photos and the vivid impressions of being there can only be recalled and not re-experienced. Interestingly, the third kind of collocation for 'the beach is' to be found in the BNC is the nominal phrase of possession, such as 'my back yard' or 'all mine'. This is the closest, grammatically, to 'the beach is photos' and the sense of possession that capturing our holidays on film gives us may also be present here.

In lines 2–3, we have 'the leaves / let go', which has the phrasal verb 'let go' employing an inanimate subject in place of its usual animate subject. Both in its literal and metaphorical meaning, this verb normally requires a subject (such as an animal or human being) which has self-determination, and the leaves become personified as a result of being placed in such a position. It could be debated (in a class) as to whether they 'let go' their chlorophyll to become colourful, 'let go' the branches to fall to the ground or 'let go' in the sense of 'let their hair down'. The verb is used intransitively here, so the question of what they let go of is left open. Stylistics does help us describe more precisely how effects are achieved linguistically, but it doesn't – and shouldn't – close down the meaning potential of poems and other literature.

Another selectional restriction broken here is in 'relight autumn'. The verb 'relight' would normally be expected to occur with a concrete, and probably inanimate object. A search in the BNC reveals only 11 examples of this verb, but in each case the object was something associated with fire, such as 'his pipe', 'the candle' or 'the burner'. There were no examples of abstract objects like 'autumn' and none of the objects was even a general inanimate concrete noun like 'table' or 'house'. This, presumably, is because the verb is an intentional one: we only relight things that we want to burn. The choice here of 'relight' rather than 'light' now becomes more interesting than the semantic addition brought by the morpheme 're-' which establishes the circularity of the seasons and reminds us of the fact that autumn has been 'lit' before. What we learn by examining the collocational tendencies of this word is that 'relight' is a deliberate act and on reflection the verb 'light' is commonly used in non-animate contexts such as 'the moon lit up the trees'. The metaphor – autumn as fire – is not difficult for competent readers to see in the poem. The stylistic analysis brings some understanding of how the metaphor is constructed and what the specific effects might be in this situation.

The phrase 'scented colours' (line 4) is produced by breaking the usual collocational tendency of the adjective 'scented'. The BNC shows it as occurring almost exclusively as the modifier of words for flowers and plants. Examples include 'flowers', 'buttercups', 'roses', 'lilies', 'pine woods', 'rambler' and so on. The exceptions to this are the frequent occurrence of 'soap' and other human-made items which tend to borrow fragrance from the natural world. Also, there are occasional references to food (e.g., 'molasses') as 'scented'. What is clear from this is that the adjective 'scented' carries with it the association of its normal range of collocates, which are usually flowers. The 'colours', then, is a shorthand way of referring to the whole gamut of bedding plants that can be bought in garden centres and it has the added advantage of connecting the main senses that are attracted by bright summer flowers; sight and smell. The additional unusual collocation of these 'colours' (an abstract noun) with the verb 'are loaded' breaks the selectional restriction on that verb which normally requires it to have a concrete object (in this case the subject of a passive form). Thus the transition of the abstract noun 'colours' to having not only concrete but specific reference (to flowers) is completed by the two collocations discussed here.

Lines 5–6 have another pair of interesting collocations in the prepositional phrase (and its relative clause) 'In parks / that saw offices undress for lunch'. These are clearly broken selectional restrictions on the verbs, with 'saw' normally requiring an animate (higher animal) actor and 'undress' being restricted to human actors on the whole. The collocations here create the place (the park) as a kind of all-seeing witness to the goings-on within its borders. This is not an uncommon conceit in literature of course, but it is helpful to be able to pinpoint how it comes about. The other collocation here is metonymic, since the 'office' refers of course to the people from offices who have taken off their restrictive 'uniforms' for a lunchtime in the sun.

The second stanza also has some foregrounded examples of interesting collocations. In line 15, the swans are said to 'disprove the moon they paddle through'. Here, the swans have already been endowed with the ability to reason by being collocated with the verb 'disprove' which is normally restricted to human actors. The goal (in this case grammatical object) of the verb is also restricted to something abstract resembling an argument or a theory, and the moon is thus positioned as an idea, rather than something concrete, which of course it is in this case, being no more than a reflected image of the moon. The final collocation of interest here is the use of the verb and preposition 'paddle through' which would usually have something liquid, specifically a body of water like a lake or pond or sea, as their goal. Here, it is a solid, concrete object, the moon, which is being paddled through, except of course the other collocations have already intimated that it is not in fact the moon, but an idea of the moon (disproved) or rather an image of it. This combination of collocations, then, provides the reader with not just a scene of swans on a river disturbing the perfect reflection of the moon but with a sense that the swans have intelligence, that the moon seems to be concrete until disturbed and that it becomes not a broken image but itself becomes liquid. There may be further effects of these two lines, but the lexical combinations certainly make up the richness of the imagery here.

Later in the stanza (lines 16–17) the rowing boat is defined as 'a temptation you decline'. Here, the verb 'decline' seems to be slightly unusually collocated with 'temptation'. The BNC has no way of searching for the sense of 'decline' that is synonymous with 'reject' and the very many examples that it gives of this word form are mainly those relating to the sense of 'lowering', as in 'economic decline' or 'terminal decline'. Whilst these are not related to the sense in the poem, the argument of those researching semantic prosody is that such a common and over-whelmingly negative sense of a word is bound to affect its reception, even in other senses. This may be why there is something of a regretful or sad connotation of its use here. Moreover, the verb 'decline' is an intentional action, usually communicated to another sentient being, but here it is not an explicit 'offer' from another that is declined; rather it is an inanimate object which is portrayed as tempting the protago-nist ('you'). It is worth mentioning here, too, that 'decline' is a verb which connotes politeness and there is possibly also something old-fashioned about it. This may connect with the poem's dedication (does it reflect something of the old-fashioned gentlemanly about Stanley Cook, even though we may only recognize this through his relatively old-fashioned-sounding name?) or it may contribute to the wistful nos-talgia that seems to emanate from the poem as a whole. Again, I would remind those new to stylistics that nothing in the aim of linguistic analysis is about closing down meanings. Rather it is aimed at enhanc-ing the appreciation and understanding of the meaning potential of texts, including poems.

One of the clearest examples of a restricted collocation being evoked, but not used, is in line 19 where the protagonist is said to take 'the long cut to the car park'. Without knowledge of the very common phrase 'the short cut', this phrase would be incomprehensible, and it therefore relies on knowledge about the 'norms' of the language for us to work out that this route shares some of the features of a short cut – that is, it is a diversion from a normal route – but differs in that it is longer than the normal route. This very succinct phrase, then, manages to refer the reader to a phenomenon that is probably quite familiar, that of choos-ing a preferred route despite it being longer than the norm.

Before we look at more structural aspects of this poem, there are two more lexical items whose nature is worth considering. Though they are not collocated here in particularly striking ways, the words 'drag' and 'viscous' both seem to have meaning that goes beyond their denotation or reference. Thus, 'drag' seems to have an ominous connotation which may arise from its semantic prosody – in other words, its tendency to be used in contexts where there is a threat from drowning. Similarly, 'viscous' seems ominous, and this is confirmed by its 179 occurrences in the BNC, many of which appear to be descriptions of fictional horror events. The following is typical:

> something that could have been an eye popped loudly and viscous yellow fluid streamed down the corpse's ravaged face

In addition to these horror-related uses, the word is also used a great deal in engineering and scientific texts, with a neutral evaluation, rather than the negative one we see here. The only other, neutral, use of the word in the BNC is found in a poem by Fleur Adcock where she defines happiness in the following way:

> Too jellied, viscous, floating a condition to inspire more action than a sigh

What does all this tell us about the application of 'viscous' to the water in 'Summer Evening'? It helps to explain to readers who have a sense of unease why they might do so (perhaps they are big readers of horror?). It also tells us that a positively evaluated use is possible in poetry, since clearly Adcock's use is describing something valued highly by human beings. It leaves open the possibility that alongside the other connotations and collocations in this poem, there is something just slightly uneasy about its use here. The water is calm and peaceful, but it also threatens.

Syntax

The syntax in this poem reflects the relaxing pleasure of a summer's evening, mainly by the use of long clause elements in the final (focal) position of clauses, which being after the verbal element, can be extensive but without holding up comprehension. The first sentence illustrates this well. It is made up of an adverbial, giving the sense of regularity 'Every summer' followed immediately by the main verb 'comes'. Note that this is unusual in English where the subject would normally be expected to come before the verb. The subject is in fact postponed to the final position, after the verb, and this means that it is the focus of the sentence, and introduces the new information. It is also rather long: 'an opaque evening / before the beach is photos and the leaves let go to relight autumn'. I have assumed that the postposition of the subject means that the conjoined prepositional phrases, 'before the beach is photos and the leaves let go to relight autumn' form part of the noun phrase, defining what kind of evening it is. It would also be possible to see these phrases as further adverbials, adding to the 'every summer' of the opening as background information, though the latter analysis would normally expect there to be a comma after 'evening'. Either way, there is a long 'right-branching' tail to the structure, which means that the verb is accessed early, and the syntax is therefore relatively easy to follow. However, the long end to the sentence creates a lack of urgency in getting on to the next part of the description of this summer evening and to this extent, I would argue, is iconic of the atmosphere of this moment.

When we get to it, the next sentence is structurally, as well as semantically, a great contrast. The clause 'It's brisk in Wickes' not only has the phonological abruptness noted earlier, it is also completed very quickly, being only four words or five morphemes long. The bustle of a Do-It-Yourself store on a summer evening is portrayed by this lack of long clause elements, the quick arrival at the verb element ('s) and the single syllable words with short vowels and a cluster of plosive and fricative consonants. The shopping being carried out at the garden centre by contrast is more dreamy and relaxed. The longish subject 'the garden centre's scented colours' delays the verb 'are loaded' longer than we might expect, just as the shoppers might linger over the plants and the passive form of this verb allows the poet to not mention directly the people doing the loading, producing a relatively impressionistic view of this scene, as if seen from a distance.

Similar effects can be seen in the next sentence, where the initial adverbial 'in parks / that saw offices undress for lunch' sets the scene and delays the first obligatory clause element, the subject, 'lads' a little, almost taking up the time that an imagined camera or viewing persona might take to sweep across the park and notice the football game going on. The subject of this clause is short, so that once the 'lads' have been noted, their activity is soon recognized too. The next clause is different as it has a longish subject, 'wood after deliberate wood' which delays the resolution of the verbal element 'finds' and emphasizes the repetition of the actions in a bowling game viewed from the outside by repeating the word 'wood' rather than using a more conventional plural form such as 'woods'. The separation of the repeated noun is also iconic, of course, in reflecting the time gap that occurs between the woods being bowled.

The following sentence (lines 10–13) has a slightly unusual structure, as its grammatical subject, 'Everywhere' is more normally encountered as an adverbial, giving the setting of the main action, whereas here it is much more grammatically central to the structure and is behaving in a nominal kind of way. This means that the complement ('couples, and pushchairs / that make sense of last year or last but one') is being equated with 'everywhere', so that the people described become the place itself. Note that this sentence, like many others in this poem, arrives quickly at the verb ('is') which means that although the sentence continues for a long time after this, it is not an 'uncomfortable' read, as it might be, for example, with a string of initial adverbials or a very long subject. In this case, the complement is quite long, as we have seen, and it is followed by adverbial elements in lines 12 and 13, which might be two separate adverbials, or could be seen grammatically as one long adverbial. The reason for this ambiguity is that the second one, 'laughing like it might last', is not clearly linked to a particular antecedent. Usually, when there is a non-finite subordinate clause like this, the subject of the non-finite verbal element will be unambiguous, as in, for example: 'I could see all the people round the pub tables, laughing like it might last'. In the poem, there is no human antecedent mentioned, though the presence of human beings is implicit in the 'pubs overflow', and the syntax is ambiguous as there are a few noun phrases ('pubs', continental tables', 'main roads') which are potential antecedents within the adverbial clause structure. It is not difficult to conclude that 'pubs' is the best semantic fit, as it is also the subject of its subordinate clause and is thus higher in the structure than the other candidates.

The final adverbial, 'laughing like it might last', is wistful and introduces the first clear sign that the jolly scene being played out does not represent unalloyed happiness. I asked groups of students to paraphrase this phrase and found that on the whole they saw something either short-lived or insincere in the laughter described by this phrase. This exercise, using the student body as a testing ground of consensus in the interpretation of a poem, can be of use to demonstrate both the variation and the overlap in readers' reactions. This in itself can be helpful for the more nervous student of poetry.

The opening sentence of the second stanza, unusually for this poem, has a relatively delayed verb ('disprove') which follows the opening adverbial ('Sooner or later') and the subject ('swans on a river'). Whilst not uncomfortably late, the verb position still seems to enact the time lag that is implied by the adverbial and its anticipation makes the unusual collocation of this verb all the more foregrounded too.

The final six and a half lines (16–22) of the poem constitute the final sentence. The main clause in this sentence is over by the end of line 17, and the remaining five lines are one long adverbial subordinate clause introduced by the subordinator 'though' in line 18 and whose subject and verb are 'you imagine' at the end of line 19. There is thus some material intervening between the subordinator and the main clause elements. This material is probably best analysed as an adverbial noun phrase incorporating a reduced relative clause and an adverbial clause respectively:

- all the time (that) you walk
- taking the long cut to the car park

Notice that these are subordinate to the already subordinate clause starting at 'though'. Their semantics, which relates to time and diversion ('long cut'), is thus reflected in the delay that they create between the evident start of a clause ('though') and the subject and verb of that sentence. The final three lines of the poem add to this effect of wandering in both mind and body, by contributing the grammatical object to this subordinate clause, which consists of a three-part list:

- being out on that water
- the drag and viscous ripples as you pull
- then shipping oars and just letting it drift

This list is a combination of a noun clause, a noun phrase with another level of subordinate clause within it ('as you pull') and a pair of conjoined noun clauses in the final part. The three-part list, of course, is regularly described as being a symbolically 'complete' list, and this one, therefore, works against the otherwise endless meanderings of the syntax to bring some kind of closure to the poem.

Before we consider more contextual and cognitive aspects of the style of this poem, it is important to recognize the syntactic ambiguity that is a feature of this poem, but is also very common in other contemporary poems. I would argue that this is one of the poet's main methods for undermining the reader's impulse to define the absolute meaning of a poem. The ambiguity here is not particularly detrimental to understanding, but it possibly introduces a little uncertainty in the processing. So, for example, the two interruptions to this final subordinate clause ('all the time you walk, taking / the long cut to the car park,') have been presented above as independently qualifying the clause ('you imagine') but they could be seen as a single subordinate structure, with the latter part further subordinated to the former. The difference in meaning is slight, with 'taking the long cut' either being a modification and expansion of 'all the time you walk', or being an independent modification to the main action (imagining). The effect is similar in the mind's eye – the person (you) is either walking *whilst* taking a long way round or walking *and* taking a long way round. The combination of these possibilities is a cognitive one – the slight disorientation of the reader.

A similar effect is seen in the final three lines which I have described above as a three-part list forming the object of the verb 'imagine'. Whilst it is certain that the whole of these three lines form the object, the internal analysis could be different. The second and third parts of the list, for example, could be seen as subordinate to the first ('being out on that water'), rather than directly subordinate to the imagining itself.

It is undeniably true that for students of stylistics, syntactic analysis is the most difficult of all to grasp. This is for a number of reasons, including the fact that English grammar still presents difficulties of analysis for the most advanced scholars, but also because of these ambiguities that I have been discussing. It is unlikely that many undergraduate level students will get to the point where they can discuss all the syntax of a poem, particularly where there is a great deal of complexity, as in the last sentence discussed here. Later, I will address some of the ways in which we can get students engaging with even these harder parts of the syllabus. Before I do that, I would like to consider recent developments in stylistics which may be of help to the analysis of poetry.

Developing fields of stylistics – cognitive approaches

Other chapters in this book will address the recent exciting trend towards corpus approaches to stylistics and this is an approach which can be used towards poetry as much as any other text-type or genre. Here, however, I will focus on a development which has been applied more readily to poems than corpus methods. This is the development of a cognitive slant on stylistics, which concerns itself with theories which attempt to explain something of the process by which readers create meaning in interaction with texts. Whilst these theories inevitably produce explanations which are not open to direct observation, their development has led to some interesting collaborations between stylisticians and psychologists and has helped to counter (mostly unfounded) criticisms of stylistics on the grounds that it privileges textual meaning.

Rather than trying to introduce theories fully here, I will address them as they seem relevant to the poem analysed above. There are certain linguistic features which I haven't mentioned so far, and which align with one or other of these more reader-oriented theories.

These include the verb tenses – mainly present indicative, the very late use of the second-person pronoun 'you' (in lines 17, 19 and 21), the adverbial of time 'last year' (line 11) and place 'there' (line 17) and the use of a demonstrative adjective '*that* water' (line 20). All of these

features of the text demonstrate its deixis, which is the
that positions the reader in a particular viewpoint. So, th
especially following the iterative 'Every summer', is ar
much of what is in the poem is repeated and generic ar
to be familiar to the reader. The abundant detail appears to ᴜᴄ.
generalizing tendency, since it seems to be telling a specific story about
a particular evening. However, as is common in contemporary poems,
the general and the particular meet in the deictic centre of the poem.
Note that some of the other deictic expressions help to centre the reader
in this point of view. Thus, 'last year' confirms the reader's position in
time, which is by default within 'this year' and the distal adverbs, such
as 'the rowing boat / moored *there*' help to position the mind's eye in
the scene, but some distance (physical or psychological) from the boat
and '*that* water' uses a distal demonstrative to again distance the viewpoint (narrator/reader/combination?) from the river. Note also that
the composite narrator/reader is allowed to develop by the absence of
specific human actors in much of the poem, which makes the viewing
point seem somewhat ghostlike as it threads its way through the scenes
described without interacting with them. This narratorial viewing position is confirmed as both potentially a particular person and also the
reader (in generic mode) by the use of the ambiguous 'you' pronoun,
here seeming to indicate 'one' as a version of 'I' but also likely to draw
the reader's attention as if it were second person and thus referring to
them. For more on point-of-view, see Simpson (1993) and for an introduction to the use of deixis in stylistic analysis, see Green (1995).

The creation of a world in which the reader can be said to 'deictic shift'
(see, for example, McIntyre 2006) into different viewpoints in this way
is explained by some as creating a 'possible world' or a 'text world' (see
Werth 1999). Possible world theory is an attempt to explain how readers can interact with texts which are clearly not 'true' in any absolute
sense, and text world theory elaborated and adapted this idea to trace
the various world types that arise in complex narratives. Although they
are abstract, students can find such theories attractive in explaining the
process of reading literature. If we are not to lose the advantages of rigour
and explicitness that stylistics claims, however, it is important that students are trained to use the detailed analysis of the language, including
deixis, modality, transitivity and so on to support their descriptions of
text worlds and sub-worlds. This means being able to get into the detail
of the language and unfortunately, there is no short cut to that skill.

Schema Theory (see Semino 1997) is another borrowing from psychology to explain how we bring our world knowledge into the process

understanding texts. Thus, in the poem I have been analysing, readers' knowledge of the nature of home improvement stores and garden centres, including the way that people behave in them, is a necessary aspect of understanding the poem. Similarly, understanding something about the game of bowls, and how it is played will help us visualize the scenes described. This world-knowledge is only part of the picture of course, though a poem which is so specific in time and place might be difficult for readers to comprehend if their backgrounds provide them with significantly different schemata for summer evenings.

How to go about stylistic analysis of poems

In this section I will address some general questions about how to teach some of what I have introduced in this chapter. I will leave aside the question of whether (like me) you wish to assume that students will acquire linguistic knowledge separately and then apply it or (like Mick Short, Chapter 2 in this volume) you want to introduce linguistic knowledge as part of the teaching of stylistics. This question depends upon the kind and level of students you teach. It will, of course, have an impact on the process of teaching, but I think there are also some general techniques of teaching stylistics which can be applied to both situations.

One of the ways to enthuse students about stylistic analysis is to use exposition as a demonstration of its effectiveness. The lecture (or similar) format can be used to 'perform' an analysis of a short text. Poems of course are ideal for this purpose. A similar effect can be achieved in written form, when a single poem is analysed thoroughly. Alternatively, the lecture or written analysis can focus on one aspect of analysis, using extracts from a pool of poems that the students can develop familiarity with over the weeks. What this exposition can do is to demonstrate the kind of insights that a linguistic approach can bring. What it cannot be is the only teaching of stylistics that takes place, since the skills of analysis require hands-on experience and repeated practice to master.

Once students have been motivated to want to do stylistic analysis, I have found that it helps if the first stage in developing their skills is not analysis at all, but synthesis. Usually this is a mainly non-poetic activity, but a reminder of linguistic structures and features for those who know, or an introduction to them for those who don't. So, for example, the best way to introduce topics in phonology is to get students writing their own phrases, or paragraphs, using particular concentrations of sounds.

The final stage in a student's developing skill is analysis, and it usually helps to follow exercises encouraging synthesis with a poem where they can discover the same kinds of feature that they have just been synthesizing. I would encourage teachers to use whole poems where possible so that students can relate their observations to the context in which they occur. One way to avoid overloading them is to revisit the same poems a number of times in relation to different topics (phonology, syntax, etc.).

Here is one example of the kind of work sheet (Figure 7.1) that I have used with second-year stylistics students, in a mixed group of language and literature students. For students not already familiar with basic

---

WEEK 3: SOUNDS

'Alliteration'
1. Choose a 'manner of articulation'. Write its name down here:
2. Write down all the English consonants which use this manner - in phonemic script, of course!:
3. In pairs/groups, make a list of a lot of words with these sounds in (at the beginning, middle and end). Write them below in normal orthography:
4. Write a sentence or two using some of your words and adding other words, but keeping a high concentration of your manner of articulation. Play with effects so that your finished sentences use the sounds:

   (a) musically
   (b) symbolically

Assonance
1. Write down 6 words with long vowels. Put the phonemic symbol in brackets after the word.
2. Put the words into some kind of order or pattern (open to closed, closed to open, back vs. front etc.). The result doesn't have to make sense! Read them out loud and notice the patterning in the vowel sounds.
3. Write a sentence or two using the sounds in one of the orders (you may change the words at this stage)
4. Repeat steps. 1–3 with short vowels.
5. The sentences you have written will have musical effects as a result of the patterning of vowels. Now see if you can change some of your sentences to make the vowel patterning symbolic i.e. meaningful, in some way. (NB closed vowels = high pitch, small etc.)
6. Now look at the following poem and mark four musical and meaningful uses of sounds you find. Be prepared to explain the meaningful ones to the class.

   [*There follows a poem which is rich in phonological features.*]

Figure 7.1   Example work sheet

articulatory phonetics, a short introduction, or required reading would be helpful, and there is also scope for the tutor to help students individually whilst others get on with the exercises.

Conclusions

What I have tried to do in this chapter, using the analysis of a single poem, is to demonstrate that the detailed stylistic analysis of a poem is a very valuable way into the meaning of such a text, though all sorts of other factors, including the readers' own background and experience of reading will also play a part in any single reading process. In my own research into poetic style, I have personally moved through stages where the textual analysis was my main aim (see, for example, Jeffries 1993) to a point where I am trying to get closer to describing the reader's experience through the language of the text (see Jeffries 2000, 2001, 2008).

From my experience of teaching the stylistics of poetry to undergraduates over a number of years, I would counsel against getting into the more cognitive aspects of theory until the students have mastered some basic textual analysis. The danger of inviting students to consider how involved they are with a text or what aspects of their background knowledge are relevant to a poem's interpretation is that their ability to be as objective as possible, and certainly as rigorous as possible, will be pushed to the background. Once the skills of analysis are acquired, they are better able to explicate the ways in which text and reader's cognition can – and do – interact with each other.

Note

1. Note that in corpus studies it is often appropriate to search for strings of items that do not form units grammatically or lexically. This is one case, since the string 'the beach is' consists of subject and predicator, but no predicate itself. The term 'string' is useful as a general label for any sequence of items that is formally consistent, whether or not it is linguistically complete.

References

Adcock, F. (1991) *Time-Zones*. Oxford: Oxford University Press.
Carter, R. A. (2004) *Language and Creativity: The Art of Common Talk*. London: Routledge.
Ehrlich, V. (1965) [1955] *Russian Formalism: History and Doctrine*. The Hague: Mouton.
Green, K. (1995). *New Essays in Deixis: Discourse, Narrative, Literature*. Amsterdam: Rodopi.

Jeffries, L. (1993) *The Language of Twentieth Century Poet* Macmillan.

Jeffries, L. (2000) 'Point of view and the reader in the poet Duffy', in Jeffries, L. and Sansom, P. (eds), *Contemporary Poe Approaches*, pp. 54–68. Huddersfield: Smith-Doorstop.

Jeffries, L. (2001) 'Schema theory and White Asparagus: Cultural multilingualism among readers of texts', *Language and Literature* 10(4): 325–43.

Jeffries, L. (2006) *Discovering Language: The Structure of Modern English*. Basingstoke: Palgrave Macmillan.

Jeffries, L. (2008) 'The role of style in reader-involvement: Deictic shifting in contemporary poems', *Journal of Literary Semantics* 37(1): 69–85.

Jeffries, L. (2010a) *Opposition in Discourse*. London: Continuum.

Jeffries, L. (2010b) *Critical Stylistics*. Basingstoke: Palgrave Macmillan.

Jeffries, L. and McIntyre, D. (2010) *Stylistics*. Cambridge: Cambridge University Press.

Jeffries, L., McIntyre, D. and Bousfield, D. (eds) (2007) *Stylistics and Social Cognition*. Amsterdam: Rodopi.

Laws, S. (1993) *Darkfall*. Sevenoaks: New English Library.

Leech, G. (2008) *Language in Literature: Style and Foregrounding*. London: Pearson Education.

McIntyre, D. (2006) *Point of View in Plays: A Cognitive Stylistic Approach to Viewpoint in Drama and Other Text-types*. Amsterdam: John Benjamins.

Sansom, P. (2001) *Point of Sale*. Manchester: Carcanet.

Saussure, F. de (1959) [1916] *Course in General Linguistics*. New York: McGraw-Hill.

Semino, E. (1997) *Language and World Creation in Poems and Other Texts*. London: Longman.

Simpson, P. (1993) *Language, Ideology and Point of View*. London: Routledge.

Steen, G. J. (1994) *Understanding Metaphor in Literature: An Empirical Approach*. London: Longman.

Steen, G. J. (2007) *Finding Metaphor in Grammar and Usage*. Amsterdam: John Benjamins.

Van Peer, W. (1986) *Stylistics and Psychology: Investigations of Foregrounding*. London: Croom Helm.

Van Peer, W. (ed.) (2007) *Language and Literature, Special Issue: Foregrounding*. 16(2): 99–224.

Werth, P. (1999) *Text Worlds: Representing Conceptual Space in Discourse*. London: Longman.

8
Teaching the Stylistics of Drama

Beatrix Busse

Editors' preface

Beatrix Busse's chapter focuses on drama, traditionally the genre which has attracted the least attention from stylisticians. She introduces a number of tools particularly useful for analysing dramatic texts, as well as discussing the debate concerning what constitutes the object of study in the stylistic analysis of drama. Busse also makes suggestions about the sequence in which analytical techniques might best be introduced to students.

Introduction

Before the advent of pragmatics and sociolinguistics it was assumed that there were no stylistic tools suitable for the analysis of dramatic texts. Stylisticians were also not used to investigating pieces of texts longer than lyric poems. Moreover, spoken language – which is what is imitated in plays – was generally seen as stylistically and aesthetically debased in comparison with, for example, poetry.

  Carter (2004), among others, has addressed the latter objection by showing that the distinction between literary and non-literary language is a myth. No matter which genre is investigated, literary and non-literary language is a continuum, a cline of 'literariness'. Nevertheless, stylistic investigations of dramatic dialogue were not pursued as frequently as analyses of narrative fiction or lyric poetry until fairly recently. Now, there has developed an extensive focus on the stylistic analysis of dramatic dialogue, and, with the potential of the interdisciplinary character of stylistics firmly acknowledged, the stylistic tool kit for the analysis of dramatic dialogue has been considerably broadened, embracing, for example, pragmatic, corpus, cognitive and multimodal stylistic approaches. Among the range of topics that have been covered stylistically are, for example, the role of language in characterization (Culpeper 2002), speech acts (Short 1996, 2007a; Toolan 2000), pragmatic principles (Leech 2008 [1992]), (im-)politeness (Bousfield 2007; Culpeper 1998, 2005), key words (Culpeper 2002; Leech 2008) and specialized investigations of linguistic features or applications of modern pragmatic-stylistic approaches to explain dramatic texts originating from older stages of the English language (Busse 2007). In this chapter I focus particularly on how stylistic tools can be used in teaching to help students understand and appreciate drama, particularly drama of the Early Modern period.

Many literary critical investigations of play-texts have focused not so much on the systematic linguistic analysis of the language of plays or on performative aspects, but, for example, on themes displayed in the textual material. Stylisticians have stressed that the dramatic text itself is a more stable object of analysis than performance (Short 1981). Most recently, however, stylistic approaches to dramatic discourse have attempted to stress the importance and interplay of drama as text and performance and to enhance its systematic analysis by including the multimodality of (filmed or staged) drama as discourse (Busse 2006; Culpeper and McIntyre 2010; McIntyre 2008). This disclosure of meanings also includes the study of aesthetic questions along the roles of functional and pragmatic perspectives.

Because of stylistic approaches being hands-on, systematic, retrievable and detailed, one could argue that the studies conducted in this area carry inherent didactic implications. However, there are also a number of studies which focus explicitly on the teaching of the stylistics of drama (Boyle 1986), including those that focus on the stylistics of film and web-based stylistics. For example, Carter and Long (1991) devote attention to the teaching of the language of drama and also include such aspects as performance, reading plays and Shakespeare's dramatic works. Many of the introductions to stylistics (Short 1996, Simpson 2004, Toolan 1997) include hands-on tasks for the analysis of drama. Focusing on discourse analysis, Montoro (2007) discusses the interfaces between literature and film adaptations and their contextualized and aesthetic communicative activities in the classroom. Short's (2007b) web-based introduction to stylistics includes a section on the stylistics of drama in which a variety of interactive performative activities focus on such features as turn-taking, language, power and characterization, the realization of speech acts and so on (see also Plummer and Busse 2006; Short et al. 2006).

This chapter aims to outline and exemplify the main tenets of teaching the stylistics of drama as text and performance. It first describes some historical features which form the basis for the development of drama. This description is followed by a brief discussion of drama as text *and* performance and the importance of the theory of foregrounding. It then outlines the classic stylistic tool kit used to analyse play-texts. The final sections are devoted to more state-of-the art approaches to the analysis of play-texts. The chapter illustrates the usefulness of a corpus methodology for the investigation and teaching of play-texts. In an example analysis, it identifies the primings of the concept of *welcome* and their unusual or foregrounded collocations in the corpus of Shakespeare plays as well as exploring their meaning-making potential in the context of drama as text *and* performance. Each section will be accompanied by suggestions as to how the topic covered can be taught. The examples that I discuss could be used in seminars with students, and with this in mind the general pedagogical points that I make are exemplified through specific examples.

At a time when 'the place of literature in the foreign language classroom as custodian of style and culture, as a guide to moral good conduct, as a warrant of authenticity, or as a mirror to history is universally being questioned' (Carter 2007: x), I stress the importance of literature for language analysis, understanding and aesthetic appreciation. Due to its interdisciplinary character, stylistics (and the stylistics of drama) is particularly suited to draw on students' experiences with new representational and poetic/aesthetic/literary clines in a virtual and also multimodal world, because students become aware of the basic stylistic concept of how meaning is created in and through language and other modes in context.

To get you going – the bread and butter of (the language of) play-texts

Aristotle's *Poetics* (trans. Hubbard 1972; rpt. 1989) describes six elements that most often characterize a play. According to Aristotle, these are 'spectacle, the *mimesis* of character, plot, verbal expression, song, and the *mimesis* of intellect' with *mimesis* meaning people 'doing things' (Aristotle 1989: 52–3, my emphasis) in order to represent (i.e., imitate) life (Aristotle 1989: 59, taken from Munkelt 2010). Aristotle anticipates what is today often referred to as the multimodal character of a performance in which the words uttered by actors interrelate with their mime, gesture and voice pitch or the stage, and, in film adaptations, with the camera angle chosen; this is Bakhtin's (1984) polyphony of voices at its best, or a mega-show of modes directed at the audience.

Munkelt (2010) explains that the interpretative role of the observer is necessary and highlighted by Shakespeare. It entails active, intellectual participation. The understanding of play-texts is often facilitated when the interaction draws on conventions – linguistic, social, cultural and so on – familiar to the spectator. Of the three elements – action, speech and perception – one can be foregrounded in play-texts to varying degrees (Munkelt 2010). While Pfister (1993: xv) elevates dialogue to be the fundamental mode of presentation in play-texts and Short (1996) calls it the 'conversational genre', Munkelt (2010) somewhat heretically – though challengingly – explains 'that the generic function of action is superior to that of speech, but that speech and language lend depth to action and character in a play'.

The origins of English drama can be seen in classical play-texts as well as medieval liturgical drama (Munkelt 2010). Both have a religious base and rely on the audience's familiarity with the respective myths and stories on which they were based (Munkelt 2010). Medieval liturgical plays can be seen as transformations of a narrative into short speeches delivered in front of the altar. While medieval liturgical plays do not really show character development, Renaissance drama moved from the general to the personal, demonstrating the presentation of consciousness by characters who show emotions. Through linguistic interaction interpersonal relations are created and play-texts become mimetic (re-)presentations of life.

Without answering the question of which of the generic functions in play-texts – action or speech – is superior in stylistic analysis, it can be said that a stylistic analysis of dramatic discourse takes as fundamental the interaction between action, speech and perception because stylistics focuses on how texts and (filmed or staged) performance mean what they do in context, how meaning is created and how language, interactional strategies and characterization interact. The notion of context may, of course, include various aspects: for example, what Schiffrin (1987) has described as the physical, personal and cognitive context, or what we would generally understand as social, cultural, linguistic, authorial or editorial contexts of production and reception. Reading and watching a play are also influenced and guided by the readers'/spectators' own encyclopaedic knowledge, personal values and information about the author; that is, what Toolan describes as the 'colouring in' (2009: 7) by the reader, which also allows him or her to draw implicatures. Most recently, cognitive stylistics has further embraced the attention towards the reader/audience and focus on the cognitive processes that are at work when readers consume literature (Burke 2006; Gavins and Steen

2003; Semino and Culpeper 2002; Stockwell 2002), although, again, dramatic discourse is somewhat neglected here, especially the interplay between drama as texts and performance (see Hakemulder 2007).

In order to understand the discourse architecture of prototypical dramatic texts, Short (1996) outlines at least two different levels of discourse: one is that between playwright and reader (or audience if we are referring to a performance), the other is embedded and captures the discourse exchanged between character and character (see Figure 8.1). In a more abstract vein this, then, also alludes to the six functions of language which Jakobson (1960) elaborates on and which also have been the guiding framework for Halliday's ideas (1994, 2003). However, it remains to be discussed whether actors in a performance are the mediators of the reading material because the playwright transfers that task to them.

The constant interplay between text/performance and reader/audience and the characters or actors in dialogic interaction is a semiotic process, which creates meaning. The meaning-making and the inference of meaning is based on norms and conventions which are also built upon in dramatic dialogue and which can be exploited. Intra- and inter-textual norms need to be established by the stylistician in order to detect, for example, foregrounded usage of politeness markers, irony, satire, over-decorous greetings – that is, linguistic elements which contribute to characterization (Culpeper 2002) in plays.

It goes without saying that all works of literature, including plays, are constructed. In other words, the principles of social interaction are built upon: 'Dramatic action [...] becomes meaningful in relation to the "authenticating conventions" that are drawn from the wider world of affairs in which the dramatic activity is embedded' (Herman 1995: 6, cited in Simpson 1998: 41). This process carries a specific potential in the case of play-texts originating from older stages of the English

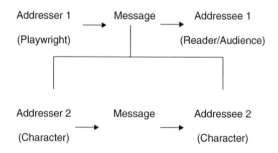

Figure 8.1 Short's (1996) model of dramatic discourse

language, because for ease of understanding it is helpful to reconstruct past communicative habits (see Busse 2010, for the challenges of a new historical stylistic approach to stylistics). Knowledge of norms and deviations or overuses of those can also be used to measure and describe staging trends and techniques as well as ways of strategies of filming.

Generally speaking, my experience in the classroom has shown that there is enormous didactic potential in the stylistics of drama, and that consequently it is a popular topic with students. As preludes to stylistic investigations, play-texts can be acted out and performances/film adaptations can be watched, although Carter and Long (1991: 124) draw our attention to the dangers of this (notably that performances are unstable objects of study). The genre is also particularly accessible to students because they can draw on their knowledge of spoken interaction in everyday communication (this is not to say that dramatic discourse is always similar to spoken conversation; in historical play-texts this is not necessarily the case). This interest is a useful starting point and helps to highlight the multi-levelled, multimodal interactive nature of drama.

The complex discoursal aspects of drama and of action, speech and perception need to be studied by students. They can be brought closer to the student by stating the obvious and drawing on their communicative realities of everyday life. For example, the concept of mimesis and representation can be introduced by asking students to collect and then describe a number of the functional interactive elements of web-based social networks, such as Facebook, or the virtual world *Second Life*. Although these platforms cannot be compared with drama on a one-to-one basis, the different clines of *mimesis* of the variety of modes interacting can be introduced through those platforms, especially because they are so frequently used by students. In Facebook, for example, users create a particular image of themselves through online connections they show with so-called friends and the language they use to communicate with them. They present themselves, which, in turn, is interpreted by onlookers and friends. Similarly, in *Second Life* users are part of a new virtual world with all its interpersonal and experiential facets. Having customized an avatar, users can connect and communicate with others, change their appearance, use different voices, buy land or even study together. In effect, *Second Life* is an interactive drama, and drawing students' attention to this can be helpful in allowing them to transfer concepts from this domain into the analysis of more conventional dramatic texts.

In order to embark on studying the specific linguistic and multimodal characteristics of particular text types, students can be asked to write a paragraph on a particular topic for a Facebook entry or for a newspaper article or a poem. This is also a good means of introducing the theory of foregrounding. Students will have recognized that there are particular norms that create or construe spoken fictional and non-fictional conversation, be it web-based or face-to-face. They will become sensitive to the fact that even what is generally considered to be close to real-life spoken interaction in dramatic discourse will have to be seen as existing on a cline of literariness. They will also recognize that there are norms and that deviations from these along with other semiotic choices are meaning-making in context. As mentioned earlier, the suggestions here are for introductory tasks, preceding systematic stylistic analysis and raising the students' awareness of general aspects of drama. However, these issues may well be taken up again in a concluding session at the end of the course.

Dramatic discourse as text and performance

The classic tool kit

This section begins with a hands-on textual analysis of four lines from a Shakespeare play. It then broadens the analysis to a reader/performance-oriented and corpus-based approach. The following example from Shakespeare's *Hamlet* (1604–5) illustrates the inherent nature of conversation as exchange.

> **King** But now, my cousin Hamlet, and my son,
> **Ham**   [Aside] A little more than kin and less than kind
> **King** How is it that the clouds still hang on you?
> **Ham**   Not so, my lord, I am too much in the sun.
>
> (*Hamlet* 1.2.64–7)

Here there are four turns by two speakers. One of these turns, as the stage directions from the edition taken – the *Riverside Shakespeare* (Evans and Tobin 1997) – informs us, is an 'aside' which conventionally indicates that it is spoken by the actor so that the audience can hear it but not the character. Further linguistic indicators mark the interactive nature of these turns: the use (and non-use) of nominal and pronominal address, such as 'my cousin Hamlet', 'my son', 'you' and 'my lord', is a case in point. The variety of lexical choices in this example illustrates what, in an earlier study (Busse 2006), I explained to be the potential of vocatives for becoming experiential, interpersonal and textual markers going beyond selecting the next speaker only. King Claudius selects a personal name, 'Hamlet', and two kinship terms 'my cousin' and 'my son'; Hamlet only resorts to the conventional title 'my lord'. Even if we did not know the social relations between Hamlet and Claudius, their choice of address formulae would – at least superficially – allow us to infer that Claudius's position is higher up the social ladder than that of Hamlet because he addresses Hamlet by his personal name and kinship terms and Hamlet resorts to the – in Early Modern English – rather neutral and generalized 'my lord'. The number of vocative forms used by each speaker and attributed to the respective addressee allows us, however, to draw the conclusion that despite Claudius's desperate attempts at gaining favour with Hamlet, Hamlet remains rather disillusioned and cynical and is not affected by these addresses. The King alludes to both of Hamlet's roles within his nuclear family: that of being the King's nephew and his son, a kinship relation which results from Claudius's marriage with Gertrude, Hamlet's mother. Hamlet's severe moral criticism of their marriage and his sadness about his father's murder is also expressed by the pun on the homophony of 'son' and 'sun', which means that he is too much in the light of the present King ('sun' being the royal emblem). This highlights the need for including contextual information in the analysis and interpretation process (Busse 2010) – here of Early Modern England and Early Modern English – which embraces what we would generally understand as social, cultural, editorial, authorial, linguistic and political.

The notion of a 'turn' is one of the central concepts of interaction, and conversation analysts of the ethnomethodological school (Sacks, Schegloff and Jefferson 1978) have illustrated that, against our expectations, in ordinary conversation turn-management is systematic and rule-governed. The order of turns depicted in the quoted example illustrates that this is the case for Shakespeare's play as well because we can see an almost regular exchange between two speakers. Yet from casual conversation we also know that there may be disequilibrium amongst speakers, for example, with the speaking-time of one interlocutor being at the expense of another's. Therefore, when analysing turn-taking management as a means of characterization and creating power relations between participants, it is important to ask who has most turns, who has the longest turns, who interrupts, who is interrupted, who allocates turns to whom, who initiates, who responds and how, who uses which kind of speech acts (like questioning, commanding, demanding on the one hand, and agreeing, giving in and apologizing on the other), who controls the topic of talk, who uses which forms of address (Short 1996, 2007b). All of these are useful questions to ask of students. As Short (1996) explains, asking small and specific questions breaks down the interpretative and analytical task for students, making it more manageable. For example, in the *Hamlet* passage, through the use of forms of address, King Claudius switches the topic and the speaker, while Hamlet undermines, though covertly, Claudius's address by the aside. If spoken to the audience, the aside would get another dimension of meanings and would realign Hamlet as a commentator in the Brechtian sense. For a more comprehensive analysis of the entire play it could be suggested that the number of words for each turn, the number of turns, the number of interruptions for each speaker could be counted in order to base the analysis on a sounder footing.

Pragmatic aspects

Grice's (1975) 'cooperative principle' assumes that conversation is goal-directed and that these goals are usually fulfilled because interlocutors attempt to be cooperative in communication. We follow the maxims of quantity (give the right amount of information), quality (do not say what you believe to be false), manner (be clear) and relation (be relevant), and ideally it is because of the observation of these maxims that conversation is successful. Yet speakers may often be indirect, ironic or polite, which – overtly or covertly – represent incidences of failing to observe one of those maxims. In order to understand the irony of Hamlet's reply in 'I'm too much in the sun', it is useful to explain how the maxim of quality is flouted on the discourse level of playwright and audience and violated on the character–character level, when seen from Claudius's perspective. Claudius must perceive Hamlet's reply as uncooperative because Hamlet does not initially confirm that he is mourning his father's death. On the contrary, his reference to the sun superficially refers to him as being allegedly in good spirits. For the audience, this utterance implies a harsh criticism of Claudius's usurpation of the throne of fatherhood, and, more importantly, shows the extent to which Claudius is held in abhorrence.

The stylistic application of Grice's (1975) 'cooperative principle' frequently goes hand in hand with the identification of politeness strategies. Among the frequently used models are Brown and Levinson's (1987) work on politeness. Claudius's choice of vocative forms is directed at both Hamlet's positive and negative face (the need to be liked and the need to be unimpeded, respectively) because their inclusive and in-group character are supposed to flatter him. At the same time, the vocatives – in initial position – represent a mitigation of the face-threatening interrogative which seems to suggest that Hamlet's grief for his deceased father should now be over. Hamlet's use of 'my lord' is formulaic, non-committal and neither addresses Claudius's public role as King or his private role as uncle and father. The form of 'my lord' is one of the most frequently used forms of address in Shakespeare's plays (Busse 2006) and also undergoes a process of semantic generalization.

What are further possible strategies for teaching the 'cooperative principle' and politeness theory in relation to the *Hamlet* example? It is clear that their theoretical base has to be taught to students at some point and that students have to be given time to read about the major tenets of these theories for themselves. Therefore, my advice would be to begin with the hands-on analysis of the example itself, ask the students to read out loud or even act out the drama, have them write down their initial impressions of the text and provide them with enough linguistic and literary knowledge to understand the exchanges within an Early Modern English context. To fulfil this task, enough time has to be attributed because students need to overcome their focus on pronouncing the passages correctly when acting them or reading them out loud so that they can concentrate on the linguistic and performative effects of the text. I asked my own students to rewrite the *Hamlet* exchange into Modern English in order to simply show their understanding of this exchange and to raise their awareness of the stylistic notion of meaning as choice. It was only then that I began with a more detailed introduction of the theoretical frameworks employed.

Further interactive stylistic tools

The incorporation of different specific analytical frameworks to the analysis of the stretch from Shakespeare's *Hamlet* implies the need for a *comprehensive* investigation of dramatic discourse that is not restricted to one particular perspective only. It is also important to observe that linguistic texture and other semiotic modes always involve a cognitive dimension. The meaning-making process always comprises an interaction between the text and the audience. Cognitive stylistic (or cognitive poetic) approaches try to answer questions such as how readers or spectators process literature, for example 'what do people do when they read?' and 'what happens to people when they read?' (Burke 2006: 218). Approaches that are generally drawn on and have their base in cognitive linguistics or cognitive psychology are blending theory (Dancygier 2005, 2006), conceptual/cognitive metaphor theory (Steen 1994), contextual frame theory (Emmott 1997), schema theory (Cook 1994; Semino 1997), deictic shift theory (McIntyre 2006) and text world theory (Gavins 2007; Werth 1999).

Every interactive event involves, for example, an activation of schemas we draw on in order to make sense of it. Schemas embrace background knowledge that has been accumulated about a particular domain in life or a particular aspect of the world. Covering a cognitive notion, scripts, which are particular kinds of schemas, then 'handle stylized everyday situations [… a] script is a predetermined, stereotyped sequence of actions that define a well-known situation' (Schank and Abelson 1977: 41). According to Schank and Abelson schemas/scripts consist of a number of slots which need to be filled with a variety of elements. The two main processes involved in the activation of schemas or scripts are known as bottom-up or stimulus-driven processes and top-down or conceptually-driven processes. In the former, the linguistic texture activates a mental world. These triggers are called headers (Rumelhart and Ortony 1977: 128). Conceptually driven processes are then able to mobilize the multitude of background knowledge of which the reader is already in possession.

As readers of the passage from *Hamlet* we have to rely on our own reconstructions of the past and the meanings of past stages of the English language displayed in the example, because it is no longer possible to ask a contemporary audience. But Suzanne Romaine (1982) offers a way out of that dilemma. By invoking what she calls the 'uniformitarian principle' she stresses that 'we accept that the linguistic forces which operate today and are observable around us are not unlike those which have operated in the past' (Romaine 1982: 122). Therefore, we can activate our own knowledge and argue, for example, that forms of address like Claudius's 'cousin' and 'son', which are supposed to serve as headers, activate the family schema, which then immediately evokes the kinship relations between father and mother, uncle and aunt, as well as a certain (ideally happy) image of a family. However, this header also preconditions a 'natural' father-role, which, as we know, Claudius cannot fulfil because he has only appropriated fatherhood through an overhasty marriage. Therefore, it is here where the violation of the existent family schema takes place and where the audience is able to understand that both Hamlet's aside and his reply to Claudius must be ironic. As such, it is also necessary to discuss the extent to which play-texts (and screenplays; see McIntyre 2008) contain inherent information about the ways in which a particular scene needs to be performed (filmed or staged) (Busse 2006). In my 2006 study, for example, I argue that vocative forms can serve as stage directions or as a stage-directing device (Busse 2006: 413ff.).

This cognitive dimension is even further enhanced by other modes that are used and constructed in dramatic discourse as performance. These relate, for example, to the intonation, gestures, body movement and posture actors may be using in uttering those words, and the costumes they are wearing, and also to scenery as well as lighting. More specifically, it may involve the ways in which Claudius phonologically introduces his selection of Hamlet as his new addressee and how the audience perceives this: for example, will Claudius change his body movement or his voice, as indeed he does in a recording with Derek Jacobi as Claudius and Kenneth Branagh as Hamlet by the Renaissance Theatre Company (Lancaster 1992)? How, on the stage (in the round theatre), will Hamlet physically indicate, for example – through mimic, gesture and body movement – that 'A little more than kin and less than kind' is an aside? In the recording just mentioned, he whispers those lines. For teaching purposes, it also turns out to be highly interesting to the students to investigate entries from prompt books. Particular scenes can be further illustrated with the help of production postcards (provided, for example, by the RSC) or photographs. Indeed, it is necessary to discuss what the interplay is between the printed text, the screenplay and the performance or the film. In Illustration 8.1, for example, the welcome scene of the new king is displayed as a huge and pompous gathering at court with Gertrude and Claudius in the front of the stage. Hamlet is not part of this display of regal power but stands on the left-hand side, dressed in black and turning away from the couple. The ghost of Hamlet's father is symbolized through the soldier figure, which darkens the scene and overpowers it from behind possibly as a reminder of death and murder and as an icon and symbol of ideal fatherhood and kingship, which is multimodally directed at the audience to remind them of the crimes committed.

In Illustration 8.2, Hamlet (Kenneth Branagh) is heckled by Claudius and Gertrude, who surround him. To keep up appearances the newlywed couple wear white clothes while Hamlet is dressed in black. The diametrically opposed colours of their dress not only visualize Hamlet's melancholy (one of the four humours usually portrayed in black, but also alluding to his outfit referred to in the text as 'inky cloak') and the farce of the purity of marriage between Gertrude and Claudius, but also represent the staged texts multimodally. These images are one way of highlighting the performative aspects of dramatic discourse. They can also be used as starting points for a stylistic analysis. In addition, it is important to have students watch a number of different productions so that they understand that performances may vary although they may use the same printed text. This can also prefigure a discussion of the relative stability of texts and performances as objects of study, and of the methodological difficulties that can ensue when analysing performance stylistically.

Corpus-based approaches to the analysis of play-texts

Claudius's address to Hamlet can also be seen as a way of avoiding a (conventional) greeting formula. Although this is the first time he

Illustration 8.1 Hamlet by Shakespeare; set design: John Gunter, costumes: Liz da Costa, director: Richard Eyre. Front left centre: Daniel Day-Lewis (Hamlet), centre, making an entrance: Judi Dench (Gertrude), John Castle (Claudius). Olivier Theatre/National Theatre, London SE1, 16 March 1989. Photo Reg Wilson

Illustration 8.2 Hamlet, 1992, directed by Adrian Noble, designed by Bob Crowley. Claudius (John Shrapnel), Hamlet (Kenneth Branagh), Gertrude (Jane Lapotaire), RSC. Photo Reg Wilson

speaks to Hamlet – he has spoken to everybody else before – he does not welcome him in the same way that he welcomes, for example, Laertes in 'And now, Laertes, what's the news with you?' (*Ham.* 1.2.42) a few lines earlier. Claudius does not establish phatic communion to get the conversation going but immediately begins *in medias res*.

The following section illustrates linguistic realizations of the expressive speech act of a greeting in Shakespeare's plays by focusing mainly on the *welcome* schema. This section will illustrate how Hoey's (2005) corpus-based theory of lexico-grammatical priming can be applied to older stages of the English language to illustrate the meaning-making interplay between lexis and grammar in the context of dramatic discourse. At the same time, I will illustrate more specifically the extent to which the analysis and interpretation of elements allegedly restricted to the phatic only, may in dramatic discourse carry interpersonal and textual potential because of the complex multi-levelled interplay between norms and deviations from those norms.

I suggest that teachers might begin with the analysis of examples first before the corpus-stylistic framework of this section is outlined in general and Hoey's (2005) theory and its applicability to dramatic dialogue is explained in particular. In order to introduce students to what a *welcome* schema entails I start with either playing or singing the first stanza of the welcome song from the musical *Cabaret*.

> Willkommen, bienvenue, welcome!
> Fremde, étrangers, strangers.
> Glücklich zu sehen, je suis enchanté,
> Happy to see you, bleibe, reste, stay.
> Willkommen, bienvenue, welcome
> Im Cabaret, au Cabaret, to Cabaret

> (Allen, Jay P. 'Willkommen', *Cabaret*, 1972)

In a brainstorming session students will be asked to reflect upon the conditions of a welcoming scene in terms of the presence of a host, visitors, a particular occasion. In the conventional schema of a welcoming scene, the host is familiar with the place while the people he welcomes are strangers. Usually, the situation of a welcome is a happy occasion, because a visitor or a stranger may have received an invitation, or may just be attracted by the special events that take place.

This introductory section to the *welcome* schema could then continue with a more detailed discussion of the linguistic characteristics of the type *welcome*, that is, the parts of speech it may take on, its syntactic and pragmatic functions and the accompanying constituents. Students can be introduced to the etymological base of *welcome* through a first glance at the lemmata (i.e., base forms) of *welcome* in the *Oxford English Dictionary* (*OED*). They will see that the *OED* displays four lemmata – two verbs, one noun and another noun out of which the interjection and the adjective emerge. They can be set the task of studying the etymology of 'welcome, n1, int., and a'. in order to understand the etymological relatedness of *welcome* in French (*bienvenue*), German (*willkommen*) and English (*welcome*) that are used in the stanzas from *Cabaret* to address the strangers. The students will learn that Old English *wilcuma* was also under influence from Old French *bienvenu* and that 'parallel developments appear in the cognate languages [...]' (*OED* 1.), such as Middle Low German, for example. Such a task exemplifies the necessity of linguistic contextual information in the study of older types of drama.

The next section aims at a systematic investigation of the use of *welcome* in the Shakespeare corpus. Students can be given a sample of collocations of *welcome* taken from Spevack's (1968–80) concordances as illustrated in Figure 8.2.

The concordance entry illustrates a sample of lines for *welcome* in the Shakespeare plays, with specific information about the right and left contexts of *welcome* and the plays in which these lines occur. Students should learn from this that *welcome* appears 338 times in the Shakespeare corpus with a relative frequency of 0.0427, which means it is not a high-frequency item like the definite article *the* or the auxiliary *must*.

As soon as the students read through those examples, it should be clear to them that the concordance entries of *welcome* cover different word classes, such as noun and adjective in predicative and attributive usage, and that the concordance lines reflect the type (i.e., the schema) *welcome* but not the respective parts of speech. For the purpose of what I would like to outline, the fact that I do not deal with a concordance of *welcome* which is tagged or sorted according to parts of speech is not crucial at the moment. The focus here is on identifying the primings, that is, repetitive lexico-grammatical patterns, as well as functions that *welcome* may take on in the contexts of the dialogues exhibited in Shakespeare's plays.

For the investigation of the semantic, syntactic and pragmatic associations of *welcome*, students can be asked to perform a more detailed and systematic analysis and answer the following questions, which are based on the concordance lines taken from Spevack (1968–80):

(a) Describe the word classes in which *welcome* may appear and the elements it collocates with (use of adverbs, use of forms of address).
(b) Describe the contextual situation

The students' answers can be supported and verified with the help of the *OED* entries. These describe, for example, the adjectival use of the construction *welcome to* via recourse to the *OED* 'n1, int. and a'. (1.B.), in which the predicative usage of *welcome* is described as passing into an adjective. I would also expect them to understand the frequent co-occurrence of address forms – as in 'Gentlemen, you are welcome to Elsinore' (*Hamlet*. 2.2.370) – with *welcome to* and a reference to a place or a spatial adverbial. The attributive usage of welcome in 'And he hath brought us smooth and welcome news' (*Henry IV Part 1*, 1.1.66) should equally be recognized.

It is not at this stage that Hoey's (2005) concept of lexical priming should be introduced because students should first get used to the analysis of the co-text of words and their contextual functions. The following examples from Shakespeare's plays can be presented to the students as a printed text and as an audio file.

(a) *King Lear* (1605)
   Lear: You are welcome hither.
                    (*Lr.* 5.3.290)

(b) *Hamlet* (1600)
   Hamlet: Gentlemen, you are welcome to Elsinore.
                    (*Ham.* 2.2.370)

(c) *King Edward III* (1595)
   Countess: O happy comfort, welcome to our house!
                    (*E3* 1.2.74)

(d) *Love's Labour's Lost* (1594)
   King: Fair Princess, welcome to the court of Navarre.
                    LLL (2.1.90)

Here it should be stressed that the constructions in (a) and (b) are similar to those encountered so far. The grammatical realizations are the following:

Verb *to be* + *welcome* (adj.) + *to* + noun indicating a place

or

Verb *to be* + *welcome* (adj.) + adverbial of space

```
WEIGHT                                   THE COMPLETE WORKS                                   WELCOME

  STOOP WITH OPPRESSION OF THEIR PRODIGAL WEIGHT:          3.04.'31
  I NEED NO MORE WEIGHT THAN MINE OWN BOWELS.         1H4 5.03. 35P
  LEND TO THIS WEIGHT SUCH LIGHTNESS WITH THEIR       2H4 1.01.122
  THE WEIGHT OF A HAIR WILL TURN SCALES BETWEEN           2.04.253P
  HIM, OF SOME THINGS OF WEIGHT | THAT TASK OUR       H5  1.02.  5
  MERIT, | ACCORDING TO THE WEIGHT AND WORTHINESS.        2.02. 35
  WHICH IN WEIGHT TO RE-ANSWER, HIS PETTINESS             3.06.128P
  I MEAN, IN BEARING WEIGHT OF GOVERNMENT, | WHILE 3H6 4.06. 51
  THOU ART NO ATLAS FOR SO GREAT A WEIGHT:                5.01. 36
  AND HEAVE IT SHALL SOME WEIGHT, OR BREAK MY BACK        5.07. 24
  AND STILL, AS YOU ARE WEARY OF THIS WEIGHT,         R3  1.02. 31
  SUDDENLY AN ANSWER | IN SUCH A POINT OF WEIGHT,     H8  3.01. 71
  THERE WAS THE WEIGHT THAT PULL'D ME DOWN.               3.02.407
  LAY ALL THE WEIGHT YE CAN UPON MY PATIENCE, | I         5.02.101
  OF THEIR OBSERVANT TOIL THE ENEMIES' WEIGHT --      TRO 1.03.203
  MIGHT BE AFFRONTED WITH THE MATCH AND WEIGHT            3.02.166
  SCRUPLE | OF HER CONTAMINATED CARRION WEIGHT,           4.01. 72
  LOVE, | SO MUCH BY WEIGHT HATE | HER DIOMED.            5.02.168
  THY MADNESS SHALL BE PAID WITH WEIGHT | /TILL       HAM 4.05.157
  THE WEIGHT OF THIS SAD TIME WE MUST OBEY,           LR  5.03.324
  IT SHALL BE FULL OF POISE AND DIFFICULT WEIGHT,     OTH 3.03. 82
  THOUGH THOU DENY ME A MATTER OF MORE WEIGHT:        ANT 1.02. 69P
  WE DO BEAR | SO GREAT WEIGHT IN HIS LIGHTNESS.          1.04. 25
  O HAPPY HORSE, TO BEAR THE WEIGHT OF ANTONY!            1.05. 21
  THE WEIGHT WE MUST CONVEY WITH 'S WILL PERMIT,          3.01. 36
  GONE INTO HEAVINESS, | THAT MAKES THE WEIGHT.           4.15. 34
  AND YOU BEAR IT | AS ANSWERING TO THE WEIGHT.           5.02.102
  HOW MUCH THE QUANTITY, THE WEIGHT AS MUCH, | AS     CYM 4.02. 17
  UPON THIS MIGHTY MORR-- -- OF MICKLE WEIGHT --      TNK 3.05.118
  NEVER FAINTING | UNDER THE WEIGHT OF ARMS;              4.02.130
  BY A HALFPENNY LOAF A DAY, TROY WEIGHT.             STM II.C.  7P
  ONCE SET ON RINGING, WITH HIS OWN WEIGHT GOES:      LUC     1494
  PLODS /DULLY ON, TO BEAR THAT WEIGHT IN ME, | AS SON     50. 6
WEIGHTIER                     3 FREQ  0.0003 REL FR     3 V       0 P
  IN WEIGHTIER THINGS YOU'LL SAY A BEGGAR NAY.        R3  3.01.119
  TO YOUR EAR | MUCH WEIGHTIER THAN THIS WORK.        H8  5.01. 18
  CONTAIN THEE, | ATTEND OUR WEIGHTIER JUDGMENT.      TIM 3.05.101
WEIGHTLESS                    1 FREQ  0.0001 REL FR     1 V       0 P
  THAT LIGHT AND WEIGHTLESS DOWN | PERFORCE MUST      2H4 4.05. 33
WEIGHTS                       2 FREQ  0.0002 REL FR     2 V       0 P
  WHAT PASSION HANGS THESE WEIGHTS UPON MY TONGUE? AYL 1.02.257
  FROM WHOSE SO MANY WEIGHTS OF BASENESS CANNOT       CYM 3.05. 88
WEIGHTY                      13 FREQ  0.0014 REL FR    13 V       0 P
  SUFFICETH MY REASONS ARE BOTH GOOD AND WEIGHTY.     SHR 1.01.248
  MADE ME ACQUAINTED WITH A WEIGHTY CAUSE | OF            4.04. 26
  DID LOOK NO BETTER TO THAT WEIGHTY CHARGE.          1H6 2.01. 62
  THIS WEIGHTY BUSINESS WILL NOT BROOK DELAY,         2H6 1.01.170
  WITH THY CONFEDERATES IN THIS WEIGHTY CAUSE.            1.02. 86
  WHAT COUNSEL GIVE YOU IN THIS WEIGHTY CAUSE?            3.01.289
  WITH LIES WELL STEEL'D WITH WEIGHTY ARGUMENTS,      R3  1.01.148
  NOW | THAT BEAR A WEIGHTY AND A SERIOUS BROW,       H8  PR  .  2
  THIS SECRET IS SO WEIGHTY, 'TWILL REQUIRE | A           2.01.144
  THERE YE SHALL MEET ABOUT THIS WEIGHTY BUSINESS.        2.02.139
  HOW YOU STAND MINDED IN THE WEIGHTY DIFFERENCE          3.01. 58
  WORDS CANNOT CARRY | AUTHORITY SO WEIGHTY.              3.02.234
  THE COMMON EYE | FOR SUNDRY WEIGHTY REASONS.        MAC 3.01.125
WEIRD                         6 FREQ  0.0006 REL FR     5 V       1 P
  THE WEIRD SISTERS, HAND IN HAND, | POSTERS OF       MAC 1.03. 32
  BEFORE, THESE WEIRD SISTERS SALUTED ME, AND             1.05.  8P
  I DREAMT LAST NIGHT OF THE THREE WEIRD SISTERS:         2.01. 20
  AS THE WEIRD WOMEN PROMIS'D, AND I FEAR | THOU          3.01.  2
  (AND BETIMES I WILL) TO THE WEIRD SISTERS.              3.04.132
  SAW YOU THE WEIRD SISTERS?                              4.01.136
WELCOM'D                      5 FREQ  0.0005 REL FR     4 V       1 P
  FROM HOME, WELCOM'D HOME WITH IT WHEN I RETURN:     ERR 4.04. 36P
  HER SISTER KATHERINE WELCOM'D YOU WITHAL?           SHR 3.01.  3
  WELCOM'D ALL, SERV'D ALL:                           WT  4.04. 57
  TYRE, | WELCOM'D AND SETTLED TO HIS OWN DESIRE.     PER 4.CH.  2
  WELL WAS HE WELCOM'D BY THE ROMAN DAME, | WITHIN LUC          51
/WELCOME                      1 FREQ  0.0001 REL FR     1 V       0 P
  /BUT /THAT'S /NO /WELCOME.                          TRO 4.05.165
WELCOME                     378 FREQ  0.0427 REL FR   326 V      52 P
  THEE AND THY COMPANY I BID | A HEARTY WELCOME.      TMP 5.01.111
  WELCOME, MY FRIENDS ALL!                                5.01.125
  WELCOME, SIR;                                           5.01.165
  WELCOME HIM THEN ACCORDING TO HIS WORTH --          TGV 2.04. 83
  WELCOME, DEAR PROTEUS!                                  2.04.100
  CONFIRM HIS WELCOME WITH SOME SPECIAL FAVOR.            2.04.101
  HIS WORTH IS WARRANT FOR HIS WELCOME HITHER,            2.04.102
  YOU ARE WELCOME TO A WORTHLESS MISTRESS.                2.04.113
  THAT YOU ARE WELCOME?                                   2.04.115
  ONCE MORE, NEW SERVANT, WELCOME;                        2.04.118
  LAUNCE, BY MINE HONESTY, WELCOME TO /MILAN.             2.05.  1P
  NOT THYSELF, SWEET YOUTH, FOR I AM NOT WELCOME.         2.05.  4P
  NOR NEVER WELCOME TO A PLACE TILL SOME CERTAIN          2.05.  5P
  SHOT BE PAID AND THE HOSTESS SAY "WELCOME."             2.05.  7P
  OF LOVE, | WARRANT ME WELCOME TO MY PROTEUS.            2.07. 71
  YOUR GRACE IS WELCOME TO A MAN DISGRAC'D,               5.04.123
  WIFE, BID THESE GENTLEMEN WELCOME.                  WIV 1.01.194P
  SUCH /BROOKS ARE WELCOME TO ME, THAT O'ERFLOWS           2.02.151P
  YOU'RE WELCOME.                                         2.02.158P
  HE'S WELCOME.                                           3.01. 28P
  AS I AM A TRUE SPIRIT, WELCOME!                         5.05. 29P
  Y' ARE WELCOME;                                     MM  2.02. 26
  COME IN, THE WISH DESERVES A WELCOME.                   3.01. 45
  AND VERY WELCOME.                                       3.01. 49
  WELCOME, HOW AGREED?                                    4.01. 64
  WELCOME, FATHER.                                        4.02. 72
  GAVE HEALTHFUL WELCOME TO THEIR SHIPWRACK'D         ERR 1.01.114
  THAT NEVER TOUCH WELL WELCOME TO THY HAND,              2.02.116
  ANSWER MY GOOD WILL AND YOUR GOOD WELCOME HERE.         3.01. 20
  YOUR DAINTIES CHEAP, SIR, AND YOUR WELCOME DEAR.        3.01. 21
  A TABLE FULL OF WELCOME MAKES SCARCE ONE DAINTY         3.01. 23
  AND WELCOME MORE COMMON, FOR THAT'S NOTHING BUT         3.01. 25
  CHEER AND GREAT WELCOME MAKES A MERRY FEAST.            3.01. 26
  HERE IS NEITHER CHEER, SIR, NOR WELCOME:                3.01. 66
  AT THE DOOR, MASTER, BID THEM WELCOME HITHER.           3.01. 68
  AND TO THAT END, SIR, I WILL WELCOME YOU.               4.04. 17
  LET ME BID YOU WELCOME, MY LORD, BEING              ADO 1.01.154P
  WELCOME, SIGNIOR, YOU ARE ALMOST COME TO PART           5.01.113P

  AND THEREFORE WELCOME THE SOUR CUP OF PROSPERITY LLL 1.01.313P
  FAIR PRINCESS, WELCOME TO THE COURT OF NAVARRE.         2.01. 90
  YOU BACK AGAIN, AND "WELCOME" I HAVE NOT YET.           2.01. 91P
  AND WELCOME TO THE WIDE FIELDS TOO BASE TO BE           2.01. 93P
  YOU SHALL BE WELCOME, MADAM, TO MY COURT.               2.01. 95
  I WILL BE WELCOME THEN -- CONDUCT ME THITHER.           2.01. 96
  MEAN TIME RECEIVE SUCH WELCOME AT MY HAND | AS          2.01.168
  O, YOU ARE WELCOME, SIR, ADIEU.                         2.01.213
  FAREWELL TO ME, SIR, AND WELCOME TO YOU.                2.01.214
  WELCOME, PURE WIT!                                      5.02.484
  WELCOME, MARCADE, | BUT THAT THOU INTERRUPTEST          5.02.716
  WELCOME, WANDERER.                                  MND 2.01.247
  WELCOME, GOOD ROBIN.                                    4.01. 46
  HAVE BROKE OFF, | NOT PAYING ME A WELCOME.              5.01. 99
  OUT OF THIS SILENCE YET I PICK'D A WELCOME:             5.01.100
  I COULD BID THE FIFT WELCOME WITH SO GOOD HEART  MV  1.02.127P
  THEN FAREWELL HEAT, AND WELCOME FROST!                  2.07. 75
  LORENZO AND SALERIO, WELCOME HITHER, | IF THAT          3.02.220
  INT'REST HERE | HAVE POWER TO BID YOU WELCOME.          3.02.222
  FRIENDS AND COUNTRYMEN, | SWEET PORTIA, WELCOME.        3.02.224
  SO DO I, MY LORD, | THEY ARE ENTIRELY WELCOME.          3.02.225
  NERISSA, CHEER YOND STRANGER, BID HER WELCOME.          3.02.237
  BID YOUR FRIENDS WELCOME, SHOW A MERRY CHEER --         3.02.312
  YOU ARE WELCOME, TAKE YOUR PLACE.                       4.01.170
  THIS DEED WILL BE WELL WELCOME TO LORENZO.              4.02.  4
  SOME WELCOME FOR THE MISTRESS OF THE HOUSE.             5.01. 38
  DEAR LADY, WELCOME HOME!                                5.01.113
  YOU ARE WELCOME HOME, MY LORD.                          5.01.132
  GIVE WELCOME TO MY FRIEND:                              5.01.133
  SIR, YOU ARE VERY WELCOME TO OUR HOUSE.                 5.01.139
  GRIEVE NOT YOU, YOU ARE WELCOME NOTWITHSTANDING.        5.01.239
  ANTONIO, YOU ARE WELCOME, | AND I HAVE BETTER           5.01.273
  AND IN MY VOICE MOST WELCOME SHALL YOU BE.          AYL 2.04. 87
  SIT DOWN AND FEED, AND WELCOME TO OUR TABLE.            2.07.105
  WELCOME.                                                2.07.167
  WELCOME, FALL TO.                                       2.07.171
  LIVING IN YOUR FACE, | BE TRULY WELCOME HITHER.         2.07.195
  MAN, | THOU ART RIGHT WELCOME AS THY /MASTER IS.        2.07.198
  GOOD MY LORD, BID HIM WELCOME.                          5.04. 40P
  O MY DEAR NIECE, WELCOME THOU ART TO ME!                5.04.147
  EVEN DAUGHTER, WELCOME, IN NO LESS DEGREE.              5.04.148
  WELCOME, YOUNG MAN;                                     5.04.166
  NOW, FELLOWS, YOU ARE WELCOME.                      SHR IN.1. 79
  AND GIVE THEM FRIENDLY WELCOME EVERY ONE.               IN.1.103
  MASTER, SOME SHOW TO WELCOME US TO TOWN,                1.01. 47
  HOUSE AND PLY HIS BOOK, WELCOME HIS FRIENDS,            1.01.196
  Y' ARE WELCOME, SIR, AND HE, FOR YOUR GOOD SAKE.        2.01. 61
  I KNOW HIM WELL; YOU ARE WELCOME FOR HIS SAKE.          2.01. 70
  WELCOME, GOOD CAMBIO.                                   2.01. 84P
  I MAY HAVE WELCOME 'MONGST THE REST THAT WOO,           2.01. 96
  YOU ARE VERY WELCOME, SIR.                              2.01.105
  YOU ARE PASSING WELCOME, | AND SO I PRAY YOU ALL        2.01.112
  YOU ARE WELCOME, SIR.                                   3.02. 88
  WELCOME HOME, GRUMIO!                                   4.01.106P
  WELCOME, YOU;                                           4.01.111P
  ARE THOSE" -- | SIT DOWN, KATE, AND WELCOME.            4.01.142
  COME, KATE, AND WASH, AND WELCOME HEARTILY.             4.01.154
  YOU ARE WELCOME.                                        4.02. 72
  WELCOME!                                                4.04. 70
  I THINK I SHALL COMMAND YOUR WELCOME HERE:              5.01. 12
  MY FAIR BIANCA, BID MY FATHER WELCOME, | WHILE I        5.02.  4
  WHILE I WITH SELF-SAME KINDNESS WELCOME THINE.          5.02.  5
  FEAST WITH THE BEST, AND WELCOME TO MY HOUSE.           5.02.  8
  YOU ARE WELCOME ALL.                                    5.02. 48
  WELCOME TO PARIS.                                   AWW 1.02. 22
  WELCOME, COUNT, | MY SON'S NO DEARER.                   1.02. 75
  REST | UNQUESTION'D WELCOME AND UNDOUBTED BLEST.        2.01.208
  WELCOME SHALL THEY BE:                                  3.01. 19
  Y' ARE WELCOME, GENTLEMEN.                              3.02. 91
  LORD THE KING, | WE'LL BE BEFORE OUR WELCOME.           4.04. 14
  TO WHOSE TRUST | YOUR BUSINESS WAS MORE WELCOME.        4.04. 16
  THE BITTER PAST, MORE WELCOME IS THE SWEET.             5.03.334
  WELCOME, ASS. NOW LET'S HAVE A CATCH.               TN  2.03. 18P
  YOUR MISDEMEANORS, YOU ARE WELCOME TO THE HOUSE:        2.03. 99P
  O, WELCOME, FATHER!                                     5.01.150
  AND SAY, "THRICE WELCOME, DROWNED VIOLA!"               5.01.241
  THOU LOV'ST US, SHOW IN OUR BROTHER'S WELCOME:      WT  1.02.174
  YOU BID | THESE UNKNOWN FRIENDS TO 'S WELCOME,          4.04. 65
  ON, | AND BID US WELCOME TO YOUR SHEEP-SHEARING,        4.04. 69
  SIR, WELCOME.                                           4.04. 70
  YOU'RE WELCOME, SIR.                                    4.04. 72
  BE TO YOU BOTH, | AND WELCOME TO OUR SHEARING!          4.04. 77
  Y' ARE VERY WELCOME.                                    4.04.108
  PLEAS'D WITH MADNESS, | DO BID IT WELCOME.              4.04.485
  MOST DEARLY WELCOME!                                    5.01.130
  WELCOME HITHER, | AS IS THE SPRING TO TH' EARTH.        5.01.151
  EMBRACE HIM, LOVE HIM, GIVE HIM WELCOME HITHER.     JN  2.01. 11
  I GIVE YOU WELCOME WITH A POWERLESS HAND, | BUT         2.01. 15
  WELCOME BEFORE THE GATES OF ANGIERS, DUKE.              2.01. 17
  LET THEM BE WELCOME THEN, WE ARE PREPAR'D.              2.01. 83
  AND WILL NOT LET ME WELCOME THIS GOOD NEWS.             5.03. 15
  AND WELCOME HOME AGAIN DISCARDED FAITH.                 5.04. 12
  AND WHAT HEAR THERE FOR WELCOME BUT MY GROANS?      R2  1.02. 70
  RETURN WITH WELCOME HOME FROM BANISHMENT.               1.03.212
  WHY I SHOULD WELCOME SUCH A GUEST AS GRIEF,             2.02.  7
  WELCOME, MY LORDS.                                      2.03. 59
  NOR FRIENDS, NOR FOES, TO ME WELCOME YOU ARE:           2.03.170
  MORE WELCOME IS THE STROKE OF DEATH TO ME | THAN        3.01. 31
  WELCOME, MY LORD.                                       3.02. 63
  WELCOME, HARRY.                                         3.03. 20
  HIS NOBLE COUSIN IS RIGHT WELCOME HITHER, | AND         3.03.122
  WELCOME, BULLINGBROOK!"                                 5.02. 17
  NO JOYFUL TONGUE GAVE HIM HIS WELCOME HOME,             5.02. 29
  WELCOME, MY SON!                                        5.02. 46
  WELCOME, MY LORD, WHAT IS THE NEWS?                     5.06.  5
  AND HE HATH BROUGHT US SMOOTH AND WELCOME NEWS.  1H4 1.01. 66
  SHILLINGS AND SIXPENCE," AND "YOU ARE WELCOME,"         2.04. 26P
  WELCOME, JACK, WHERE HAST THOU BEEN?                    2.04.113P
  MY COUSIN VERNON, WELCOME, BY MY SOUL!                  4.01. 86
  PRAY GOD MY NEWS BE WORTH A WELCOME, LORD.              4.01. 87

                                        -3816-
```

Figure 8.2 Concordance lines for *welcome* in the Shakespeare Corpus (Spevack 1968–80)

WELCOME — THE COMPLETE WORKS — WELCOME

<table>
<tr><td>HE SHALL BE WELCOME TOO.</td><td></td><td>4.01. 94</td></tr>
<tr><td>WELCOME, SIR WALTER BLUNT:</td><td></td><td>4.03. 32</td></tr>
<tr><td>HOME, | MY FATHER GAVE HIM WELCOME TO THE SHORE:</td><td></td><td>4.03. 59</td></tr>
<tr><td>WELCOME, ANCIENT PISTOL.</td><td>2H4</td><td>2.04.111P</td></tr>
<tr><td>BY MY TROTH, WELCOME TO LONDON.</td><td></td><td>2.04.292P</td></tr>
<tr><td>LIGHT FLESH AND CORRUPT BLOOD, THOU ART WELCOME.</td><td></td><td>2.04.295P</td></tr>
<tr><td>WELCOME, GOOD SIR JOHN.</td><td></td><td>3.02. 84P</td></tr>
<tr><td>YOUR GOOD WORSHIP IS WELCOME.</td><td></td><td>3.02. 91P</td></tr>
<tr><td>DID WITH THE LEAST AFFECTION OF A WELCOME | GIVE</td><td></td><td>4.05.172</td></tr>
<tr><td>KIND MASTER BARDOLPH, AND WELCOME, MY TALL</td><td></td><td>5.01. 58P</td></tr>
<tr><td>MYSELF | TO WELCOME THE CONDITION OF THE TIME,</td><td></td><td>5.02. 11</td></tr>
<tr><td>WAGS ALL, | AND WELCOME MERRY SHROVE-TIDE.</td><td></td><td>5.03. 35</td></tr>
<tr><td>HONEST BARDOLPH, WELCOME.</td><td></td><td>5.03. 55P</td></tr>
<tr><td>WELCOME, MY LITTLE TINY THIEF, AND WELCOME</td><td></td><td>5.03. 57P</td></tr>
<tr><td>MY LITTLE TINY THIEF, AND WELCOME INDEED TOO.</td><td></td><td>5.03. 57P</td></tr>
<tr><td>WHY, HERE IT IS, WELCOME THESE PLEASANT DAYS!</td><td></td><td>5.03.141</td></tr>
<tr><td>WOULD THE PEACEFUL CITY QUIT, | TO WELCOME HIM!</td><td>H5</td><td>5.PR. 34</td></tr>
<tr><td>NOW WELCOME, KATE:</td><td></td><td>5.02.357</td></tr>
<tr><td>BASTARD OF ORLEANCE, THRICE WELCOME TO US.</td><td>1H6</td><td>1.02. 47</td></tr>
<tr><td>AND HE IS WELCOME. WHAT? IS THIS THE MAN?</td><td></td><td>2.03. 14</td></tr>
<tr><td>WELCOME, HIGH PRINCE, THE MIGHTY DUKE OF YORK!</td><td></td><td>3.01.176</td></tr>
<tr><td>WELCOME, BRAVE DUKE, THY FRIENDSHIP MAKES US</td><td></td><td>3.03. 86</td></tr>
<tr><td>WELCOME, BRAVE CAPTAIN AND VICTORIOUS LORD!</td><td></td><td>3.04. 16</td></tr>
<tr><td>TO BID HIS YOUNG SON WELCOME TO HIS GRAVE?</td><td></td><td>4.03. 40</td></tr>
<tr><td>WELCOME, BRAVE EARL, INTO OUR TERRITORIES!</td><td></td><td>5.03.146</td></tr>
<tr><td>WELCOME, QUEEN MARGARET. | I CAN EXPRESS NO</td><td>2H6</td><td>1.01. 17</td></tr>
<tr><td>LORDS, WITH ONE CHEERFUL VOICE WELCOME MY LOVE.</td><td></td><td>1.01. 36</td></tr>
<tr><td>WELL SAID, MY MASTERS, AND WELCOME ALL.</td><td></td><td>1.04. 13P</td></tr>
<tr><td>WELCOME IS BANISHMENT, WELCOME WERE MY DEATH.</td><td></td><td>2.03. 14</td></tr>
<tr><td>WELCOME IS BANISHMENT, WELCOME WERE MY DEATH.</td><td></td><td>2.03. 14</td></tr>
<tr><td>WELCOME, LORD SOMERSET. WHAT NEWS FROM FRANCE?</td><td></td><td>3.01. 83</td></tr>
<tr><td>WELCOME, MY LORD, TO THIS BRAVE TOWN OF YORK.</td><td>3H6</td><td>2.02. 1</td></tr>
<tr><td>WELCOME, BRAVE WARWICK!</td><td></td><td>3.03. 46</td></tr>
<tr><td>THEN, GENTLE CLARENCE, WELCOME UNTO WARWICK,</td><td></td><td>4.02. 6</td></tr>
<tr><td>WELCOME UNTO WARWICK, | AND WELCOME, SOMERSET:</td><td></td><td>4.02. 7</td></tr>
<tr><td>BUT WELCOME, SWEET CLARENCE, MY DAUGHTER SHALL</td><td></td><td>4.02. 12</td></tr>
<tr><td>WELCOME, SIR JOHN! BUT WHY COME YOU IN ARMS?</td><td></td><td>4.07. 42</td></tr>
<tr><td>O, WELCOME, OXFORD, FOR WE WANT THY HELP.</td><td></td><td>5.01. 66</td></tr>
<tr><td>NOW WELCOME MORE, AND TEN TIMES MORE BELOV'D,</td><td></td><td>5.01.103</td></tr>
<tr><td>WELCOME, GOOD CLARENCE, THIS IS BROTHER-LIKE.</td><td></td><td>5.01.105</td></tr>
<tr><td>WELL ARE YOU WELCOME TO /THE OPEN AIR.</td><td>R3</td><td>1.01.124</td></tr>
<tr><td>WELCOME DESTRUCTION, BLOOD, AND MASSACRE!</td><td></td><td>2.04. 53</td></tr>
<tr><td>WELCOME, SWEET PRINCE, TO LONDON, TO YOUR</td><td></td><td>3.01. 1</td></tr>
<tr><td>WELCOME, DEAR COUSIN, MY THOUGHTS' SOVEREIGN,</td><td></td><td>3.01. 2</td></tr>
<tr><td>I WANT MORE UNCLES HERE TO WELCOME ME.</td><td></td><td>3.01. 6</td></tr>
<tr><td>WELCOME, MY LORD. WHAT, WILL OUR MOTHER COME?</td><td></td><td>3.01. 25</td></tr>
<tr><td>HER | TO MEET YOU AT THE TOWER AND WELCOME YOU.</td><td></td><td>3.01.139</td></tr>
<tr><td>WELCOME, MY LORD!</td><td></td><td>3.07. 56</td></tr>
<tr><td>THE AID | OF BUCKINGHAM TO WELCOME THEM ASHORE.</td><td></td><td>4.04.439</td></tr>
<tr><td>YOUR WIVES SHALL WELCOME HOME THE CONQUERORS:</td><td></td><td>5.03.260</td></tr>
<tr><td>A GENERAL WELCOME FROM HIS GRACE | SALUTES YE</td><td>H8</td><td>1.04. 1</td></tr>
<tr><td>FIRST, GOOD COMPANY, GOOD WINE, GOOD WELCOME,</td><td></td><td>1.04. 6</td></tr>
<tr><td>Y' ARE WELCOME, MY FAIR GUESTS.</td><td></td><td>1.04. 35</td></tr>
<tr><td>THIS, TO CONFIRM MY WELCOME, | AND TO YOU ALL</td><td></td><td>1.04. 37</td></tr>
<tr><td>GOOD LORD CHAMBERLAIN, | GO, GIVE 'EM WELCOME:</td><td></td><td>1.04. 57</td></tr>
<tr><td>AND ONCE MORE | I SHOW'R A WELCOME ON YE.</td><td></td><td>1.04. 63</td></tr>
<tr><td>WELCOME ALL!</td><td></td><td>1.04. 63</td></tr>
<tr><td>YOU'RE WELCOME, | MOST LEARNED REVEREND SIR,</td><td></td><td>2.02. 75</td></tr>
<tr><td>AND ONCE MORE IN MINE ARMS I BID HIM WELCOME,</td><td></td><td>2.02. 98</td></tr>
<tr><td>THAT CRANMER IS RETURN'D WITH WELCOME,</td><td></td><td>3.02.400</td></tr>
<tr><td>YOU GO, | AND FIND THE WELCOME OF A NOBLE FOE.</td><td>TRO</td><td>1.03.309</td></tr>
<tr><td>THE WELCOME EVER SMILES, | AND FAREWELL GOES OUT</td><td></td><td>3.03.168</td></tr>
<tr><td>IN HUMANE GENTLENESS, | WELCOME TO TROY!</td><td></td><td>4.01. 22</td></tr>
<tr><td>NOW, BY ANCHISES' LIFE, | WELCOME INDEED!</td><td></td><td>4.01. 23</td></tr>
<tr><td>WELCOME, SIR DIOMED!</td><td></td><td>4.04.109</td></tr>
<tr><td>MOST DEARLY WELCOME TO THE GREEKS, SWEET LADY.</td><td></td><td>4.05. 18</td></tr>
<tr><td>ACHILLES BIDS YOU WELCOME.</td><td></td><td>4.05. 25</td></tr>
<tr><td>THAT GIVE A COASTING WELCOME ERE IT COMES, | AND</td><td></td><td>4.05. 59</td></tr>
<tr><td>AS WELCOME AS TO ONE | THAT WOULD BE RID OF SUCH</td><td></td><td>4.05.163</td></tr>
<tr><td>FROM HEART OF VERY HEART, GREAT HECTOR, WELCOME.</td><td></td><td>4.05.171</td></tr>
<tr><td>YOU BRACE OF WARLIKE BROTHERS, WELCOME HITHER.</td><td></td><td>4.05.175</td></tr>
<tr><td>AND, WORTHY WARRIOR, WELCOME TO OUR TENTS.</td><td></td><td>4.05.200</td></tr>
<tr><td>WELL, WELCOME, WELCOME!</td><td></td><td>4.05.210</td></tr>
<tr><td>WELL, WELCOME, WELCOME!</td><td></td><td>4.05.210</td></tr>
<tr><td>MOST GENTLE AND MOST VALIANT HECTOR, WELCOME!</td><td></td><td>4.05.227</td></tr>
<tr><td>THAT THIS GREAT SOLDIER MAY HIS WELCOME KNOW.</td><td></td><td>4.05.276</td></tr>
<tr><td>WELCOME, BRAVE HECTOR, WELCOME, PRINCES ALL.</td><td></td><td>5.01. 70</td></tr>
<tr><td>WELCOME, BRAVE HECTOR, WELCOME, PRINCES ALL.</td><td></td><td>5.01. 70</td></tr>
<tr><td>GOOD NIGHT AND WELCOME, BOTH /AT /ONCE, TO THOSE</td><td></td><td>5.01. 77</td></tr>
<tr><td>TELL VALERIA | WE ARE FIT TO BID HER WELCOME.</td><td>COR</td><td>1.03. 44</td></tr>
<tr><td>WELCOME TO ROME, RENOWNED CORIOLANUS!</td><td></td><td>2.01.166</td></tr>
<tr><td>WELCOME TO ROME, RENOWNED CORIOLANUS!</td><td></td><td>2.01.167</td></tr>
<tr><td>O, WELCOME HOME:</td><td></td><td>2.01.181</td></tr>
<tr><td>AND WELCOME, GENERAL, AND Y' ARE WELCOME ALL.</td><td></td><td>2.01.182</td></tr>
<tr><td>AND WELCOME, GENERAL, AND Y' ARE WELCOME ALL.</td><td></td><td>2.01.182</td></tr>
<tr><td>WELCOME!</td><td></td><td>2.01.184</td></tr>
<tr><td>YET WELCOME, WARRIORS:</td><td></td><td>2.01.189</td></tr>
<tr><td>WELCOME HOME.</td><td></td><td>3.01. 20</td></tr>
<tr><td>YOU WILL BE WELCOME WITH THIS INTELLIGENCE,</td><td></td><td>4.03. 29P</td></tr>
<tr><td>MOST WELCOME!</td><td></td><td>4.05.147</td></tr>
<tr><td>REPEAL HIM WITH THE WELCOME OF HIS MOTHER.</td><td></td><td>5.05. 5</td></tr>
<tr><td>CRY, "WELCOME, LADIES, WELCOME!"</td><td></td><td>5.05. 6</td></tr>
<tr><td>CRY, "WELCOME, LADIES, WELCOME!"</td><td></td><td>5.05. 6</td></tr>
<tr><td>WELCOME, LADIES, | WELCOME!</td><td></td><td>5.05. 6</td></tr>
<tr><td>WELCOME, LADIES, | WELCOME!</td><td></td><td>5.05. 7</td></tr>
<tr><td>MOST WELCOME!</td><td></td><td>5.06. 8</td></tr>
<tr><td>YOU ARE MOST WELCOME HOME.</td><td></td><td>5.06. 60</td></tr>
<tr><td>AND WITH LOUD 'LARUMS WELCOME THEM TO ROME.</td><td>TIT</td><td>1.01.147</td></tr>
<tr><td>AND WELCOME, NEPHEWS, FROM SUCCESSFUL WARS,</td><td></td><td>1.01.172</td></tr>
<tr><td>WELCOME, AEMILIUS, WHAT'S THE NEWS FROM ROME?</td><td></td><td>5.01.155</td></tr>
<tr><td>COME DOWN AND WELCOME ME TO THIS WORLD'S LIGHT:</td><td></td><td>5.02. 33</td></tr>
<tr><td>I AM, THEREFORE COME DOWN AND WELCOME ME.</td><td></td><td>5.02. 43</td></tr>
<tr><td>WELCOME, DREAD FURY, TO MY WOEFUL HOUSE:</td><td></td><td>5.02. 82</td></tr>
<tr><td>RAPINE AND MURTHER, YOU ARE WELCOME TOO.</td><td></td><td>5.02. 83</td></tr>
<tr><td>BUT WELCOME AS YOU ARE:</td><td></td><td>5.02. 91</td></tr>
<tr><td>WELCOME, MY LORD:</td><td></td><td>5.03. 26</td></tr>
<tr><td>WELCOME, DREAD QUEEN:</td><td></td><td>5.03. 26</td></tr>
<tr><td>WELCOME, YE WARLIKE GOTHS:</td><td></td><td>5.03. 27</td></tr>
<tr><td>WELCOME, LUCIUS:</td><td></td><td>5.03. 27</td></tr>
<tr><td>AND WELCOME, ALL.</td><td></td><td>5.03. 28</td></tr>
<tr><td>AMONG THE STORE | ONE MORE, MOST WELCOME, MAKES</td><td>ROM</td><td>1.02. 23</td></tr>
<tr><td>MY HOUSE AND WELCOME ON THEIR PLEASURE STAY.</td><td></td><td>1.02. 37</td></tr>
<tr><td>WELCOME, GENTLEMEN!</td><td></td><td>1.05. 16</td></tr>
<tr><td>WELCOME, GENTLEMEN!</td><td></td><td>1.05. 21</td></tr>
<tr><td>YOU ARE WELCOME, GENTLEMEN!</td><td></td><td>1.05. 25</td></tr>
<tr><td>WELCOME THEN.</td><td></td><td>3.03. 80</td></tr>
<tr><td>COME, DEATH, AND WELCOME!</td><td></td><td>3.05. 24</td></tr>
<tr><td>WELCOME FROM MANTUA!</td><td></td><td>5.02. 3</td></tr>
<tr><td>PAINTING IS WELCOME.</td><td>TIM</td><td>1.01.156</td></tr>
<tr><td>MOST WELCOME, SIR!</td><td></td><td>1.01.247</td></tr>
<tr><td>RIGHT WELCOME, SIR!</td><td></td><td>1.01.253</td></tr>
<tr><td>MORE WELCOME ARE YE TO MY FORTUNES | THAN MY</td><td></td><td>1.02. 19</td></tr>
<tr><td>O, APEMANTUS, YOU ARE WELCOME.</td><td></td><td>1.02. 23</td></tr>
<tr><td>YOU SHALL NOT MAKE ME WELCOME.</td><td></td><td>1.02. 24</td></tr>
<tr><td>TH' ART AN ATHENIAN, THEREFORE WELCOME.</td><td></td><td>1.02. 36P</td></tr>
<tr><td>THEY'RE WELCOME ALL, LET 'EM HAVE KIND</td><td></td><td>1.02.128</td></tr>
<tr><td>MUSIC, MAKE THEIR WELCOME!</td><td></td><td>1.02.129</td></tr>
<tr><td>THEY ARE FAIRLY WELCOME.</td><td></td><td>1.02.176</td></tr>
<tr><td>O, NONE SO WELCOME.</td><td></td><td>1.02.217</td></tr>
<tr><td>YOU ARE VERY RESPECTIVELY WELCOME, SIR.</td><td></td><td>3.01. 8P</td></tr>
<tr><td>WELCOME, GOOD BROTHER.</td><td></td><td>3.04. 7</td></tr>
<tr><td>BLESS THEM, AND TO NOTHING ARE THEY WELCOME.</td><td></td><td>3.06. 84P</td></tr>
<tr><td>FEAST | WHEREAT A VILLAIN'S NOT A WELCOME GUEST.</td><td></td><td>3.06.103</td></tr>
<tr><td>THINE EARS (LIKE TAPSTERS THAT BADE WELCOME)</td><td></td><td>4.03.215</td></tr>
<tr><td>NOTHING LIVING BUT THEE, THOU SHALT BE WELCOME.</td><td></td><td>4.03.356P</td></tr>
<tr><td>HE IS WELCOME HITHER.</td><td>JC</td><td>2.01. 94</td></tr>
<tr><td>HE IS WELCOME TOO.</td><td></td><td>2.01. 95</td></tr>
<tr><td>THEY ARE ALL WELCOME.</td><td></td><td>2.01. 97</td></tr>
<tr><td>AND SUCH SUFFERING SOULS | THAT WELCOME WRONGS;</td><td></td><td>2.01.131</td></tr>
<tr><td>WELCOME, PUBLIUS.</td><td></td><td>2.02.109</td></tr>
<tr><td>BUT HERE COMES ANTONY. WELCOME, MARK ANTONY!</td><td></td><td>3.01.147</td></tr>
<tr><td>WELCOME, GOOD MESSALA.</td><td></td><td>4.03.163</td></tr>
<tr><td>SHALL BE AS WELCOME TO THE EARS OF BRUTUS | AS</td><td></td><td>5.03. 77</td></tr>
<tr><td>WELCOME HITHER!</td><td>MAC</td><td>1.04. 27</td></tr>
<tr><td>WHOSE CARE IS GONE BEFORE TO BID US WELCOME:</td><td></td><td>1.04. 57</td></tr>
<tr><td>BEAR WELCOME IN YOUR EYE, | YOUR HAND, YOUR</td><td></td><td>1.05. 64</td></tr>
<tr><td>TO MAKE SOCIETY | THE SWEETER WELCOME, WE WILL</td><td></td><td>3.01. 42</td></tr>
<tr><td>AT FIRST | AND LAST, THE HEARTY WELCOME.</td><td></td><td>3.04. 2</td></tr>
<tr><td>BUT IN BEST TIME | WE WILL REQUIRE HER WELCOME.</td><td></td><td>3.04. 6</td></tr>
<tr><td>FRIENDS, | FOR MY HEART SPEAKS THEY ARE WELCOME.</td><td></td><td>3.04. 8</td></tr>
<tr><td>WHILE 'TIS A-MAKING, | 'TIS GIVEN WITH WELCOME.</td><td></td><td>3.04. 34</td></tr>
<tr><td>MAY KINDLY SAY | OUR DUTIES DID HIS WELCOME PAY.</td><td></td><td>4.01.132</td></tr>
<tr><td>SUCH WELCOME AND UNWELCOME THINGS AT ONCE | 'TIS</td><td></td><td>4.03.138</td></tr>
<tr><td>MY EVER GENTLE COUSIN, WELCOME HITHER.</td><td></td><td>4.03.161</td></tr>
<tr><td>WELCOME, HORATIO, WELCOME, GOOD MARCELLUS.</td><td>HAM</td><td>1.01. 20</td></tr>
<tr><td>WELCOME, HORATIO, WELCOME, GOOD MARCELLUS.</td><td></td><td>1.01. 20</td></tr>
<tr><td>AND THEREFORE AS A STRANGER GIVE IT WELCOME.</td><td></td><td>1.05.165</td></tr>
<tr><td>WELCOME, DEAR ROSENCRANTZ AND GUILDENSTERN!</td><td></td><td>2.02. 1</td></tr>
<tr><td>WELCOME, MY GOOD FRIENDS!</td><td></td><td>2.02. 58</td></tr>
<tr><td>MOST WELCOME HOME!</td><td></td><td>2.02. 85</td></tr>
<tr><td>HE THAT PLAYS THE KING SHALL BE WELCOME -- HIS</td><td></td><td>2.02.319P</td></tr>
<tr><td>GENTLEMEN, YOU ARE WELCOME TO ELSINORE.</td><td></td><td>2.02.370P</td></tr>
<tr><td>THEN, TH' APPURTENANCE OF WELCOME IS FASHION AND</td><td></td><td>2.02.371P</td></tr>
<tr><td>YOU ARE WELCOME:</td><td></td><td>2.02.375P</td></tr>
<tr><td>YOU ARE WELCOME, MASTERS, WELCOME ALL.</td><td></td><td>2.02.421P</td></tr>
<tr><td>YOU ARE WELCOME, MASTERS, WELCOME ALL.</td><td></td><td>2.02.421P</td></tr>
<tr><td>WELCOME, GOOD FRIENDS.</td><td></td><td>2.02.422P</td></tr>
<tr><td>MASTERS, YOU ARE ALL WELCOME.</td><td></td><td>2.02.429P</td></tr>
<tr><td>YOU ARE WELCOME TO ELSINORE.</td><td></td><td>2.02.547P</td></tr>
<tr><td>YOU ARE WELCOME.</td><td></td><td>3.02.313P</td></tr>
<tr><td>YOUR LORDSHIP IS RIGHT WELCOME BACK TO DENMARK.</td><td></td><td>5.02. 81</td></tr>
<tr><td>YOUR GRACES ARE RIGHT WELCOME.</td><td>LR</td><td>2.01.129</td></tr>
<tr><td>WHOSE WELCOME I PERCEIV'D HAD POISON'D MINE --</td><td></td><td>2.04. 39</td></tr>
<tr><td>YOU YET, NOR AM PROVIDED | FOR YOUR FIT WELCOME.</td><td></td><td>2.04.233</td></tr>
<tr><td>THOU SHALT MEET | BOTH WELCOME AND PROTECTION.</td><td></td><td>3.06. 92</td></tr>
<tr><td>WELCOME THEN, | THOU UNSUBSTANTIAL AIR THAT |</td><td></td><td>4.01. 6</td></tr>
<tr><td>WELCOME, MY LORD!</td><td></td><td>4.02. 1</td></tr>
<tr><td>/YOU ARE WELCOME HITHER.</td><td></td><td>5.03.290</td></tr>
<tr><td>THE WORSER WELCOME:</td><td>OTH</td><td>1.01. 95</td></tr>
<tr><td>WELCOME, GENTLE SIGNIOR, | WE LACK'D YOUR</td><td></td><td>1.03. 50</td></tr>
<tr><td>GOOD ANCIENT, YOU ARE WELCOME.</td><td></td><td>2.01. 96</td></tr>
<tr><td>WELCOME, MISTRESS.</td><td></td><td>2.01. 96</td></tr>
<tr><td>WELCOME, IAGO: WE MUST TO THE WATCH.</td><td></td><td>2.03. 12P</td></tr>
<tr><td>WELCOME TO CYPRUS.</td><td></td><td>4.01.221</td></tr>
<tr><td>YOU ARE WELCOME, SIR, TO CYPRUS.</td><td></td><td>4.01.263</td></tr>
<tr><td>YOUR HONOR IS MOST WELCOME.</td><td></td><td>4.03. 4</td></tr>
<tr><td>WELCOME, MY GOOD ALEXAS.</td><td>ANT</td><td>1.05. 66</td></tr>
<tr><td>WELCOME TO ROME.</td><td></td><td>2.02. 28</td></tr>
<tr><td>WELCOME FROM EGYPT, SIR.</td><td></td><td>2.02.171P</td></tr>
<tr><td>TO SICILY AND DID FIND | HER WELCOME FRIENDLY.</td><td></td><td>2.06. 46</td></tr>
<tr><td>ENOBARBUS, WELCOME!</td><td></td><td>2.07. 86</td></tr>
<tr><td>WELCOME HITHER!</td><td></td><td>3.06. 78</td></tr>
<tr><td>WELCOME TO ROME, | NOTHING MORE DEAR TO ME.</td><td></td><td>3.06. 85</td></tr>
<tr><td>BEST OF COMFORT, | AND EVER WELCOME TO US.</td><td></td><td>3.06. 90</td></tr>
<tr><td>WELCOME, LADY.</td><td></td><td>3.06. 90</td></tr>
<tr><td>WELCOME, DEAR MADAM.</td><td></td><td>3.06. 91</td></tr>
<tr><td>SISTER, WELCOME.</td><td></td><td>3.06. 97</td></tr>
<tr><td>GOOD MORROW TO THEE, WELCOME.</td><td></td><td>4.04. 18</td></tr>
<tr><td>BID THAT WELCOME | WHICH COMES TO PUNISH US, AND</td><td></td><td>4.14.136</td></tr>
<tr><td>ALL STRANGE AND TERRIBLE EVENTS ARE WELCOME,</td><td></td><td>4.15. 3</td></tr>
<tr><td>O, COME, COME, COME, | AND WELCOME, WELCOME!</td><td></td><td>4.15. 38</td></tr>
<tr><td>O, COME, COME, COME, | AND WELCOME, WELCOME!</td><td></td><td>4.15. 38</td></tr>
<tr><td>THANKS, GOOD SIR, | YOU'RE KINDLY WELCOME.</td><td>CYM</td><td>1.06. 14</td></tr>
<tr><td>YOU ARE AS WELCOME, WORTHY SIR, AS I | HAVE</td><td></td><td>1.06. 29</td></tr>
<tr><td>I WAS GOING, SIR, | TO GIVE HIM WELCOME.</td><td></td><td>1.06. 55</td></tr>
<tr><td>YOU'RE VERY WELCOME.</td><td></td><td>1.06.210</td></tr>
<tr><td>WELCOME, SIR.</td><td></td><td>2.04. 29</td></tr>
<tr><td>THOU ART WELCOME, CAIUS.</td><td></td><td>3.01. 68</td></tr>
<tr><td>HIS MAJESTY BIDS YOU WELCOME.</td><td></td><td>3.01. 77P</td></tr>
<tr><td>ALL THE REMAIN IS "WELCOME!"</td><td></td><td>3.01. 85</td></tr>
<tr><td>BOYS, BID HIM WELCOME.</td><td></td><td>3.06. 68</td></tr>
<tr><td>AND SUCH A WELCOME AS I'LD GIVE TO HIM | (AFTER</td><td></td><td>3.06. 72</td></tr>
<tr><td>MOST WELCOME!</td><td></td><td>3.06. 73</td></tr>
<tr><td>TO TH' OWL AND MORN TO TH' LARK LESS WELCOME.</td><td></td><td>3.06. 93</td></tr>
<tr><td>MOST WELCOME, BONDAGE!</td><td></td><td>5.04. 3</td></tr>
<tr><td>LORD THALIARD FROM ANTIOCHUS IS WELCOME.</td><td>PER</td><td>1.03. 30</td></tr>
<tr><td>WELCOME IS PEACE, IF HE ON PEACE CONSIST;</td><td></td><td>1.04. 83</td></tr>
<tr><td>YOUR GRACE IS WELCOME TO OUR TOWN AND US.</td><td></td><td>1.04.106</td></tr>
<tr><td>WHICH WELCOME WE'LL ACCEPT;</td><td></td><td>1.04.107</td></tr>
<tr><td>AND FLAP-JACKS, AND THOU SHALT BE WELCOME.</td><td></td><td>2.01. 83P</td></tr>
</table>

-3817-

Figure 8.2 Continued

The examples (b), (c) and (d) from the Shakespeare plays also show the *to*-construction, but are realized by what the *OED* 'n1, int. and a. c.1'. calls the interjection linked with a vocative form. The speech act conventionally associated with a welcome scene is a greeting in a happy situation. Examples (c) and (d) follow these conventional pragmatic associations. In examples (a) and (b) the situational context is needed in order to understand that these examples are expressed on rather unhappy occasions. Example (a) is Lear's resigned expression of gratefulness to Kent after he has lost both his public and private roles as king and father, that is, his 'body politic' and his 'body natural' (Kantorowicz 1957). Again, this resignation will also find its multimodal expression in the way Lear in performance utters those words, moves his body or uses his voice. Example (b) is Hamlet's ironic address to Rosencrantz and Guildenstern because he has realized that the two cooperate with Claudius. As such, the speech act is nothing more than a polite but empty formula, which, however, may be shaped by Hamlet's voice.

In the next session, the students can also be asked to explore the attributive usage of *welcome*, which came into the language in Early Modern English:

> *The First Part of King Henry IV* (1596)
> King: And he hath brought us smooth and welcome news.
> (1H4 1.1.66)

The following questions could be asked:

(a) What are the grammatical associations of *welcome* in this example? (Also, observe the collocation of *welcome* with *smooth*.)
(b) Check the *OED* for this use of *welcome*.
(c) Which semantic associations of the predicative usage have been kept?

Welcome is used attributively in those examples. An *OED* search reveals that the semantic associations of a happy occasion are transferred to this attributive usage. Other usages can be highlighted within this framework as well, such as the construction *you are welcome to* do something.

Once students have completed these tasks, it is possible to introduce them to Hoey's (2005) theory of lexico-grammatical priming. Hoey impressively shows that the way we use language can be compared to a complex linguistic weaving that is both quantitatively and qualitatively connected on all levels of language. Hoey's theory embraces 'a general theory of expected co-occurrence at every level from the lexical to the generic' (Toolan 2009: 16). He sets out from the lexico-grammatical interface and argues that a number of lexical items or words take on specific collocational patterns and that speakers 'have strong tacit expectations, reflected in extensive discourse evidence, about the words with which those items tend to co-occur' (Toolan 2009: 16). Following the psycholinguistic notion of priming, Hoey argues that words tend to occur not only with specific other words, but also in specific sentence patterns, semantic and pragmatic roles, and even in particular text types. The concept of collocational priming does not refer to an automatic or strict sequence of words, but refers to 'a looser bonding of discoursal chunks such that, when we hear or read part of that chunk, the remainder is expectable' (Toolan 2009: 17). A collocation may be defined as:

> the far-greater-than-chance tendency of particular words to co-occur (adjacently or within a few words of another). These co-occurrence tendencies have text-constructional and semantic implications. Proficient native language users are equipped, by their communicational experience, with the commoner collocational tendencies and implications.
>
> (Toolan 2009: 19)

The tendencies of particular units to co-occur in particular grammatical constructions are often summarized under the heading of *colligation*. *Collocation* and *colligation* are often mentioned in tandem. Colligation describes the tendency of grammatical units to co-occur with specific lexical items.

Hoey (2005: 8) points out that every word is 'mentally primed for collocational use', which means that there seems to be a mental awareness of the repetition of words in particular sequences. Following Romaine's (1982) 'uniformitarian principle', we may assume that similar to modern English these collocational patterns existed in older stages of the English language or appear in higher than regular frequency, and more importantly, are primed towards – or indicative of – particular pragmatic contexts. Hoey's notion that words, phrases and textual segments, uttered or written, first prime the occurrences of those that occur later is also cognitively based and not purely textual. As such, it can help us to position the lexico-grammatical patterns characteristic of different collocations (here in Shakespeare's plays) on a broader contextual framework in which a particular form not only construes a scheme, character or situation, but also points to one.

Students can acquire the knowledge of Hoey's theory through initial instruction as well as through a reading of his work. Their attention should also be drawn to the fact that there are other models of collocational patterning and theory, such as Biber's notion of 'lexical bundles' (Biber et al. 1999; Biber et al. 2004). These observations carry a clear performative potential as well. It has been shown that a welcome scene is associated with particular pragmatic associations, which can then also entail direction advice or serve as a direction device.

This can be further elaborated on because an additional task could be to focus on obvious deviations from a welcome scene (similar to the one we have encountered in the address to Hamlet) and other possible greeting strategies. For example, the students could be asked to analyse two more examples from Shakespeare:

(a) A Midsummer Night's Dream (1595)
    Enter the King of Fairies [Oberon] at one door with his TRAIN, and
        the Queen [TITANIA] at another with hers.
    Oberon: Ill met by moonlight, proud Titania.
    Titania: What, jealous Oberon? [Fairies], skip hence –

(MND 2.1.609)

(b) *Othello* (1604)
    Othello: Once more, well met at Cyprus.

(Oth. 2.1.212)

Students can be asked to carry out are the following tasks:

(b) Search the adverb *well* and the construction *well met* in the *OED* and try to identify their meanings. Also pay attention to the stage directions that are given in the example from *MND*.
(c) Investigate the semantic, grammatical, and pragmatic associations of *ill met*.

Students will discover in the *OED* that *well met* is a fixed expression of a greeting which often co-occurs with 'Hail friend!' The stylistic foregrounding of *ill met* is remarkable because it is only through the reversal of the positive construction of *well met* and the additional adjunct *by moonlight* that (a) Oberon's jealousy is conveyed, (b) the anti-climax of a romantic situation is transferred, and (c) the audience encounters the contrast of a welcome scene. It is alluded to in the stage directions because Titania and Oberon enter from two different sides.[1] The collocation 'Ill met' only occurs once in the Shakespeare corpus, while 'well met' is used 25 times; much less frequently than the collocations with *welcome*.

To conclude, the linguistic realizations of the type *welcome* can be illustrated via recourse to examples from the Shakespeare corpus. These realizations should be systematically described so that it becomes clear that there are some repetitive lexico-grammatical patterns of *welcome* which acquire particular functions in context. Students can learn about the semantic associations of *welcome* with place, with movement, with positive emotions and pleasure as well as with its pleasing application to people and things. As regards grammatical associations of the concept of *welcome* in Shakespeare it can be used as:

(a) an adjective with a relational clause, which is the predicative usage:

(optional adverbial) + copula verb *be* + *welcome* +
                                     (to + NP) (especially *you are welcome*)
                                     (Adverbs) (*hither, right heartily*)
                                     (in + NP)

(b) an interjection which co-occurs with forms of address, the *to* construction, and usually in sentence initial function.

The functions can be related to the general schema associated with a welcome situation, but some of the examples discussed also deviate functionally from an established norm and move towards irony and insincerity. These observations need to be theoretically explained by reference to Hoey's theory. Students should learn that the theory can also be applied to older stages of the English language and that the lexis-grammar interface is not only crucial on a textual basis but also from a more pragmatic and multi-modal view. In addition, they should understand the usefulness of combining quantitative with qualitative observations in order to be able to establish, measure and describe norms and deviations from these or aspects of style (of a character, a situation, a scene and an act). The usefulness of concordance lines should be pointed out for systematic and precise analysis.

Conclusions

The main ingredients for teaching the stylistics of drama are various and range from a historical focus on the development of drama and Aristotle's approach to action, speech and perception to the multimodal aspects of dramatic discourse as text and performance, which includes the text, the context and the reader/audience. The stylistic toolkit applied to dramatic discourse needs to account for this. It should combine classic approaches, such as analyses of implicature, turn-taking or politeness, as well as more multimodal aspects that account for the performative aspect of drama.

Studying the stylistics of drama allows students to explore and analyse the analytical, linguistic, aesthetic, pedagogic, social and cultural challenges of drama as text and performance. Linguistic structures may serve as triggers for the activation of particular concepts, schemas and performance techniques, while, at the same time, an image may bring to light new, additional meanings or reinforce them. Correlating this to the social and intellectual worlds of students, we can say that the complex dramatic framework also enables students to explore both the literary and the creative in drama. These analytical abilities can be transferred to fiction in general, the new media and virtual worlds to explore 'fiction and reality, speech and writing, texture and visuality' (Carter 2007: x).

Note

1. I thank Marga Munkelt for drawing my attention to this passage from *MND*.

References

Allen, J. P. (1972) 'Willkommen', *Cabaret*. Music by John Kander, directed by Bob Fosse. http://www.ibdb.com/index.php (accessed 21 April 2010).

Aristotle, trans. Hubbard, M. E. (1972; rpt. 1989), *'Poetics'*, in Russell, D. A. and Winterbottom, M. (eds), *Classical Literary Criticism*, pp. 51–90. Oxford and New York: Oxford University Press.

Bakhtin, M. M. (1984), in Holquist, M (ed.), Emerson, C. and Holquist, M. (trans.), *The Dialogic Imagination: Four Essays*. Austin: University of Texas Press.

Biber, D., Conrad, S. and Cortes, V. (2004) '"If you look at...": Lexical bundles in university teaching and textbooks', *Applied Linguistics* 25(3): 371–405.

Biber, D., Johannsson, S., Leech, G., Conrad, S. and Finegan, E. (1999) *Longman Grammar of Spoken and Written English*. London: Longman.

Birch, D. (1991) *The Language of Drama*. Basingstoke: Macmillan.

Bousfield, D. (2007) '"Never a truer word said in jest": A pragmastylistic analysis of impoliteness as banter in *Henry IV, Part I*', in Lambrou, M. and Stockwell, P. (eds), *Contemporary Stylistics*, pp. 209–20. London and New York: Continuum.

Boyle, J. P. (1986) 'Testing language with students of literature in ESL situations', in Brumfit, C. J. and Carter, R. A. (eds), *Literature and Language Teaching*, pp. 199–207. Oxford: Oxford University Press.

Brown, P. and Levinson, S. C. (1987) *Politeness: Some Universals in Language Usage*. Cambridge: Cambridge University Press.

Burke, M. (2006) 'Cognitive stylistics', in Brown, K. (ed.), *Encyclopaedia of Language and Linguistics*, pp. 218–21. Amsterdam: Elsevier Science.

Burton, D. (1980) *Dialogue and Discourse: A Sociolinguistic Approach to Modern Drama Dialogue and Naturally Occurring Conversation*. London: Routledge & Kegan Paul.

Busse, B. (2006) *Vocative Constructions in the Language of Shakespeare*. Amsterdam and New York: John Benjamins.

Busse, B. (2007) 'The stylistics of drama: *The Reign of King Edward III*', in Lambrou, M. and Stockwell, P. (eds), *Contemporary Stylistics*, pp. 232–43. London and New York: Continuum.

Busse, B. (2010) 'Recent trends in new historical stylistics', in McInytre, D. and Busse, B. (eds), *Language and Style*. Basingstoke: Palgrave Macmillan.

Carter, R. (2004) *Language and Creativity: The Art of Common Talk*. London: Routledge.

Carter, R. (2007) 'Foreword', in Watson, G. and Zyngier, S. (eds), *Literature and Stylistics for Language Learners: Theory and Practice*. Basingstoke: Palgrave Macmillan.

Carter, R. and Long, M. N. (1991) *Teaching Literature*. Harlow: Longman.

Cook, G. (1994) *Discourse and Literature: The Interplay of Form and Mind*. Oxford: Oxford University Press.

Culpeper, J. (1998) '(Im)politeness in drama', in Verdonk, P., Short, M. and Culpeper, J. (eds), *Exploring the Language of Drama: From Text to Context*, pp. 83–95. London: Routledge.

Culpeper, J. (2002) 'Computers, language and characterisation: An analysis of six characters in *Romeo and Juliet*', in Melander-Marttala, U., Ostman, C. and Kytö, M. (eds), *Conversation in Life and in Literature: Papers from the ASLA Symposium, Association Suedoise de Linguistique Appliquée (ASLA)*, Volume 15, pp. 11–30. Universitetstryckeriet: Uppsala.

Culpeper, J. (2005) 'Impoliteness and entertainment in the television quiz show: *The Weakest Link*', *Journal of Politeness Research: Language, Behaviour, Culture* 1: 35–72.

Culpeper, J. and McIntyre, D. (2010) 'Activity types and characterisation in dramatic discourse', in Schneider, R., Jannidis, F. and Eder, J. (eds), *Characters in Fictional Worlds: Interdisciplinary Perspectives*. Berlin: Mouton de Gruyter.

Culpeper, J., Short, M. and Verdonk, P. (eds) (1998) *Exploring the Language of Drama: From Text to Context*. London: Routledge.

Dancygier, B. (2005) 'Blending and narrative viewpoint: Jonathan Raban's travels through mental spaces', *Language and Literature* 14(2): 99–127.

Dancygier, B. (2006), 'What can blending do for you?', *Language and Literature* 15(1): 5–15.

Darby, D. (2001), 'Form and context: An essay in the history of narratology', *Poetics Today* 22(4): 829–52.

Emmott, C. (1997) *Narrative Comprehension: A Discourse Perspective*. Oxford: Oxford University Press.

Evans, B. G. and Tobin, J. J. M. (eds) (1997) *The Riverside Shakespeare*, 2nd edn. Boston, MA: Houghton Mifflin.

Evans, G. (1974) *The Riverside Shakespeare*. Boston, MA: Houghton Mifflin.

Facebook http://www.facebook.com (accessed 21 April 2010).

Gavins, J. (2007) *Text World Theory: An Introduction*. Edinburgh: Edinburgh University Press.

Gavins, J. and Steen, G. (eds) (2003), *Cognitive Poetics in Practice*. London and New York: Routledge.

Grice, H. P. (1975) 'Logic and conversation', in Cole, P. and Morgan, J. (eds), *Syntax and Semantics 3: Speech Acts*, pp. 41–58. New York: Academic Press.

Hakemulder, J. (2007) 'Tracing foregrounding in responses to film', *Language and Literature* 16(2): 125–40.

Halliday, M. A. K. (1994) *An Introduction to Functional Grammar*, 2nd edn. London, New York, Sydney and Auckland: Arnold.

Halliday, M. A. K. (2003) *An Introduction to Functional Grammar*, 3rd edn, with C. Matthiessen. London: Edward Arnold.

Herman, V. (1995) *Dramatic Discourse: Dialogue as Interaction in Plays*. London: Routledge.

Hoey, M. (2005) *Lexical Priming: A New Theory of Words and Language*. London: Routledge.

Hunter, L. (2005) 'Echolocation, figuration and tellings: Rhetorical strategies in *Romeo and Juliet*', *Language and Literature* 14(3): 259–78.

Jakobson, R. (1960) 'Closing Ssatement: Linguistics and poetics', in Sebeok, T. A. (ed.), *Style In Language*, pp. 350–77. Cambridge, MA: MIT Press.

Kantorowicz, E. H. (1957) *The King's Two Bodies*. Princeton, NJ: Princeton University Press.

Lancaster, R. (1992) *The Tragedy of Hamlet Prince of Denmark*. Perf. Renaissance Theatre Company. Audiocassette. New York: Random House Audiobooks.

Leech, G. ([1992] 2008) *Language in Literature: Style and Foregrounding*. London: Longman.

Mandala, S. (2007) 'Solidarity and the Scoobies: An analysis of the –y suffix in the television series *Buffy the Vampire Slayer*', *Language and Literature* 16(1): 53–73.

McIntyre, D. (2003) 'Using foregrounding theory as a teaching methodology in a stylistics course', *Style* 37(1): 1–13.

McIntyre, D. (2006), *Point of View in Plays: A Cognitive Stylistic Approach to Viewpoint in Drama and other Text-Types*. Amsterdam: John Benjamins.

McIntyre D. (2008) 'Integrating multimodal analysis and the stylistics of drama: A multimodal perspective on Ian McKellen's *Richard III*', *Language and Literature* 17(4): 309–34.

Montoro, R. (2007) 'Analyzing literature through films', in Watson, G. and Zyngier, S. (eds), *Literature and Stylistics for Language Learners: Theory and Practice*. Basingstoke: Palgrave Macmillan.

Munkelt, M. (2010) 'The stylistics of drama', in McIntyre, D. and Busse, B. (eds), *Language and Style*. Basingstoke: Palgrave Macmillan.

OED (*Oxford English Dictionary* [online]) Available at: http://www.oed.com (accessed 20 April 2010).

Pfister, M. (trans. Halliday, J., 1993 [1988]) *The Theory and Analysis of Drama*. Cambridge: Cambridge University Press.

Plummer, P. and Busse, B. (2006) 'E-learning and *Language and Style* in Mainz and Münster'. *Language and Literature* 15(3): 257–76.

Plummer, P. and Busse, B. (2007) 'Mick Short (Lancaster University) in discussion with Patricia Plummer (University of Mainz) and Beatrix Busse (University of Mainz)', *Anglistik* 18(1): 135–51.

Romaine, S. (1982) *Socio-Historical Linguistics: Its Status and Methodology*, Cambridge Studies in Linguistics 34. Cambridge: Cambridge University Press.

Rumelhart, D. E. and Ortony, A. (1977) 'The representation of knowledge in memory', in Anderson, R. C., Spiro, R. J., and Montague W.E. (eds), *Schooling and the Acquisition of Knowledge*, pp. 99–135. Hillsdale, NJ: Lawrence Erlbaum Associates.

Sacks, H., Schegloff, E. and Jefferson, G. (1978) 'A simplest systematics for the organization of turn-taking for conversation', in Schenkein, J. (ed.), *Studies in the Organization of Conversational Interaction*, pp. 7–55. New York: Academic.

Schank, R. C. and Abelson, R. P. (1977) *Scripts, Plans, Goals and Understanding: An Enquiry into Human Knowledge Structures*. Hillsdale, NJ: Lawrence Erlbaum.

Schiffrin, D. (1987) *Discourse Markers*. Cambridge: Cambridge University Press.

Scott, M. (2004) *WordSmith Tools*. Oxford: Oxford University Press.

Second Life www.secondlife.com (accessed 21 April 2010).

Semino, E. (1997) *Language and World Creation in Poems and Other Texts*. London: Longman.

Semino, E. and Culpeper, J. (eds) (2002) *Cognitive Stylistics: Language and Cognition in Text Analysis*. Amsterdam and New York: John Benjamins.

Short, M. (1981) 'Discourse analysis and the analysis of drama', *Applied Linguistics* 11(2): 180–202.

Short, M. (ed.) (1989) *Reading, Analysing and Teaching Literature*. Harlow: Longman.

Short, M. (1991) 'Discourse analysis in stylistics and literature pedagogy', *Annual Review of Applied Linguistics (ARAL)*, Volume 11, pp. 181–95. Cambridge: Cambridge University Press.

Short, M. (1996) *Exploring the Language of Poems, Plays and Prose*. London: Longman.

Short, M. (1998) 'From dramatic text to dramatic performance', in Culpeper, J., Short, M. and Verdonk, P. (eds), *Exploring the Language of Drama: From Text to Context*, pp. 6–18. London: Routledge.

Short, M. (2007a) 'How to make a drama out of a speech act: The speech act of apology in the film *A Fish Called Wanda*', in Hoover, D. and Lattig, S. (eds), *Stylistics: Retrospect and Prospec*, pp. 169–89. Amsterdam and New York: John Benjamins.

Short, M. (2007b), 'Language and Style – A web-based course', http://www.lancs.ac.uk/fass/projects/stylistics/

Short, M. (2007c) 'Thought presentation twenty-five years on', *Style* 42(2): 227–43.

Short, M., Busse, B. and Plummer, P. (eds) (2006) *Language and Literature*. Special Issue: *The Language and Style: Pedagogical Investigations* 15(3): 219–328.

Simpson, P. (1998) 'Odd talk: Studying discourses of ambiguity', in Culpeper, J., Short, M. and Verdonk, P. (eds), *Exploring the Language of Drama: From Text to Context*, pp. 34–53. London: Routledge.

Simpson, P. (2004) *Stylistics: A Resource Book for Students*. London: Routledge.

Spevack, M. (1968–80) *A Complete and Systematic Concordance to the Works of Shakespeare*. Hildesheim: Georg Olms.

Steen, G. (1994) *Understanding Metaphor in Literature: An Empirical Approach*. London: Longman.

Stockwell, P. (2002) *Cognitive Poetics: An Introduction*. London: Routledge.

Toolan, M. (1997) *Language in Literature: An Introduction to Stylistics*. London: Hodder.

Toolan, M. (2000). '"What makes you think you exist?": A speech move schematic and its application to Pinter's *The Birthday Party*', *Journal of Pragmatics* 32(2): 177–201.

Toolan, M. (2009) *Narrative Progression in the Short Story: A Corpus Stylistic Approach*. Amsterdam and New York: John Benjamins.

Werth, P. (1999) *Text Worlds: Representing Conceptual Space in Discourse*. London: Longman.

9
Teaching the Stylistics of Prose Fiction[1]

Michael Toolan

Editors' preface

Michael Toolan's chapter challenges a common perception that the key to understanding works of prose fiction, particularly from remote historical periods, is the possession of specific cultural knowledge in order to interpret allusions and intertextual references. Toolan argues that just as important is an ability to process complex sentence structure in order to deduce relations between participants, processes and circumstances.

Dear Reader,

So you've reached, in your scaling of the higher peaks of the English novel, George Eliot's *Middlemarch*, judged by many to be the greatest novel in English literature? Congratulations, enjoy, I want to say. Lucky you! You are like someone about to hear a live performance of Bach's *St Matthew Passion* or see Rembrandt's actual painting of 'The Night Watch' for the first time.

And now you find how this greatest English novel begins:

PRELUDE

Who that cares much to know the history of man, and how the mysterious mixture behaves under the varying experiments of Time, has not dwelt, at least briefly, on the life of Saint Theresa, has not smiled with some gentleness at the thought of the little girl walking forth one morning hand-in-hand with her still smaller brother, to go and seek martyrdom in the country of the Moors? Out they toddled from rugged Avila, wide-eyed and helpless-looking as two fawns,

178

but with human hearts, already beating to a national idea; until domestic reality met them in the shape of uncles, and turned them back from their great resolve. That child-pilgrimage was a fit beginning. Theresa's passionate, ideal nature demanded an epic life: what were many-volumed romances of chivalry and the social conquests of a brilliant girl to her? Her flame quickly burned up that light fuel; and, fed from within, soared after some illimitable satisfaction, some object which would never justify weariness, which would reconcile self-despair with the rapturous consciousness of life beyond self. She found her epos in the reform of a religious order.

That Spanish woman who lived three hundred years ago, was certainly not the last of her kind. Many Theresas have been born who found for themselves no epic life wherein there was a constant unfolding of far-resonant action; perhaps only a life of mistakes, the offspring of a certain spiritual grandeur ill-matched with the meanness of opportunity; perhaps a tragic failure which found no sacred poet and sank unwept into oblivion. With dim lights and tangled circumstance they tried to shape their thought and deed in noble agreement; but after all, to common eyes their struggles seemed mere inconsistency and formlessness; for these later-born Theresas were helped by no coherent social faith and order which could perform the function of knowledge for the ardently willing soul. Their ardour alternated between a vague ideal and the common yearning of womanhood; so that the one was disapproved as extravagance, and the other condemned as a lapse.

Some have felt that these blundering lives are due to the inconvenient indefiniteness with which the Supreme Power has fashioned the natures of women: if there were one level of feminine incompetence as strict as the ability to count three and no more, the social lot of women might be treated with scientific certitude. Meanwhile the indefiniteness remains, and the limits of variation are really much wider than any one would imagine from the sameness of women's coiffure and the favourite love-stories in prose and verse. Here and there a cygnet is reared uneasily among the ducklings in the brown pond, and never finds the living stream in fellowship with its own oary-footed kind. Here and there is born a Saint Theresa, foundress of nothing, whose loving heart-beats and sobs after an unattained goodness tremble off and are dispersed among hindrances, instead of centring in some long-recognizable deed.

How was that for you? Are you hooked, on this first encounter? Was this Prelude easy to read? Is your appetite whetted for the 750 pages of presumably similar writing that you can see are to follow? Perhaps your answers to these questions are something less than an ecstatic 'Yes!' Mine were – at least initially. The business of life in the early twenty-first century, this world of contrapuntal multi-tasking so unlike the 'plain-chant' steady focus that Eliot's nineteenth-century reader could deploy, perhaps makes you feel not lucky but oppressed and daunted by all that dense prose lying ahead of you, before journey's end. Still, at this point you might simply read on, appetite unwhetted, engagement less than full, undertaking the reading as *work*, reminding yourself that (everyone says) this is a great novel and that you *ought* to be able to appreciate its greatness, and carrying forward the hope that things will 'pick up'. But it is much better, in my view, *not* to read on regardless, but to pause, reflect and ask why this Prelude is in places difficult, confusing, even off-putting (if, like me, you find it to be so).

Middlemarch is not an easy read; like much great literature (or the climbing of great mountains), its difficulty is one of its sources of value. What I will suggest below, as stylistic tips on how to 'condition' your reading muscles in preparation for reading this novel, will not I think change the reading and make it 'easy'. But these tips may adjust your frame of mind as you set about the activity (it is not a 'passivity') of reading this most demanding, and relatedly most rewarding, of novels. All my comments are oriented to the very beginning and end of the novel, its first three and final three paragraphs.

You may very reasonably ask why I believe stylistics is particularly useful to the appreciation of *Middlemarch*, and I will come back to that question at the end of this chapter. But as a preliminary answer I want to emphasize that stylistics is useful in many different ways in the reading of literature, ways that often relate to understanding how those hugely varied texts work, regardless of whether the texts are an easy or difficult read. Here I am concentrating on just one important use of stylistics: the preliminary grasp of a style of prose writing which is fairly demanding, and so must be coped with before fuller appreciation is possible. For this kind of adjustment to the complex language of a text, a stylistic approach is, I believe, the most useful analytical approach available.

The difficulties of this opening may have multiple sources and I do not want simply to *assume* that they will all be explicable stylistically. Instead I propose to go again at this Prelude as a kind of common-sense 'ordinary' reader from the early twenty-first century, a secular reader, not deeply versed in religion or Greek mythology or Spanish history, identifying if I can what the main difficulties might be for many readers, in the belief that this is a crucial step on the way to making adjustments and developing the necessary redressive reading *strength*. Or to put this in other terms, I think that as early as the Prelude of *Middlemarch*, the reader can and should identify the kinds of things they need to be suitably equipped with in order to read the novel intently, appreciatively, and as it were, 'from the inside'. The stylistic approach here attempted tries to identify some of the main linguistic characteristics of the writing, to cope with which a 'gearing up' may prove useful, the better for one to engage with the novel. While considering the comments offered below, it will be good continually to look back to the text of the Prelude itself, given above.

Complexity of structure and sense

If the first sentence of the Prelude is at all indicative, to read *Middlemarch* fluently you have to be able to cope with sentences that are quite complexly structured. That first sentence is of a kind that is rarely encountered in English writing today, literary or otherwise. The whole thing is a rhetorical rather than a genuine question, and so convoluted in structure, with its discontinuous elements, such as the subject *Who* separated from its verb *has not dwelt* by two lines of text which themselves contain complicated ideas in complexly connected structures known as relative clauses (*that cares much to know the history of man and [that cares much to know] how the mysterious mixture behaves under the varying experiments of Time*). Lengthy though these embedded relative clauses are, they are about a topic so general – 'the history and adaptability of man' – as to raise a doubt whether mention of it was intended to excite interest or depress it.

This material also contains some testingly unfamiliar characterizations of familiar topics (familiar, in particular, in 'authoritative' overviews at the openings of nineteenth-century novels). Thus the phrase *mysterious mixture* is used to refer to 'man' or 'humankind', and this is said to be subject to *the varying experiments of Time*, a phrase that plays with scientific usage while implying the odd idea that *Time*, like a human scientist, can be the agent of 'experiments'. And then there is the implication of the whole sentence, whose sincerity we might be unsure of: the rhetorical question's implication that anyone who has thought about 'humankind' and its shaping by time and events will not only have known and thought about Saint Theresa and her brother when they were children, but also 'smiled' at what they did. A complex kind of involving of the reader is being attempted here, but the reader is quite likely *not* to feel that they are the kind of implied reader that the narrator has in mind, due to gaps in assumed shared knowledge; by the same token, therefore, that reader is not in the narrator's estimation someone who cares much about the history of man (even though ones who do are the ones that the narrator evidently wishes to have as his or her readers).

Filling background knowledge gaps

That first, 'Who has not...?' sentence promises to include us all, all we reflective intelligent people of the sort that are at home reading 'serious' novels. But it at once has the effect of *excluding* us from that supposedly large fraternity – because, we know, we *don't* know about Saint Theresa as a young girl going and seeking martyrdom from the Moors, therefore have *not* 'smiled with some gentleness' at the thought or picture of it. Many of us, in fact, have not even heard of Saint Theresa, let alone know details of her recorded life; and some of us may not be too clear who the Moors were (Wasn't Othello a Moor? Why would men like Othello want to harm Theresa? But Othello was in Shakespeare, so perhaps that made him different....).

There is a background knowledge gap here, and some readers who are aware of the gap may feel their immediate response should be to act to prevent the gap causing an irretrievable breakdown in understanding. That is an entirely reasonable reaction, but I think a mistaken one. Here, first I will try 'acting' to fill the gap; and then I will argue that worrying about filling out background knowledge is largely unnecessary, and that knowledge gaps are not at the core of the text's difficulty.

If I do believe that my modern ignorance of Saint Theresa and her story is a problem requiring priority treatment, at least I have the consolation of getting help via the internet far more easily than the 'ignorant reader' of any earlier time (it is almost as if George Eliot wrote knowing we would be able to effect this remedy). I can type 'Saint Theresa' into the Google enquiry panel, and be taken, top hit, to the Wikipedia entry on 'Teresa of Ávila' (accent on A, no antecedent *Saint*). The entry tells me she lived from 1515 to 1582 and was raised a pious Christian:

> Teresa was fascinated by accounts of the lives of the saints, and ran away from home at age seven with her brother Rodrigo to find martyrdom among the Moors. Her uncle stopped them as he was returning to the city and spotted the two outside the city walls.
>
> (http://en.wikipedia.org/wiki/Teresa_of_%C3%81vila
> (accessed 6 October 2009)

As a reader of the *Middlemarch* Prelude, I find this information helpful at first; and then upon reflection not really of much help at all, for reasons I will try to clarify.

Is having such general knowledge as the above, or taking steps to acquire it if you do not, really crucial to the reading of the Prelude? At its extreme, anxiety about lack of background knowledge can lead the self-doubting reader to a *profoundly* disenfranchising conclusion: 'I can't even *read* these paragraphs until I first know [all?] about Saint Theresa, Avila, the Moors, Spain, and whether cygnets have oary feet!'. And how much, in practice, have the Wikipedia facts enlarged what we had already gleaned from the *Middlemarch* paragraph? Wikipedia tells us Theresa 'ran away from home' to find martyrdom; but we already knew that from the novel (or, actually, something subtly more fitting – that she walked forth 'hand-in-hand' with her brother to seek martyrdom). Similarly Wikipedia tells us that the uncle stopped the children; but again, the novel has already told us that: *domestic reality ... in the shape of uncles ... turned them back*. The Wikipedia information (and by extension, all background researching) comforts us in its confirmations, but it tells us almost nothing relevant that was not already given in the literary text itself. It is therefore usually redundant. Or it is missing: I have tried quite hard to seek confirmation that cygnets have oar-shaped feet while ducks do not, with limited success; such searches become a distraction, time spent away from the language of the actual text which I wish to read. The Prelude has already told me that cygnets not ducks have oar-shaped feet, and without any reason to suspect irony or unreliability in the narrator, it might be as well to trust the text.

A reader's gaps in background knowledge, knowledge not explicit in or retrievable indirectly from the text itself, cannot and should never be decisive in adjudging whether the literary text has been 'properly appreciated'. To support this claim, let me present *Middlemarch's* opening sentences again, but now with the specific historical or cultural allusions amended:

Who that cares much to know the history of man, and how the mysterious mixture behaves under the varying experiments of Time, has not dwelt, at least briefly, on the life of Wong Wei Lan, has not smiled with some gentleness at the thought of the little girl walking forth one morning hand-in-hand with her still smaller brother, to go and seek martyrdom in the country of the Yuba? Out they toddled from rugged Hao Bei, wide-eyed and helpless-looking as two fawns, but with human hearts, already beating to a national idea; until domestic reality met them in the shape of uncles, and turned them back from their great resolve.

Something is lost here of course, as a result of the changes; but surely none of the central themes and effects of these sentences and this text is lost. Some things are different, too (my names are inventions), with interestingly different, Chinese, resonances. But all the important elements and texture are unchanged; this is still the opening of *Middlemarch* (infinitely more so than even the most attuned filmic adaptation). The truth is, *Middlemarch* is not about Theresa or Avila or Antigone. It is overwhelmingly about Dorothea and Lydgate and Bulstrode and the Midland town they inhabit, and there is no background knowledge about *them*, to be gleaned beforehand from external researches, that is an even remotely appropriate supplement to the knowledge you will acquire about them in the course of immersing yourself in the language of this novel.

Voicing sentences

While the opening sentence is complex, its punctuation offers the reader some assistance. There are six commas here, but none is of the easy-to-process kind used in lists. I believe that with a sentence this long and complex, there is a very considerable 'processing load' and some danger that the reader will fail to grasp the full sense, as intricately presented here all within the confines of one period. In fact, psycholinguistic research has amply confirmed that memory/processing tasks that are very long or complex, or both, cause reader difficulties or mistakes that short simple structures do not, but I do not have the space to rehearse that copious, intuition-confirming evidence. The implication, for the present text, is that the reader must proceed carefully, so as to pick out the main sense from the 68-word whole. (I think we can assume that Eliot realized all this – realized, for example, that she could have rewritten this sentence and many that follow as three or four much simpler ones, albeit ones where the claims would not be so tightly bound together; realizing this, she still chose the style she has chosen.)

I suggest the main sense is:

> Who that cares... has not dwelt... on the life of Saint Theresa, has not smiled... at the thought of the little girl walking forth... to go and seek martyrdom?

How do you do this sorting of main sense, as a reader? You do it in part by *voicing* or enunciating the sentence, even if sub-vocally, so that you 'hear' the rise and fall of the intonation, and the marking of potential turns or dips in the sense at each mark of punctuation. So, I suggest, if you are a new reader of the novel, you have to get into the habit of 'vocalizing' the Middlemarch sentences, as you read them, to help get the shape of the complex sense they contain. The voicing of

> *Who <u>that cares much to know the history of man, and how the mysterious mixture behaves under the varying experiments of Time</u>, has not dwelt, <u>at least briefly</u>, on the life of Saint Theresa…*

helps you as reader to 'push down' or hold to one side everything from *that cares much* to *experiments of Time* (underlined above), so as to prioritize, as sense continuation of the opening *Who*, the sequence *has not dwelt on the life of Saint Theresa*. The same voicing equally helps us to subordinate or demote the comma-flanked qualification *at least briefly*, as secondary to the main rhetorical question. Even within that main first question – *Who has not dwelt on the life of Saint Theresa?* – a plausible voicing of the stress and intonation will confirm to us that *the life of* is slightly subordinate here to the naming of the saint. Notice that punctuation helps with this promoting and pushing-down voicing, but only up to a point: it signals where the first lower-importance segment ends but not where it began. That is why a process of voicing so as to grasp the main sense, and not just a reliance on the visible punctuation, is needed. Similarly, it is hard to sort out the sense of the rhetorical question in the antepenultimate sentence of the first paragraph (*what were many-volumed romances … to her?*) unless we voice it with strong contrastive stress on the final *her*, underscoring the implied comparison with other girls – even brilliant ones – who would be fulfilled by literature and social conquests.

Returning now to the first sentence, when the main structure has been picked out, as in the quotation with ellipses above, we can more clearly notice something about the introduction of the second question, about 'smiling' at Theresa's childhood passion. There is no *and* before *has not smiled*. This is odd, since it is clear that we are intended to read the sentence as if there were a linking *and* at this point, or as if there were an ellipted second *who*, or both: 'Who has not dwelt, and who has not smiled?' But the fact is, despite the considerable length of text separating the initial *Who has not dwelt* from the second *has not smiled*, neither *and* nor *who* is present: *Who has not dwelt on…, has not smiled at…?* There is a slight awkwardness here which we might do well to recognize, taking forward an awareness that such little grammatical abridgements might appear occasionally in future paragraphs.

Objective measuring of sentence complexity

If a stylistician claims a text's sentences are complex or a comparatively difficult read, they must produce some explicit or measurable criteria as a basis for the claims. Otherwise 'complexity' and 'difficulty' remain purely subjective and impressionistic reading judgements, and you have small guarantee that others will see what you see or will evaluate the writing in the same way as you. So here are my criteria of sentence-structure difficulty, with supporting examples from the Prelude, the first steps in an explicit, testable (and contestable and falsifiable) argument about the relative difficulty of reading *Middlemarch's* sentences. Clearly there is no room here for a full argument, with counts of complexity (as defined below) across a large sample of the novel and duly compared with complexity scores for novels by Dickens, Thackeray, Mrs Gaskell and so on. But what is broached below could lead directly to a setting out of that more fully elaborated case.

My approach to sentential complexity (and therefore difficulty of reading) stems from the widely recognized phenomenon that there is a simplest presentational order within the English clause (e.g., in declarative sentences where the verb involved is transitive, the simplest presentational order is Subject-Predicate-Object), and the claim that noticeable departures from that unmarked sequence are by that fact at least slightly less simple (e.g., adopting the order Object-Subject-Predicate). This contrast is sometimes described in terms of released or loose structure (the unmarked order), contrasted with arrested or periodic structure (any less simple rearrangement). The measurable criterion of ease/simplicity vs. difficulty/complexity of structure I will propose is the following: the easiest structures to process are ones where the clause elements (commonly labelled S, P, O, C and A: Subject, Predicate, Object, Complement and Adjunct) occur in the unmarked order, and the *heads* of the required clause elements are either adjacent or minimally removed from each other (e.g., separated only by simple phrasal qualification) without interruption: <u>Mary posted</u> the <u>letter</u>; <u>Mary yawned</u>; <u>Mary slumped in</u> the *corner*; <u>Mary was tired</u> (in these examples, I have underlined the heads of the clause elements). Any departures from these simplest sequences, by means of interruption and therefore suspension of the sequence, or by means of inversion or 'fronting', or by discretionary ellipsis (as distinct from grammatically required ellipsis) add difficulty and/or slow the reading:

1. Mary, not for the first time wishing she had eaten a proper breakfast, not just an unhealthy Nuttock's marshmallow and a gulp of day-old microwave-reheated coffee which – she knew, she knew! – always gave her a godawful headache an hour later, slumped in the corner.
2. In the corner, Mary slumped.
3. Mary, in the corner, slumped.

Obviously the first of these is more complex and delaying than the second and third, but all three to differing degrees are more complex than the simplest canonical-order sequence. One can go further and argue that these grammatical variations do not merely vary the difficulty for the reader: they vary the experience. For example, the 'pictures' that readers get and make from versions 2 and 3 above are subtly different, since the verbal representations encourage subtly different responses. In (2), for example, the grammar invites us to pay a little more attention to the corner, to think of it as situationally slightly more important, than any of the other versions. These deployments of grammatical sequence can give the impression that the wording 'shows' (doesn't just 'tell') or performs (doesn't just describe) part of the sentence's meaning and may encourage a more 'felt' or experiential uptake of the text by the reader. Such phenomena fall under the topic of iconic grammar or grammatical iconicity; for a discussion of the iconic grammars of a contemporary poem and a short story, see Jeffries (2010b) and Toolan (2010) respectively.

With the above basic principles of grammar and reading kept in mind, it is clear that the Subject and Predicate in the first *Middlemarch* sentence are non-adjacent:

> <u>Who</u> that cares much to know the history of man, and how the mysterious mixture behaves under the varying experiments of Time, <u>has not dwelt</u>, at least briefly, <u>on</u> the <u>life</u> of Saint Theresa...?

Here, the writer has chosen to keep the Subject head *Who* far removed from the Predicate *has not dwelt on* to which it relates. Although the end of that Predicate is smoothly adjacent to its Object, the Predicate itself is expressed discontinuously, thanks to the intervening qualification *at least briefly*. Likewise, in the second half of this orthographic sentence, as the abridged version presented earlier suggests, there are complexity-creating disruptions of the simplest expressed sequence: there is the same main S-P-O structure, but the S (*Who*) is not re-stated and has to be 'retrieved' by the reader. The P follows immediately – *has not smiled* – but now this is detached from its Object (if we adopt an S-P-O rather than an S-P-A analysis here), *the <u>thought</u> of the little girl...* etc. by another qualification, *with some gentleness*, which again splits the bulk of the Predicate from its final element, *at*.

As noted above, this 'complexity' thesis rests not merely on the distance between the pairs of clause elements; it is also a question of whether the heads of the elements are minimally expanded (made up of one or only a few words), as in a simple phrase, or expanded by some more elaborate means, such as a clause. And in the two examples discussed here, the latter is mostly the case. In the second clause, for example, *thought* is the head of the Object, but is semantically really only the beginning of matters, which are elaborated in the long appositional phrase – all part of the Object – describing what the little girl did (everything from *of the little girl* to *country of the Moors*). Such departures from simplest sequence and simplest phrasal structure equally create reading complexity.

All the foregoing remarks about complexity propose looking at each main clause in the sentence, taken separately, as the most appropriate level at which to analyse: treating the text as a chain of main clauses (i.e., potentially sentence-length units), how much marked ordering of clause elements is there, and how much expansion – setting element heads at a distance from each other – is there? But one can additionally look for simplicity vs. complexity at the level of the whole graphological sentence, applying broadly the same principles concerning sequencing as above (and in Toolan 2010 I did so). Thus, regardless of all other factors and measures, the graphological sentence which is a simple sentence is simpler than the compound one, but both these are simpler than the complex sentence; the complex sentence containing a fronted or medial (parenthetical) Adverbial clause is more difficult yet, and so on. But such graphological-sentence-level complexity options are I believe less exploited or relevant than clause-level complexities to the distinct reading 'difficulty' effects in *Middlemarch*; they are not, in this text, a key linguistic resource in the way clausal complexity may be.

Before moving to other sources of textual complexity, let me emphasize that here I have offered only a very simple means of calibrating certain types of grammatical sentence complexity. There are all sorts of limitations to acknowledge, a first one being that sentential grammatical complexity does not automatically correlate with *textual* complexity: depending on their content, three grammatically simple sentences in a row might make an extremely complex text, while three grammatically complex sentences (with reorderings and suspensions) might still in combination yield a quite simple text. What is harder to doubt, however, is that sentential complexity tends to correlate with reading difficulty.

To all of the above, the reader not interested in the details of grammar but only in reading the text may well reply 'So what?'. My answer to that is that my proposed grammar-based rules of thumb about some of the sources of the reading difficulty enable us to understand the complexity rather than simply sense it and struggle with it. And the better one understands the phenomenon, the more able one is actively to engage with it, foresee how it may continue in later pages, and immerse oneself in the process of reading.

Lexical echoing

After the first sentence's dense evocations of Theresa's childhood venture, the second sentence summarizes 'what happened', but also evaluates and interprets the episode. Here every lexical item along the way is worth reconsidering, in relation not just to the projected text world but also in relation to all its lexical neighbours in the text. Some of the description glosses what we might have gleaned from the quoted Wikipedia lines, suitably filled out by further googling: the little girl is seven and her brother is younger, so the verb *toddling* is possible (even if on reflection we suspect that *this* Theresa, by age-seven, would already be more of a strider and a marcher than a toddler); likewise the briefest search confirms that Avila was (and is) 'rugged'. Much more interesting is the claim that Theresa's heart was beating to 'a national idea', this being immediately paired and countered by 'domestic reality'. Here these terms operate almost as antonyms: *national/domestic, idea/reality* (on the functions in discourse of conventional and constructed opposites. see Jeffries 2010a). Two lines later, there is mention of Theresa's 'ideal nature': this is not an easy phrase for the modern reader to understand out of context, who might be misled by modern usage into thinking that the description means her nature was 'just right'. But co-textual help is at hand: *ideal* is easier to construe appropriately if we are guided by the recent mention of Theresa being inflamed by an *idea*. The hackneyed modern term 'idealistic' does not do justice to the narrator's attribution to Theresa of a passionate nature inflamed by a perfect idea, an immaculate vision. And her idealism, paradoxically, sought to be real (not abstract, imagined, invented, metaphorical). The next sentence uses words from the field of literary genre and medieval physical combat (*epic, romance, chivalry, conquest*) but never at face value, always putting them under ironic erasure: Theresa 'burns up' book romances of chivalry, soon 'soars above' social conquests, in pursuit of a 'real' epic life. This in itself justifies the appearance in the final sentence of this paragraph, of the morphological root form of the just-used adjective *epic*, a form which otherwise the modern reader almost never sees: *epos*. The importance of such lexical networking to the construction and thus the reading of this novel will be returned to below.

Complex texturing by means of textual deixis and implicit co-reference

The kind of clausal complexity described in detail above is not the only kind of sentence complexity, found in the Prelude and expectable thereafter in much of the novel, to which readers need to attune themselves. Another specific kind of complexity centres on the combined use of explicit inter-sentential textual deixis, and of implicit links between one sentence and those preceding it even where explicit links are few.

For example, the opening of sentence 2, *Out they toddled ...*, straightforwardly elaborates on the brother and sister reported as *walking forth* in sentence 1 (the two formulations are almost interchangeable: sentence 1 could have had *toddling out*, sentence 2, *Forth they walked*). The succinct sentence 3 then encompasses the whole episode in the textual demonstrative *That*, and then re-describes it, not unironically, as a *child-pilgrimage*. Similarly, a deictic *that* occurs two sentences later, in the phrase *that light fuel*, as part of an extended metaphor in which Theresa's passionate nature is described as unsatisfied by book romances and social conquests. The whole sentence is worth a closer look:

> Her flame quickly burned up that light fuel; and, fed from within, soared after some illimitable satisfaction, some object which would never justify weariness, which would reconcile self-despair with the rapturous consciousness of life beyond self.

Like many sentences in this novel, this alternates between different kinds of simplicity and difficulty. Here, first, there is material that is lexically and structurally straightforward (the main clause before the semi-colon), where the main processing task is to understand the metaphor, the idea of Theresa as flame or flame-bearer, a fiery nature, *feeding* on her cultural environment, and finding much of it flimsy and soon transcended. Then, after the semi-colon, and without the help of an at least pronominal resumptive reference (e.g., *it*, 'her flame'; cf. the similarly missing repetition of *Who* before *has not smiled* in the opening sentence, noted above), we are told that her nature sought some unfailingly satisfying object. That object – and here the complexity is greatest – *would reconcile self-despair with the rapturous consciousness of life beyond self*. I do not propose to interpret this formulation, with its complex pitting of self-despair against life beyond self; I simply want to emphasize that if *soared after* is treated as a phrasal verb, then we encounter here a remarkably complex Object noun phrase (*some object which … beyond self)*, that is, a heavily nominalized and abstract style, counterposed to the direct and concrete metaphor of 'burning up'. You might say that set in contrast to the *light fuel* that can be articulated in a mere two words, the 22 words of what Theresa's flame actually soared after is eloquent, in its weight and extent, of her perdurable ambition.

As is typical of heavily nominalized long noun phrases, this one carries in condensed form many propositions and presuppositions. Among these are the indications that most objects justified Theresa's weariness, that in some way she despaired of her self, that there is a life beyond self and one can become conscious of it, that the consciousness can cause 'rapture' (another nominalization?), and that a few rare objects can actually reconcile one's self-despair with one's sense of life beyond self. The reader can get so caught up in reflecting on some of these ideas, ideas so lightly encoded in the passing phrase, that they are unprepared to switch to the much simpler and more straightforward style of the next two sentences, occurring either side of the paragraph boundary. Reading these several sentences in sequence, then, needs an extra mental agility, to negotiate the explicitly signalled cross-sentence evaluating reformulations (e.g., *that child-pilgrimage, that light fuel, That Spanish woman, these later-born Theresas,* and *these blundering lives*) which occur in alternation with several implicit cohesive connections (e.g., between the sentences mentioning *Theresa's ideal nature, her flame,* and *her epos,* between the mentions of *their struggles* and *their ardour;* and between *indefiniteness* and *hindrances*). All these linkages, overt and covert, contribute to the texture, the message and the tonality of the passage.

Linking the Prelude with the story that follows

It is only with paragraphs 2 and 3 of the Prelude that we can sense the full point of introducing Saint Theresa in the first place. In crude summary: while the saint found fulfilment in the 'epos' of reforming a whole religious order, many 'later-born Theresas' were not so lucky in their circumstances, and failed by excess or missed opportunity or lostness – according to 'common eyes'. Thus primed, the novel's reader is ready now to meet and examine one particular later-born Theresa, and see whether her life will turn out to be epic-heroic or, to use the third paragraph's first epithet, 'blundering'. There are other aspects of tone, particularly in the third paragraph, that a reader also has to keep in view: the grossly sexist or misogynist commentary on womankind, so extreme or, at times, stupid, that we assume it must be intended in some ironical way. What we are unsure of as yet, is *what* ironical way to take these remarks: the attribution of 'indefiniteness' and incompetence to all women, and of definite sameness in their coiffure and reading preferences. These sweeping idiocies are set aside in the latter half of the paragraph, however, as the focus turns to rare cygnets among ducklings, and failed Saint Theresas, as the narration advances – we can predict – towards the introduction of a particular latter-day Theresa, failed or otherwise. She, of course, is Dorothea Brooke.

There are other things that might be said about the Prelude which I must pass over quickly, given the scope of this chapter: for example, the first paragraph's linking of martyrdom, at the hands of the Moors, to a *national* idea (not a Christian one). Is this Eliotesque orientalism, understanding 'Spain' to be a Christian nation, under threat from 'foreign' Moors? Is there an echoic allusion to Joan of Arc in the nationalist depiction of Theresa (and if so, why not more fully stated)? Finally, a brief thought about the 'relevance' of *Middlemarch*, or Eliot, or Saint Theresa and Dorothea, to our very different times. There is to me an uncanny reversal of received narratives in the glimpse we get here of Theresa and her brother going to 'seek martyrdom in the country of the Moors'. Surely this resonates with shocking incidents today, of Islamic jihadists going out to seek martyrdom in the cities of the infidel West? Granted, there are differences – it is most unlikely that Theresa intended to battle the Moors by violent means, wreaking bloodshed like her Crusading contemporaries. Still, according to the text, her heart was 'beating to a national idea'. Is the young Theresa any less fundamentalist and absolute, passionately devoted to a simplified world of good and evil, than the terrorists we condemn?

The closing paragraphs

But now let us leap over that examined life, and look, 750 pages later, at the novel's close. These are *Middlemarch's* final three paragraphs:

> Sir James never ceased to regard Dorothea's second marriage as a mistake; and indeed this remained the tradition concerning it in Middlemarch, where she was spoken of to a younger generation as a fine girl who married a sickly clergyman, old enough to be her father, and in little more than a year after his death gave up her estate to marry his cousin – young enough to have been his son, with no property, and not well-born. Those who had not seen anything of Dorothea usually observed that she could not have been 'a nice woman', else she would not have married either the one or the other.

Certainly those determining acts of her life were not ideally beautiful. They were the mixed result of young and noble impulse struggling amidst the conditions of an imperfect social state, in which great feelings will often take the aspect of error, and great faith the aspect of illusion. For there is no creature whose inward being is so strong that it is not greatly determined by what lies outside it. A new Theresa will hardly have the opportunity of reforming a conventual life, any more than a new Antigone will spend her heroic piety in daring all for the sake of a brother's burial: the medium in which their ardent deeds took shape is forever gone. But we insignificant people with our daily words and acts are preparing the lives of many Dorotheas, some of which may present a far sadder sacrifice than that of the Dorothea whose story we know.

Her finely touched spirit had still its fine issues, though they were not widely visible. Her full nature, like that river of which Cyrus broke the strength, spent itself in channels which had no great name on the earth. But the effect of her being on those around her was incalculably diffusive: for the growing good of the world is partly dependent on unhistoric acts; and that things are not so ill with you and me as they might have been, is half owing to the number who lived faithfully a hidden life, and rest in unvisited tombs.

More than anything else, I want to suggest that there are extraordinary and reassuring thematic and stylistic continuities between these paragraphs and those that occurred 750 pages earlier. It is because this stylistic continuity gives us reason to expect stylistic similarity also in the intervening pages that getting 'attuned' to the style at the outset, in the way I am suggesting and trying to demonstrate, seems well worth doing.

The first paragraph reports others' judgements of Dorothea, and her actions are at least implicitly seen by them as mistakes, perversity, aberrations, rather as in the Prelude we read others' judgements – including our own – of Theresa; and one cited reason is again, as in the Prelude, inappropriateness of age (one husband too old, the next too young; cf. Theresa's and her brother's act, when much too young). Similarly, too many judging Dorothea, like those who judged Theresa, do so from ignorance (they 'had not seen anything' of her). In the second paragraph, many of the impulses cited in the characterization of Theresa reappear, disturbingly and not unambiguously: Dorothea's acts were performed in an imperfect social state where great faith often looks like illusion, or where the noble spirit may act erringly because they mistake an illusion for great faith. Only the latter alternative and quite negative interpretation, I think, can explain the presence now of the next sentence, with its warning that external forces shape or determine even the strongest selves (or 'inward beings'); there are echoes of the Darwinian zeitgeist (Darwin being Eliot's contemporary) here as there were in the Prelude's opening sentence.

In paragraph 2, perhaps most striking are the multiple generic sentences about Dorotheas as a type, beginning with the generalizations about how great feelings and great faith are often (mis)interpreted, and then the declaration about there being no scope, in the modern world, for reformers or heroines of Theresa's or Antigone's kind. Most sobering of all is the main generic judgement in the final sentence, that we insignificant people are preparing the lives of many Dorotheas (the most disturbing word here is *preparing*). In paragraph 3 we reach the final words of this greatest English novel, and that oft-quoted final sentence which can still move the reader to tears. Again there are at first unnoticed echoes and parallels with the counterpart final paragraph in the Prelude. There, there was a contrast between the duck 'trapped' in the brown pond from which it never wanders far, and the cygnet who might or might not find 'the living stream' and its own more venturesome kind. Now at the close Dorothea is compared to a type of living stream, namely a river, albeit not a famous named one but one that divides but also diffuses its energies 'in channels'. Dorothea, the text tells us in conclusion, was, finally, *unhistoric*, by the extraordinary standard identified in the Prelude (*the history of man*, we saw, was invoked in the opening line) and applied to Theresa, whose epic life rendered her historic.

But even this lowering verdict might be challenged when we realize that the Prelude implies that Dorothea might well have been 'of Theresa's kind', if only her life had been found and sung of by a 'sacred poet'. The reader can question the writer's overly modest presupposition. At the end of this extraordinary novel, we may well feel that George Eliot herself is the sacred poet deemed desirable as witness and recorder, that she has 'found' Dorothea, and that the latter's history may now survive quite as long as those of Theresa and Antigone. And why do readers find that final sentence so moving? In part, of course, for its admirable but modest sentiments, the way it succinctly articulates the best hope that most of us have for our own ultimate contribution to the lives of others. But it is also moving because of the presence of that simple, intimate phrase, *you and me*. Thanks to the easy searching of digital text, I can tell you that this phrase occurs here for the first and only time in the narrative (non-dialogue) part of the novel (it appears also within the verse epigraph to Chapter 73).

We saw that the gesture of inclusion at the opening of the Prelude (*Who that cares ... has not thought of and smiled at young Saint Theresa?*) might be felt to be quite excluding in practice. Here at the close, even as they (or we) prepare to part, there is no doubt about the bond with the reader (*you*) asserted by the writer (*me*), these two who are joint beneficiaries of the diffusive effects of so many fine-spirited, faithful hidden Dorotheas, now resting in unvisited tombs.

The kind of lexical patterning, echoing and oblique repetition we saw in the Prelude is at least as prominent here at the close of the novel. Thus the phrase *widely visible* in sentence 1 is almost paraphrased by *no great name on the earth* (both have to do with public reputation, both Complements could be replaced by the duller *were not widely known*). Lexical patterning, the kind of semantic cross-linkage that can establish textual coherence without the reader always being conscious of its presence, is not a matter of repetition and reformulation only, but is also achieved by hyponymic and antonymic linkages. Among the paired opposites here, the mention of *spirit* in sentence 1 can be set against *earth* in sentence 2 (and, as quasi synonyms, *issues* can be linked with *channels* in the same two sentences). Moving forward, *strength* and *earth* (s. 2) pair with *effect* and *world* (s. 3), respectively. And between the first and long third sentence there is the triple lexical linkage of *not ... visible*, *hidden* and *unvisited*. In these and other ways, a closer look shows there are multiple intricate linkages between the three sentences of the final paragraph, via kinds of lexical cohesion and even collocation, tying these sentences together, so that one is in part a reformulation of an earlier one, and the same point may be powerfully made, two or even three times over (but always with some adjusted value, some new inflection and suggestiveness in the reformulation: this is not prolix or redundant repetition, but a making of multiple closely related points, a texturing). The reader must be 'tuned in' to this kind of lexical echoing and reworking, the lexical networking to be found in the opening three paragraphs and, 750 pages later, the closing three paragraphs and, astonishingly, *between* the opening and closing three-paragraph spans, in order to be an 'inward' rather than a disengaged reader of the whole.

Having drawn attention to all the above kinds of stylistic complexity, let me end by reassuring any readers coming to *Middlemarch* for the first time with the good news that not every page or paragraph is as dense or wrought as the ones looked at here: there is a striking straightforwardness, for example, in the immediately following pages of Chapter 1, and their first descriptions and presentations of Dorothea and Celia Brooke.

Stylistic guidance as ear-training

In this chapter I have argued that any reader new to *Middlemarch* (whether acquainted or not with other Eliot novels) needs to adjust to the syntactic rhythm and periodicity – which can be made more palpable with a 'voiced' reading, attentive to intonation – of the opening paragraphs, their density and veiled lexical repetitions and patternings, and their passing little ironies, if they are to progress in the reading of this whole long novel. Something like a tuning of the ear to an unfamiliar – even strange – speech accent is involved. In doing so, the reader can profitably pay attention to matters of clause and sentence construction, and lexical patterning (including reformulation via either generalization or narrowing): the close attention enables you to understand some of the most distinct tendencies in the style, so that the reading of subsequent sentences, paragraphs, chapters is the more fluent and confident, and done with insider understanding.

Two remarks about method

1   Understanding technique may require some technicality

If there is one issue over which (I believe) the foregoing commentary raises questions about stylistics' pedagogical assumptions, it is the central issue of 'technicality of description'. Students and non-stylistic teachers alike voice their reservations about this along these lines:

> By all means look at the language of the text, but why must we look at the language of the text in a linguistic way, using rebarbative linguistic terms, and linguistics' overly detailed and fussy distinctions? For example, if cohesion and deixis are essentially different kinds of pointing, why not talk about 'pointing words' and be done with it?

The simplest answer, I believe, is that loose and general description does not discriminate enough, and therefore does not bring you to that position of detailed understanding necessary if you are to read the text as an insider, with insider knowledge.

2   We can't be comprehensive, and we may well not be 'elegantly economical'

A comprehensive linguistic or stylistic analysis of any text is impossible (we stylisticians tend to say). The best we can undertake is to 'do the right thing' stylistically by a representative sample (and then a little complacently we imply 'Read forth, it's all – all this play/novel/ode – similar to the scene or stanza I have just turned the stylistics floodlights onto'). I am sure I have written a disclaimer-*cum*-warranty something like that more than once. We shouldn't. The situation is more like the endlessness of heaven (something I worried about as a child): it's not that there's a bit more to be said, linguistically, about Wordsworth's *Composed upon Westminster Bridge* sonnet after which we really *will* have covered everything worth a stylistic mention, comprehensive job done; on the contrary, there is infinitely more that can be said. There is no logical end to the untying and untying, reconsidering and rede-scribing, that one might, conceivably, do, of any text – although only certain texts repay such extended attention. (For how long – how many minutes? – should I stand in the Rijksmuseum looking at Rembrandt's painting of *The Night Watch*? How long should my explanation – of anything – be?) What we stylisticians must realize and convey to our students is that, analyses being potentially, horribly endless, the best analyses are the ones that do not outstay their welcome, give enough reliable help while still drawing the reader closer to the literary work under scrutiny (rather than drawing their attention away, for example, so as to marvel at the complexity and ingenuity, perhaps even the literariness, of the analytical commentary): this is if one is interested in stylistic analyses that help illuminate the target text as a work of verbal art. Unlike the pleasure we get from suspense and warranted prolonging *in* the text, it is a cornerstone of scientific enquiry that explanations and analyses should be as concise and economical as pos-sible. The questions and difficulties that literary texts present are not, however, like the scientific questions prompted by geology or human physiology; nor are they fully amenable to scientific explanation; this is why I continue to argue that stylistics is a kind of conversation about the language of texts, and a *way* of moving through them (just as we make our way through a forest, across a sea, through a life), not a method.

Taking things further

1. When I did a very mild 're-write' of Eliot's first sentences, turning Saint Theresa into Wong Wei Lan, I was doing the kind of re-writing or interfering with the text that Rob Pope has long championed, as an aid to critical engagement and critical thinking about, especially, literary texts – and most especially, untouchable hallowed literary

texts. See, for instance, his *Textual Intervention: Critical and Creative Strategies for Literary Studies* (1995). Textual interference – if only with the eye – is something students and readers should often consider doing, for the way it helps sensitize us to what is distinctive about the writer's actual wording, the choices they have made. Consider again the wonderful final lines of Middlemarch, discussed in the chapter:

> ...for the growing good of the world is half owing to unhistoric acts; and that things are not so ill with you and me as they might have been, is partly dependent on the number who lived faithfully a hidden life, and rest in unvisited tombs.

That is finely expressed, I think. But Eliot did a little better, in fact: I have interfered with her final lines in a very small way, involving no change in the words used or scarcely in the sense, but only in where the words occur. You will soon see what I have changed around – what the text has *allowed* me to change around – and you can, then, think about what difference the change makes, and what it says about the sentence structure that such a change was possible. I doubt that I need to tell you that I find these games *fun*, and that having fun with texts on the way to understanding their special powers, is in my view highly desirable. I urge readers to do more creative interfering with the texts they are studying.

2. I wrote at some length about how complex the Prelude's first sentence is. But supposing you disbelieve me, or want a simple measure of such difficulty? A good simple 'proof' of this sentence's complexity is to try to summarize it. It is 68 words long: how hard is it, how long does it take, to produce say a 17-words-or-less (one-quarter of the length) summary of its main message? This can be developed as a more controlled group exercise, where participants collaborate on a summary that must be deemed fair and accurate by all. And the time and effort involved can be compared with that demanded to make a one-quarter length summary of, for example, the final sentence of the Prelude or the first sentence (77 words!) of the novel's antepenultimate paragraph.

3. I have argued that having, before you start reading *Middlemarch*, background knowledge about the Moors and Saint Theresa and the nature of swan's feet really is not critical, while – perhaps

obviously – knowing how to read closely (and with the help of stylistics even more closely) is. Let me just add this: if I generally believed that what was *most* crucial to the reading of complex literary texts was possession of a depth of background knowledge about the history and culture referred to in those texts, I would recommend making such specialist and rather exclusionary studies the student's first priority. But as a general principle I believe background knowledge is far less crucial to literary reading than language proficiency and language awareness, on which stylistics is predicated – and these are within reach, with a little effort but no lengthy preliminary course of study, of all modern readers. Some fundamental ideological assumptions about literature are involved here.

Note

1. With thanks to Julianne Statham and Renee Stanton for helpful comments.

References

Pope, R. (1995) *Textual Intervention: Critical and Creative Strategies for Literary Studies*. London: Routledge.

Jeffries, L. (2010a) *Opposition in Discourse: The Construction of Oppositional Meaning*. London: Continuum.

Jeffries, L. (2010b) '"The Unprofessionals": Syntactic iconicity and reader interpretation in contemporary poems', in McIntyre, D. and Busse, B. (eds), *Language and Style*. Basingstoke: Palgrave Macmillan.

Toolan, M. (2010) 'The intrinsic importance of sentence-type and clause-type to narrative effect: Or, how Alice Munro's "Circle of Prayer" gets started', in McIntyre, D. and Busse, B. (eds), *Language and Style*. Basingstoke: Palgrave Macmillan.

10
Teaching Non-Literary Stylistics
Marina Lambrou

Editors' preface

Marina Lambrou's chapter introduces a model of narrative structure drawn from sociolinguistics which she has used to analyse the oral narratives of the Greek Cypriot community in North London. Lambrou's aim is to demonstrate that narrative is not a solely literary form and that oral narratives are as highly structured as their written counterparts. Following her introduction of the model and a demonstration of how it can be applied analytically, Lambrou suggests how it might be introduced to students in order to engage them in research using their own oral narratives. Literature teachers may well find this technique useful for introducing the concept of narrative structure in prose fiction.

Introduction

This chapter sets out to describe oral narratives of personal experience by showing how stylistic techniques for the analysis of this sub-category of narratives is as applicable to non-literary forms of texts as they are to literary texts. The chapter will provide an outline of what is understood by the term 'narrative' before going on to introduce the central framework for analysis, developed in sociolinguistics. An investigation of real, narrative data based on a case study of some of my narrative research will follow, with the aim of foregrounding stylistic variation at a structural and linguistic level. These findings will provide insights into storytelling practices by showing how certain features can be correlated to the speaker and is so doing, may be useful for teachers dealing with storytelling in a classroom environment. Moreover, a close analysis of the organization of a prototypical story structure may help us to understand what is an acceptable story format as well as ask us to consider what makes an engaging and skilled narrator.

In addition to providing theoretical insights into narrative structure and narrative research, this chapter will also provide teachers with discussion pointers and ideas for activities and conducting research projects for students, both inside and outside the classroom.

We can begin with the premise that the study of narratives as a disciplinary subject is generally associated with the teaching of literary texts such as prose fiction in a literature classroom. This is usually the case in secondary schools, which are expected to adhere to the requirements of the National Curriculum. Here, the focus is on encouraging pupils to engage in a range of texts to become critical readers and users of the English language. In a literature classroom at university level, the teaching of narratives, usually through genres of fiction, aims to engage students at the level of plot, characterization and literary criticism (of social and cultural contexts) as central themes for analysis and discussion. With narratives being a key area of study in stylistics, students can also be given the linguistic *tools* to gain further insights into plot structure and characterization, for example, and engage at the level of literary form and function.

Narrative study is not only limited to stories in fictional works, however. Stylistics is also interested in non-literary text such as the form and function of everyday speech (Crystal and Davy 1966) and personal narratives about everyday experiences and real-life events. As speech events, personal narratives are part of our social discourse and are part of our everyday casual conversation (Coates 1995; Eggins and Slade 1997; Ochs and Capps 2001). They can be elicited in formal interviews (Labov and Waletzky 1967; Labov 1972a) or found in the structured format of media news stories (Bell 1991; Durant and Lambrou 2009). So, what is a narrative?

What is a narrative?

What might appear to be a straightforward question is complicated by the fact that narrative study is an interdisciplinary subject of interest to a broad range of disciplines, such as literature, linguistics and anthropology. While there are some overlapping concerns across these fields of study, there are also very specific interests, with different approaches, models and frameworks for their analysis. For example, a literary approach might want to look to models of narrative to provide insights on the prototypical roles of characters (Propp 1968 [1928]), whereas cognitive linguists may look at models of narratives to provide insights for their comprehension (van Dijk and

Kintsch 1983). A common area of interest for several disciplines such as anthropology, ethnomethodology and sociolinguistics is how narratives function to shape an individual's social reality. One suggestion is that narratives are stories concerned with 'protagonists who face and resolve problematic experiences' (Eggins and Slade 1997: 239), while another is that narratives communicate a 'socially situated' identity and 'socially situated' activity (Gee 1999). (For excellent overviews of narratives and approaches to their study, see Cortazzi 1993; Herman 2002; and Toolan 2001).

Fundamental to all disciplines is the notion of a story model or template – some sort of mental model of narrative, which allows the receiver to process or interpret a narrative based on certain schematic expectations. Otherwise, how would we recognize that what is being said is a *narrative*? To explain this point, a reader looking at a fairy tale for the first time would have no expectations as to the structure of this type of text or any expectations of the plots and characters commonly found in this genre of storytelling. As the reader reads, this information is processed and memorized. The next time the reader picks up a fairy tale, they may have certain expectations based on their prior exposure to this type of text, which is likely to be reinforced when they read the text and encounter a similar structure, characters and plot (see Mullany and Stockwell 2010). We can think of the overall organization of the text as the *macrostructure*, with the characters and specific language choices as the *microstructure*. Crucially, it is important that narratives are coherent to be able to function as complete, meaningful units that are intelligible to the reader of the text.

The notion of a narrative macrostructure and schemas will be explored further in this chapter with reference to a specific sociolinguistic model of narrative as the central case study for analysis. Before that discussion, it is useful to explore what is meant by *narrative* using examples from literature to help understand the term in both a literary and non-literary context.

A literary model of narrative

Several literary theorists including Prince (1973) and Todorov (1969, 1977) proposed that three conditions must be present in a narrative. These conditions are *temporality*, *causation* and *human interest* and are said to combine to form a minimum plot structure, with plot being 'the dynamic, sequential element in narrative literature' … 'the only indispensable skeleton', the 'most essential' but 'least variable' element of narrative (Scholes and Kellogg 1966: 207 and 238–9, cited in Cortazzi 1993: 85–6). Briefly,

> *temporality* is the temporally-ordered sequence of events, with a minimal narrative requiring three states (the beginning, middle and final state) all linked by conjunctive features of time;

> *causation* is where the middle and final state of the story are linked, that is, the events are connected by time and causation, where one thing gives rise to something else, which forms the plot (Ricouer 1981);

> *human interest* must be present, as without this there is no narrative, or at least, it is not worth telling (Bremond 1966; Prince 1973).

The novelist E. M. Forster (1927) offers a description of a narrative that foregrounds the three key conditions of *temporality, causation* and *human interest* with his example of the well-known *King and Queen* story, outlined in Table 10.1, below.

According to Forster, sentence (b) is a basic *narrative*, whereas sentence (c) provides a *plot*. This exemplification of the three conditions for the formation of a plot shows that a narrative requires more than a sequence of related actions if it is to engage a reader. But as Stubbs (1983) points out, *plot* is something we associate only with works of fiction rather than personal, non-fictional narratives as we are unlikely to say 'you won't believe what happened to me last night at the bus stop... The plot was unbelievable!'. (For a broader definition of *plot* see

Table 10.1   Forster's (1927) *King and Queen* story

(a)	*The King died. The Queen died.*	The two sentences can be read as two, separate events. They are not connected despite *King* and *Queen* prompting the reader to make one (i.e., because they are words from the same semantic field).
(b)	*The King died (i) and (ii) then the Queen died.*	The inclusion of the two conjunctions (i) and (ii) connects each sentence into a meaningful, *temporally* ordered sequence of events. The conjunction *then* also suggests *causation*.
(c)	*The King died and then the Queen died of grief.*	The addition of the prepositional phrase *of grief* makes explicit the *causation* and in doing so, provides the condition of *human interest* to engage the reader.

Wales 2001.) As to what is understood by a personal narrative, a broader discussion follows in the sections below.

A sociolinguistic model of oral narratives of personal experience

Having outlined the components of a fictional narrative according to Forster, we can turn to a definition of what constitutes a non-fictional account of real-life experiences. Oral narratives of personal experience, which are accounts of real events, must also fulfil certain conditions if they are to be considered coherent and meaningful units of language. According to the sociolinguists Labov and Waletzky, narratives can be described as 'one method of recapitulating past experience by matching a verbal sequence of clauses to the sequence of events which actually occurred' (1967: 20). In other words, the events must have actually occurred and be told in the sequence in which they happened (which rules out the use of flashbacks and flashforwards commonly found in works of fiction).

Labov and Waletzky offer their definition of narrative following an analysis of personal narratives based on *danger of death* and *fight* experiences, which they collected from members of the Black English Vernacular (BEV) community in New York in the late 1960s. They primarily set out to investigate linguistic variables, that is, differences in dialect and speech styles, by asking their informants in an interview setting to tell a story based on a personal experience. In this way, Labov and Waletzky were able to collect large amounts of discourse for analysis in their interviews.

It is worth pointing out that there were several advantages to collecting spoken data in this way, a method that was considered groundbreaking in its day. Firstly, by asking for a personal narrative, informants were able to provide large units of data for analysis rather than discrete and decontextualized vocabulary; secondly, by describing *danger of death* or *fight* experiences, informants became more emotionally engaged in telling their story and paid less attention to the fact that they were being interviewed. This had two consequences – informants were likely to automatically style-shift down to their most natural language style, the *vernacular*, which researchers investigating natural language always aim for. Furthermore, an engagement with the story reduces the occurrence of the problematic *Observer's Paradox* since 'the aim of linguistic research in the community must be to find out how people talk when they are not being systematically observed; yet we can only obtain these data by systematic observation' (Labov 1972b: 209). The paradox is that interviews and observation of language may cause informants to become inhibited or change the way they speak, which would question the authenticity and validity of the data.

When Labov and Waletzky analysed the personal stories of their informants, they identified consistent structural and linguistic patterns at both the *macrostructure* and *microstructure* levels. Specifically, they found that a fully formed narrative is composed of six stages or *schemas* which they categorized as the *abstract, orientation, complicating action, evaluation, resolution* and *coda*, and proposed this as a model of narrative. See Table 10.2, below.

Labov and Waletzky's six-schema framework provides a functional model of narrative – the *macrostructure* – where each of the six schemas describes the purpose of that section of the story – the *microstructure*. According to Labov, each section or schema is composed of 'a group of clauses of a common functional type' (1997: 403) and is recognizable by its use of specific lexical and grammatical devices. These linguistic devices form distinct sections in the narrative; for example, the *abstract* is composed of one or two clauses at the beginning of the narrative to signal what the narrative is about. Labov and Waletzky also assert that the six schemas in the model follow a fixed order as listed in Table 10.2, to form a coherent narrative. They described this kind of narrative as being 'fully formed', which has since been understood to mean all six schemas are required for a comprehensible narrative. Because Labov and Waletzky's model is accepted as providing a basic analysis of a prototypical narrative structure, it is generally accepted as universal. (One only has to map a fairy tale on to the model to find that it

Table 10.2   Labov and Waltezky's (1967) narrative model

Schema	Function
1. Abstract	signals what the story is about
2. Orientation	provides the *who?, what?, when?* and *where?* of the story; usually descriptive
3. Complicating action	provides the *what happened?* part of the story and is the core narrative category
4. Evaluation	provides the *so what?* element and highlights what is interesting to the narrator or addressee; reveals how participants in story felt
5. Resolution	provides the *what finally happened?* element of story
6. Coda	signals the end of story and may be in the form of a moral or lesson

provides the perfect story template.) The acceptance of a universal narrative structure also has implications for the existence of cultural models of storytelling because this suggests there is only *one* conventional model of narrative.

While the presence of all six schemas results in what Labov and Waletzky describe as a fully formed narrative, their model can in fact be stripped back to just one schema, the *complicating action* or core narrative category, as a basic narrative requires no more than 'a sequence of two clauses which are temporally ordered' (Labov 1972a: 360). An example of a minimum narrative is taken from Figure 10.2, *um I smashed my chin and had to go to* hospital, where two clauses are joined by the conjunction *and* to create temporality.

Labov and Waletzky also proposed that the *evaluation* schema is 'perhaps the most important element in addition to the basic narrative clause' (Labov 1972a: 366) as it signals the narrator's assessment of the events. *Evaluation* also provides the element of *human interest* as listeners will be interested in what the narrator was feeling. Linguistically, *evaluation* can be delivered through a range of strategies in one of two ways: as *internal evaluation* or *external evaluation*. These categories depend on whether the assessment appears inside the narrative, as part of the narrative clauses or whether it is found outside the narrative, where the narrator breaks off from the telling to comment on the experience. Have a look at the examples below, taken from my data, to exemplify these categories:

(a) Internal evaluation
    and it was so embarrassing and it was so funny...

(b) External evaluation
    And it wasn't at the time it wasn't THAT dangerous I suppose...

In example (a) the adverb *so* intensifies the adjectives *embarrassing* and *funny* within the telling of the narrative, whereas in example (b) the narrator breaks off from narrating his experiences in the present to reflect on the events in the past. (For the full range of *internal* and *external* *evaluation* devices, see Labov and Waletzky 1967, Lambrou, 2005.) In later studies, Labov concluded that *evaluation* appears as waves that permeate the whole narrative rather than being present as a distinct section between the *complicating action* and *resolution*.

Interestingly, Labov and Waletzky found that *evaluation* is less developed and often absent in narratives produced by children compared with those produced by adults, so the presence of this linguistic strategy can be correlated to speaker age. Not surprisingly, the use of *evaluation* is associated with skilful storytelling where it is important to engage the listener, so perhaps children are less aware of this as being a requirement. John L and his personal narrative from Labov's data is a good example of an engaging storyteller (Labov 1972a: 358–9). In a study I conducted on narrative research, part of which will be outlined below, I suggest that children have not yet acquired full competency in storytelling as certain schemas are learnt before others: a sort of *schema-acquisition*. This would help to explain why children are not fully able to *evaluate* their experiences as well as to explain the absence of the *abstract* and *coda* in some children's personal narratives. (My findings confirmed those of Labov and Waletzky, who noted differences in adult-children narratives; See Lambrou 2005, for this discussion.)

A case study: personal narratives of the London Greek Cypriot community in London

The following study describes research on oral narratives of personal experience that I conducted for scholarly purposes. However, narrative research is not only limited to academics: it could just as easily be undertaken by students in classroom-based research to gain insights into narrative structure and stylistic techniques for telling stories. In my study, I was primarily interested in testing the universal application of Labov and Waletzky's (1967) narrative model, to see how far their six-schema framework describes personal narratives from other cultural groups. (Remember that Labov and Waletzky conducted their study among the Black English Vernacular (BEV) community in New York.) By investigating a different cultural group, I set out to explore if cultural models exist. If this were the case, I wanted to identify the level at which the differences, or variations, if any, could be found, whether structurally or linguistically. Secondly, I was also interested in the idea of how people evaluate their stories and whether differences could also be correlated to social factors such as age and gender. Finally, I wanted to see how far the actual topic of the story determined story structure. In other words, if you ask someone to narrate a personal story based on a *danger of death* experience, is this more likely to result in a prototypical narrative structure described by Labov and Waletzky compared to a personal story about something *funny*? With these aims in mind, I chose the London-based Greek Cypriot community (LGC) as my alternative speech community. My choice for this group was purely practical: as a second-generation Greek Cypriot, I had a personal interest in the storytelling modes of this culture. Moreover, I had many contacts such as friends and family who would be willing to be interviewed, as well as access to a local Greek school where I was able to find willing participants amongst the parents and their children. (For classroom work, the choice of participants may have to be limited to friends and family to avoid the issue of ethics, consent and permission).

In my study I also took on the role of ethnographer, which meant that I conducted all the fieldwork such as the interviews. I hoped that as a member of the speech community, my presence would help to reduce the issue of the Observer's Paradox. (For more insights into ethnographic research, see Milroy (1987); Saville-Troike (1982). Feagin (2004) offers a comprehensive discussion of undertaking sociolinguistic research from planning and the role of the fieldworker, to ways to collect data including interviewing and other important issues related to data gathering.)

Methodology

For the purposes of my study, I identified three age groups for my informants: ages 9–11; 18–21 and 35–49. The interviews took place in one-to-one (informant and interviewer) settings or as single sex, peer group (two or more informants) interview settings. The two types of interview setting replicated the methodology of Labov and Waletzky's earlier study. I was also interested in the social dynamics of storytelling and whether peer group interviews produced differences in storytelling practices as the narrators had a ready made audience to engage with which might influence their storytelling strategies. Informants were asked to recall personal experiences about a range of topics as well as the classic *danger of death* scenario. The range of topics were:

- Happy
- Sad
- Embarrassing
- Funny
- Danger of death
- Fight

(Students working on their own data collection could decide on a different range of topics, depending on the aims of their research.)

A digital recorder was the most practical equipment for recording speech as the recording could then be downloaded on to the computer as a soundfile, which is then easier to transcribe. There was no need to develop an interview schedule as all informants were asked to respond to just one question that was framed in the same way (depending on the topic), for example:

Can you tell me about a time you thought your life was in danger?
Can you tell me about a happy experience? etc.

After gaining written consent and, in the case of children, permission from parents, I interviewed 44 informants in 26 interviews, resulting in a total of 279 personal experiences. Notice that I say 'experiences' and not 'narratives'. When the personal experiences were analysed against Labov and Waletzky's model, not all were found to be narratives as some lacked the all-important sequence of events – the *complicating action*. I categorized these types of experiences as 'recounts'. Details of this study can be found in Lambrou (2005) and in several publications that focus on different findings, such as: collaborative storytelling in peer group interviews, in Lambrou (2003); how story topic determines story structure to produce *narratives* and *recounts*, in Lambrou (2007a); and gender differences in personal narratives, in Lambrou (2007b).

Transcription

As the focus of this data is on linguistic patterns above clause and sentence level this kind of study only requires a low-level, orthographic transcription scheme. (Students wanting to investigate the use of accents, dialects or code-switching in their personal experiences may want to consider using phonemic transcription for parts of their data.) My key, which is presented in Table 10.3, was devised by adapting existing schemes, including those developed by Schiffrin (1994) and Eggins and Slade (1997) and shows a number of the basic conventions often used to transcribe speech.

To give an example of a transcribed personal narrative, Figure 10.1 is an excerpt taken from a peer group interview with 3 boys, aged 10–11. All the boys are friends, which also helped to reduce the Observer's Paradox. The excerpt is from a longer sequence of personal narratives about danger and in this excerpt, informant L takes a turn.

The narrative was analysed using Labov and Waletzky's narrative schemas, and then presented in a way as to emphasize the different narrative components against sections of the text. An additional column was created to show the narrative schemas (see Figure 10.2; CA= *complicating action*).

Table 10.3　Transcription key

?	question or uncertainty
!	surprise
WORDS IN CAPITALS	emphatic stress and/or increase in volume
' '	indicates direct speech
'italics'	captures the marked change in voice quality in direct speech of narrator or when narrator mimics another
(names and places)	names and locations not given but indicated in brackets
[ ]	non-transcribable speech
[laughs]	paralinguistic and non-verbal information
=	interruption
= =	overlap
...	pauses of under 3 seconds
(3.0)	pause of 3 seconds in utterance
[3.0]	interval between turns
–dash	false start/ restart
a-and	elongation of word

01	L	... em it's a danger one em I was riding my bike cause I was going
02		down a hill and you can't really see it cause there's another corner
03		cause me and my friends were riding bikes and we were -both
04		came out at the same time and we just -I don't know um I smashed
05		my chin and had to go to hospital and had seven stitches inside my
06		mouth and it really hurt so and I was like I didn't ride my bike for
07		another 3 or 4 months so
08	Int	did it hurt when you tried to eat or talk
09	L	yeah a bit and I -after five months I got used to it and yeah ...

Figure 10.1　Peer group interviews, males, aged 10–11. Danger of death narrative

In Figure 10.2, the informant provides a narrative that appears to be fully formed despite the tendency for children to omit evaluative strategies. Note that the *evaluation* in line 13 was prompted by the interviewer. (Had I not asked the question, perhaps this information might not have been given. This raises questions about the role of the interviewer and how far their input influences the production of the narrative – a point that is worth discussing with students.) What is also interesting in this

01	L	… em it's a danger one	*abstract*
02		em I was riding my bike cause I was going down a hill	*orientation*
03		and you can't really see it cause there's another corner	*orientation*
04		cause me and my friends were riding bikes and we were-	*orientation*
05		both came out at the same time and we just	*orientation*
06		-I don't know	*evaluation*
07		um I smashed my chin and had to go to hospital	*CA*
08		and had seven stitches inside my mouth	*resolution*
09		and it really hurt	*evaluation*
10		so and I was like I didn't ride my bike for another 3 or 4	*coda*
11		months so	*coda*
12	Int	did it hurt when you tried to eat or talk	
13	L	yeah a bit and I -after five months I got used to it and	*evaluation*
14		yeah …	*evaluation*

Figure 10.2   Peer group interviews, males, aged 10–11, showing narrative schemas

example is that despite the young age of the informant, L provides a detailed and comprehensive *orientation* to contextualize the narrative events that are about to follow for his audience. In other words, the narrator provides key information in the *orientation* section of the narrative to inform the listener, such as:

who?	*I (2), me and my friends (l.4)*
what?	*riding my bike (l.2)*
when?	Not given
where?	*down a hill (l.2)*

You could ask students what sorts of confusion might arise with gaps in the *orientation* if the *who?, what?, when?, where?* information is omitted. Does the presence or absence of this detail make someone a 'better' or 'worse' storyteller? The excerpt in Figure 10.3, which is midway through informant E's narrative, may offer some insights to this discussion.

		(Description of fight)
01	E	… and everyone's just jumped in everyone's like the next minute I just
02		see like I just went back an ambulance -it went -it was -where they
03		demolished them finished dunno I dunno who it is now I think he
04		might've I might've done it I might have broke his nose I don't even
05		know you know I was
06	A	WHAT!
07	E	yeah they really
08	A	= who the bouncers
09	E	= no no the geezer (S) he can really kick
10		the crap out of you
11	A	what he was with you?
12	E	no no I weren't with him I was with all the others I was with everyone
13		he was -he knew everyone but of cause for some reason I dunno but
14		dunno for some reason they all stood by me cause they were all my
15		friends they all stood by me but recently right what 2 year ago they did
16		not stand by me they did not stand these old and new friends did not
17		stand by me (C, S) and that lot
18	A	= Oh yeah yeah yeah
19	E	= did not stand by me
20		and they all took side and the whole [ ] took side on me
21	A	= that was over a
22		girl innit?
23	E	Yeah personally I mean it all took like they all took revenge on me an I
24		was like 'What did I do?'…

Figure 10.3 Peer group interview, males aged 18–21. Fight narrative

Essentially, if the *orientation* detail is not given in full, the listener may interrupt during the narration to ask WH-type questions in a request for clarification:

In this extract in Table 10.3, speaker A is clearly confused:

> Speaker A interrupts with specific requests for clarification on three different aspects of speaker E's experience: the *who? Who the bouncers? ...* the *what? what he was with you? ...* and the *why? that was over a girl innit? ...*

Evidently the orientation information has fallen short of what speaker A requires to fully comprehend the narrative, leading to confusion and an urgent need for clarification. Requests for clarification in this extract function as a kind of repair strategy and it is in the narrator's interest to respond with relevant answers if he wants to maintain his status as a successful storyteller (see Lambrou 2003 for a fuller discussion).

Consciously, or subconsciously, providing a detailed *orientation* at the beginning of the narrative shows an awareness of some sort of conventional model for narrative. In Figure 10.2 above, L is clearly adhering to a story template as his story maps onto a narrative framework. While the *complicating action* is fairly minimal: *um I smashed my chin and had to go to hospital* (line 7), it nevertheless fulfils Labov's description of 'a sequence of two clauses which are temporally ordered' (1972a: 360).

Another example of a narrative by a child is provided in Figure 10.4 below, by E, a female informant. In this excerpt, E's narrative may appear to be slightly less developed than the narrative in Figure 10.2 as it is composed of fewer narrative schemas. Note that the *abstract* is provided by the interviewer who prompts the narrator twice with questions in line 1 and line 5 to elicit an experience that is specifically about an argument. Because of these prompts, there is no need for the narrator to signal the topic of her story as this is already given.

In Figure 10.4, E begins narrating her experience from line 6 with a detailed *orientation* to contextualize the events. E goes on to provide the *complicating action* from line 10, but ends abruptly at line 13, with a *resolution*. Most strikingly, E does not evaluate her experiences with comments that convey how she felt at the time the narrative events took place, despite the emotive circumstances surrounding these events. Nevertheless, the narrative is coherent and meaningful to an audience especially as the *coda* provides the allegorical consequence that *if you are bad then you will lose your friends*, commonly found in stories for children.

01	Int	Okay that's great ... were you ever in a fight	
02	E	= Em	
03	Int	= at school?	
04	E	not really but I do have arguments with my friends sometimes	
05	Int	can you tell me about one particular argument that upset you	*(abstract)*
06	E	um it was I think just a few weeks ago when my friend had	*orientation*
07		told me something um she didn't want anyone to er anyone to	*orientation*
08		know and there was this -and by accident I split the word	*orientation*
09		and em another girl was spreading the word as well	*orientation*
10		my friend got really angry with me and I tried to take it back	*CA*
11		I tried to like do something to make her happy again	*CA*
12		but she wouldn't	*resolution*
13		and she kept away from from me for quite a few days em	*coda*

Figure 10.4   One-to-one interview, female aged 11. Fight/argument narrative

For a classroom activity, students could be given the above texts without the schema categories and asked to analyse them against Labov and Waletzky's narrative model. Another task is to ask students to identify the *who?, what?, when?, where?* components of the *orientation* as part of the discussion to foreground the importance of this schema at the beginning of a personal narrative.

A further example of a personal narrative is presented in Figure 10.5. The narrator is an adult and this personal narrative provides a comparison with Figures 10.2 and 10.4. The *fight* theme of the experience is exemplified by informant L's drastic physical response to the situation.

Informant L provides a concise narrative about his fight experience and is an active participant in the fight that ensues. His lengthy *orientation* is sophisticated and performs its function fully. L also provides a recognizable *coda* which, it could be argued, tries to justify his aggressive actions against the other person by saying that his behaviour is something that would only occur if provoked. In this experience, we can see that L was concerned with protecting his family as *the kids had*

01	Int	And I just wondered if um any other stories in the sort of	
02		argument danger happy sad or embarrassing kind of genre	
03		have come up at all	
04	L	Em ... fights-s ... I've only had one other experience of a	*abstract*
05		fight	*abstract*
06		and that was when someone was chasing me in a car	*orientation*
07		because apparently I'd cut him up I'd the kids in the car ...	*orientation*
08		um I parked the car outside my dad's factory he parked in	*orientation*
09		front of me walked up to the window and started staring	*orientation*
10		and started shouting at me through the window um the kids	*orientation*
11		had got scared	*orientation*
12		so I got fed up of this	*evaluation*
13		got out kicked him a couple of times... and he drove off so	*CA*
14		I phoned up the police to tell him what I've done just in	*CA*
15		case he'd gone as well	*CA*
16		and never thought anything of it.	*resolution*
17		I'm not a very violent person but I can be if I have to be	*coda*
18		em	

Figure 10.5 One-to-one interview, male aged 35–49. Fight narrative

got scared (lines 10–11). According to Labov and Waltezky, personal narratives are 'designed to place the narrator in the most favorable possible light: a function which we may call self-aggrandizement' (1967: 34). In L's personal experience, this appears to be the case: while he recognizes that his actions were wrong, he still attacks and is prepared to openly narrate these events as part of his repertoire of fight experiences. (One of the findings in my narrative research on gender differences showed that while males tend to respond physically in fight situations, female informants tend to use verbal skills to express their emotions through argument. See Lambrou 2007b.)

Another classroom activity that uses the above data would be to ask students to compare the adult-children narratives in Figure 10.5 with Figures 10.2 and 10.4 for variations or similarities at a structural and linguistic level.

Narrative analysis and classroom research

The above case study provides insights into narrative research through the different stages and processes of data collection, transcription and analysis and helps us understand how individuals tell stories. While my aims were specifically focused to investigate particular structural and linguistic features, there are a number of other levels of narrative analysis that can be investigated, some of which were mentioned above (see Lambrou 2003; 2005; 2007a; 2007b).

For classroom research into oral narratives of personal experience, what other structural, clausal, lexical and even non-linguistic features can be investigated? Students could be asked to conduct their own research and interview each other, friends or family. (Keeping it within friends and family avoids the ethical issue of consent which may be problematic if interviewing other members of the public.) As the case study showed, it is important to identify specific aims at the start to ensure there is a focus to the narrative research. Moreover, having specific aims will help to determine the interviewer's question and even the choice of transcription and key (see Graddol, Cheshire and Swann 1994).

As part of the narrative research, students could also be asked to reflect and comment on the process of data collection, which is something I ask my students to do for a greater awareness of the complexities of ethnographic study. This would include decisions on the choice of recording equipment, choice of informant, dealing with the Observer's Paradox, choosing a transcription key and so on.

Students could be asked to elicit personal narratives based on a range of topics and not just *danger of death* or *fight* and *argument* experiences, to compare differences in story structure and linguistic strategies. Interestingly, narrators of *embarrassing* experiences tend to use humour as a way to *save face* and to provide an entertaining and engaging story.

The following suggestions give some ideas for narrative research activities and coursework inside and outside the classroom:

(a) **Researching structural and linguistic differences that can be correlated to:**
  - Gender
  - Age

- Culture
- Topic

(b) **Researching linguistic strategies to engage the audience through the use of:**
  - Evaluation
  - Humour
  - Speech and thought representation
  - Paralinguistic and prosodic features
  - Other performance strategies
  - Code-switching (the use of two languages) and accents and dialects.

(c) **Researching schematic structures:**
  - Absence or presence of schemas
  - Foregrounded schemas
  - Other schematic features not discussed as part of Labov and Waletzky's findings and so on.

(d) **Consider broader questions such as:**
  - What makes a skilful storyteller: does it depend on the content of the experience or the telling of it?
  - What are some of the linguistic strategies used to 'perform' a narrative?
  - What are some of the linguistic strategies used to create humour in personal narratives? When might humour be used?
  - How do we modify the language when telling the same personal narrative to different audiences, that is, to a parent and to a friend? What might be some of the linguistic and non-linguistic differences?

The questions in (d) can be discussed in class and then students could be asked to investigate further with research – either individually or as a group project – beginning with identifying clear aims, identifying their informants, formulating their interview questions(s), collecting, transcribing, analysing and interpreting their narratives. The findings can be presented in class and compared.

In addition to collecting personal narratives, it is also possible to develop activities based on existing written accounts of experiences. One only has to think of the natural disasters and tragic events in recent years to find examples of personal experiences in media texts. Places to look for these kinds of texts include newspapers and online news sites, blogs and social networking sites. Durant and Lambrou (2009) in *Language and Media* provide an example of a media text based on a survivor's personal experience of the Indian Ocean Tsunami of 2004 and an extract of a blog of eye-witness accounts of those events with suggestions for activities to explore this topic further.

Coda

As this chapter has shown, Labov and Waltezky's (1967) sociolinguistic model of oral narratives of personal experience provides insights into personal narratives and confirms the existence of some kind of story template on to which individual's map their stories. Their prototypical framework, which is composed of six schemas – the *abstract, orientation, complicating action, evaluation, resolution* and *coda* – offers a description of a basic story template where the *complicating action* is the core narrative category and is essential if an experience is to be recognized and comprehended as a narrative (Lambrou 2007a). And, while a *fully formed* narrative is generally accepted as providing a comprehensive narrative form, a minimal narrative, such as those provided by young children, comprising just 'a sequence of two clauses which are temporally ordered' (Labov 1972a: 360), is nevertheless coherent and meaningful.

As a field of study, narrative research also offers the opportunity to conduct hands-on, ethnographic research on authentic spoken data. In this way, researchers – whether scholars or students – can gain invaluable insights into the issues that are central to collecting data for the study of narratives. The processes of collecting, transcribing, analysing and interpreting personal narratives are just some of the skills that an individual undertaking narrative research can develop. Other skills include: having to identify aims; choosing informants; considering interview techniques and issues such as the Observer's Paradox; having to decide which transcription conventions to use; as well as analysing, interpreting and presenting the results in a format that is accessible and comprehensible. The stylistic analysis of the spoken texts allows students to engage with storytelling practices which can be revealed through narrative organization and schemas. An investigation into the range of linguistic and non-linguistic choices requires an understanding of the metalanguage to be able to describe and interpret the language in front of them. A comparison of narrative texts will also give students a chance to reflect on what they consider to be a good narrative and a skilled narrator and even reflect on their own storytelling practices and those of their peers.

A further reminder of the usefulness of non-literary narratives and their relevance in stylistics can be summarized as follows. Oral narratives of personal experience provide useful insights into what makes a comprehensible narrative: they can help readers to understand the form and function of literary narratives. Put another way, one only has to look to fairy tales, the prototypical narrative structure, to realize how far this basic story structure has developed. Surely, the range of literary genres with their own complex organization beyond a simple beginning, middle and end structure, and sophisticated linguistic strategies for their telling, is evidence of this? A further project for investigation, perhaps.

References

Bell, A. (1991) *The Language of News Media*. Oxford: Blackwell.

Bremond, C. (1966) 'La logique des possibles narratifs', *Communications* 8: 60–76.

Durant, A. and Lambrou, M. (2009) *Language and Media*. Abingdon: Routledge.

Coates, J. (1995) 'The role of narrative in the talk of women friends', paper presented at the University of Technology, Sydney.

Cortazzi, M. (1993) *Narrative Analysis*. London: The Falmer Press.

Crystal, D. and Davy, D. (1966) *Investigating English Style*. London: Longman.

Eggins, S. and Slade, D. (1997) *Analysing Casual Conversation*. London: Cassell.

Feagin, C. (2004) 'Entering the community: Fieldwork', in Chambers, J. K., Trudgill, P. and Schilling-Estes, N. (eds), *The Handbook of Language Variation and Change*, pp. 20–39. Oxford: Blackwell.

Forster, E. M. (1927) *Aspects of the Novel*. Florida: Harcourt.

Gee, J. P. (1999) *An Introduction to Discourse Analysis, Theory and Method*. London: Routledge.

Graddol, D., Cheshire, J. and Swann, M. (1994) *Describing Language*. Buckinghamshire: Open University Press.

Herman, D. (2002) *Story Logic: Problems and Possibilities of Narrative*. Lincoln, NA: University of Nebraska Press.

Jeffries, L., McIntyre, D. and Bousfield, D. (2007) *Stylistics and Social Cognition*. Amsterdam: Rodopi.

Labov, W. (1972a). *Language in the Inner City: Studies in the Black English Vernacular*. Philadelphia, PA: University of Pennsylvania Press.

Labov, W. (1972b) *Sociolinguistics Patterns*. Oxford: Blackwell.

Labov, W. (1997) 'Further steps in narrative analysis', *Journal of Narrative and Life History* 7(1–4): 395–415.

Labov, W. and Waletzky, J. (1967) 'Narrative Analysis: Oral Versions of Personal Experience', in J. Holm (ed.), *Essays on the Verbal and Visual Arts*, pp. 12–44. Seattle, WA: University of Washington Press.

Lambrou, M. (2003) 'Collaborative oral narratives of general experience: When an interview becomes a conversation', *Language and Literature* 12 (2): 153–74.

Lambrou, M. (2005). *Story Patterns in Oral Narratives: A Variationist Critique of Labov and Waletzky's Model of Narrative Schemas*. Unpublished PhD thesis, Middlesex University.

Lambrou, M. (2007a) 'Oral accounts of personal experiences: When is a narrative a recount?', in Lambrou, M. and Stockwell, P. (eds), *Contemporary Stylistics*. London: Continuum.

Lambrou, M. (2007b) 'Telling stories: Males and females 'doing' gender in personal narratives about "trouble"', in Jeffries, L., McIntyre, D. and Bousfield, D. (eds), *Stylistics and Social Cognition*, pp. 125–30. Amsterdam: Rodopi.

Milroy, L. (1987). *Observing and Analysing Natural Language*. Oxford: Blackwell.

Mullany, L. and Stockwell, P. J. (2010) *Introducing English Language*. London: Routledge.

Ochs, E. and Capps, L. (2001) *Living Narratives: Creating Lives in Everyday Storytelling*. Cambridge, MA: Harvard University Press.

Prince, G. (1973) *A Grammar of Stories*. The Hague: Mouton.

Propp, V. (1968 [1928]) *Morphology of the Folktale*. Austin, TX: University of Texas Press.

Ricouer, P. (1981) 'Narrative time', in Mitchell, W. J. T. (ed.), *On Narrative*, pp. 165–86. London: University of Chicago Press.

Saville-Troike, M. (1982). *The Ethnography of Communication*. Oxford: Blackwell.

Schiffrin, D. (1994) *Approaches to Discourse*. Oxford: Blackwell.

Scholes, R. and Kellog, R. (1966) *The Nature of Narrative*. New York: Oxford University Press.

Stubbs, M. (1983) *Discourse Analysis*. Oxford: Basil Blackwell.

Todorov, T. (1969). 'Structural analysis of narrative', *Novel* 3: 70–6.

Todorov, T. (1977). *The Poetics of Prose*. Oxford: Blackwell.

Toolan, M. (1988) *Language in Literature*. London: Hodder.

Toolan, M. J. (2001) *Narrative: A Critical Linguistic Introduction*. London: Routledge.

Van Dijk, T. A. and Kintsch, W. (1983) *Strategies of Discourse Comprehension*. New York: Academic Press.

Wales, K. (2001) *A Dictionary of Stylistics*, 2nd edn. Harlow: Longman.

11
Teaching Multimodal Stylistics

Nina Nørgaard

Editors' preface

The analysis of multimodal texts is still a relatively new endeavour within English Studies. One difficulty for stylisticians is that the enormous range of dimensions to a multimodal text makes it difficult to analyse systematically. In this chapter, Nina Nørgaard suggests how the rigorous analysis of multimodal texts might be attempted. She focuses on such aspects as layout, typography and illustrations to show how a text works as a complete unit, and makes suggestions as to how techniques for analysing these features might be introduced to students.

1 Introduction

Literature is often thought of and talked about as monomodal works of art. When analysing literary texts, stylisticians as well as many other literary critics tend to concern themselves with what I will here refer to as 'wording',[1] while largely ignoring other semiotic modes which are nonetheless also at play in the complex process of meaning-making of which any literary text consists. Multimodal stylistics is a fairly new branch of stylistics which aims to extend the stylistic approach to text analysis to better accommodate texts that employ several semiotic modes such as, for example, typography, layout, colour and visual images for their semiosis. Teaching the multimodal stylistics of literature is a delightful yet challenging task. Delightful because students generally appreciate the broadening out of the object of stylistic analysis to include modes other than and in addition to wording, and typically acknowledge the usefulness of acquiring methodologies which can handle the multimodal meaning-making that is so characteristic of contemporary communication altogether. At the same time, teaching multimodal stylistics is also a challenge for a number of reasons. Most importantly, the extension of the object of analysis necessitates a significant extension of the methodological apparatus employed for analysis, the acquisition of which may be considered quite an undertaking by students and teachers alike. Added to this, multimodality and multimodal stylistics are relatively new fields of research, which means that *the* book on multimodality or multimodal stylistics to adopt for a course in the field does not yet exist. It is the aim of the present chapter to provide a brief introduction to multimodality followed by two examples of multimodal stylistic analysis, each with a different analytical focus. The chapter may thus be conceived as an appetiser to – as well as an overview of – central aspects of the field of multimodal stylistics.

2   Multimodality and multimodal stylistics

At the very heart of multimodal thinking lies the claim that all texts and all acts of communication are multimodal. While the 'mono-mode' may be a useful theoretical concept which can help us handle our practical analysis, mono-modes do, in actual fact, not exist. It must consequently be a central aim for the teaching of multimodal literary stylistics to make students aware that although the most prominent mode of literature is that of written verbal language, even the most conventional literary texts are not monomodal, since written verbal language necessarily involves the modes of typography and layout as well as wording. The analytical exercise suggested in Section 3 is conceived as a practical eye-opener in that respect.

Assuming that all communication is multimodal, the overarching (ideal) goal of multimodal theory is to develop a 'grammar of multimodality' with a common terminology for all the semiotic modes and their interaction, instead of operating with specialist grammars with specialist terminology for each semiotic mode. In reality, this is, of course, not a fully realistic goal, since some modes, such as, for example, sound and smell, are so different that all the grammatical categories of one mode are not directly applicable to the other (cf. van Leeuwen 1999: 189–93; Nørgaard 2010a), yet the work done so far indicates that certain common semiotic principles do, in fact, 'operate in and across different modes' (Kress and van Leeuwen 2001: 2):

> We seek to break down the disciplinary boundaries between the study of language and the study of images, and we seek, as much as possible, to use compatible language, and compatible terminology to

speak about both, for in actual communication the two, *and indeed many others*, come together to form integrated texts.

(Kress and van Leeuwen 2006: 177, emphasis added)

The work done by some of the most prominent proponents of multi-modality, for example, Kress and van Leeuwen (1996, 2001), Baldry and Thibault (2006), O'Toole (1994) and O'Halloran (2005),[2] builds on Michael Halliday's work on verbal language, exploring the extent to which the descriptive and analytical framework of Halliday's *Systemic Functional Linguistics* can handle meaning-making beyond verbal language. Central to Hallidayan thinking is the claim that verbal language expresses, or rather constructs, three different main kinds of meaning – the three *metafunctions* of language. According to Halliday, language thus simultaneously creates *experiential meaning*[3] to do with how we represent the world, *interpersonal meaning* concerning the interpersonal relations between interlocutors, and *textual meaning* which concerns the organization of the other two types of meaning into coherent text. Within the multimodal paradigm that springs from Hallidayan linguistics, the three metafunctions are seen as common principles across modes. As an illustration of this, the analysis in section 4 below demonstrates (among other things) how experiential meaning in terms of configurations of processes, participants and circumstances can be constructed visually as well as verbally; and how modality is not just an interpersonal linguistic resource, but also a visual one. Another principle briefly demonstrated to function across modes in Section 4 is the semiotic principle of iconicity which is here involved in the construction of meaning by the mode of typography as well as by colour.

When teaching multimodal stylistics, a central aim must be to make students aware that multimodal meaning is more complex than the mere sum of the meanings created by the different modes involved in a given text. It is thus a crucial claim that the *interaction* of different modes is semiotic in itself. In Section 4, it is demonstrated how new meaning arises as a result of the interaction between the modes of wording, typography and visual images on the book cover of a novel. The aim of this section is furthermore to illustrate how the book cover contributes to and interacts with the rest of the text in the total meaning of the novel.

The final aspect of multimodal thinking to be mentioned here is the way Kress and van Leeuwen (2001) extend their multimodal analysis to incorporate meaning-making at four different strata, or levels of articulation, which are considered semiotic in their own right, that is, *discourse, design, production, distribution*. While accounting in detail for the different strata and their meaning-making potential would be beyond the scope of the present chapter, the strata are mentioned when relevant in my analysis as appetisers for those who wish to pursue this approach to multimodality in future analyses.

3   All literature is multimodal

To get students started and to make them realize that even fairly conventional literary narratives are multimodal, one may well begin the teaching of multimodal stylistics by displaying a two-page spread of a novel, like the one presented in Figure 11.1, by means of an overhead projector or on a PowerPoint slide. In order to momentarily bypass the traditional analytical focus on wording, the presentation of the text may even be deliberately blurred by (mis-)adjusting the overhead projector or scaling down the text on the slide so that it is difficult to read the words. Alternatively, students can be asked to first look at the text with their eyes open to the extent that allows them to see only

The Historian ⤳ *563*

and my body, whom I have not seen in more than five years? We should have been speaking together all this time, a no-language of small sounds and kisses, glances, murmuring. It is so difficult for me to think about, to remember what I have missed, that I have to stop writing today, when I have only started trying.

Your loving mother,
Helen Rossi

The second was a color postcard, already fading, of flowers and urns — "*Jardins de Boboli* — The Gardens of Boboli — Boboli."

May 1962

My beloved daughter:

I will tell you a secret: I hate this English. English is an exercise in grammar, or a class in literature. In my heart, I feel I could speak best with you in my own language, Hungarian, or even in the language that flows inside my Hungarian — Romanian. Romanian is the language of the fiend I am seeking, but even that has not spoiled it for me. If you were sitting on my lap this morning, looking out at these gardens, I would teach you a first lesson: "Ma numesc . . ." And then we would whisper your name over and over in the soft tongue that is your mother tongue, too. I would explain to you that Romanian is the language of brave, kind, sad people, shepherds and farmers, and of your grandmother, whose life he ruined from a distance. I would tell you the beautiful things she told me, the stars at night above her village, the lanterns on the river. "Ma numesc . . ." Telling you about that would be unbearable happiness for one day.

Your loving mother,
Helen Rossi

Barley and I looked at each other, and he put his arm softly around my neck.

Chapter 63

Barley stood beside me in my father's hotel room, contemplating the mess, but he was quicker to see what I had missed — the papers and books on the bed. We found a tattered copy of Bram Stoker's *Dracula*, a new history of medieval heresies in southern France, and a very old-looking volume on European vampire lore.

Among the books lay papers, including notes in his own hand, and among these a scattering of postcards in a hand completely unfamiliar to me, a fine dark ink, neat and minute. Barley and I began of one accord — again, how glad I was not to be alone — to search through everything, and my first instinct was to gather up the postcards. They were ornamented with stamps from a rainbow of countries: Portugal, France, Italy, Monaco, Finland, Austria. The stamps were pristine, without postmarks. Sometimes the message on a card ran over onto four or five more, neatly numbered. Most astonishingly, each was signed "Helen Rossi." And each was addressed to me.

Barley, looking over my shoulder, took in my astonishment, and we sat down together on the edge of the bed. The first was from Rome — a black-and-white photograph of the skeletal remains of the Forum.

May 1962

My beloved daughter:

In what language should I write to you, the child of my heart

Figure 11.1   Two-page spread of Elizabeth Kostova's *The Historian*, pp. 562–3

the contours of the text (cf. Boeriis 2008 on the method of *squinting*). With the aim of eliciting an awareness of the different semiotic modes involved in the meaning-making, the following simple questions can be considered: *What* meanings are made? And *how*?

Even if respondents are unable to read the actual words, genre aware-ness and familiarity with similar texts are likely to lead to suggestions that this is a written verbal text and, more specifically, that it is prob-ably some kind of narrative which here comprises a number of inserted letters. From these observations, an investigation of the multimodal construction of the meaning 'letter' clearly invites itself and would seem to promise rewarding insights.

One of the semiotic modes that participates in creating the meaning of 'letter' is that of layout, that is, the overall spatial page design of the text. Of significance to the page design of the text displayed in Figure 11.1 is the layout resource of *framing*. Framing is a compositional[4] resource for visually connecting and disconnecting elements in a composition by means of features such as, for example, lines and white space. In the present example, it is quite clear that white space functions to divide the text into a number of separate units – what Bateman (2008) calls *layout units* – which are thus framed by means of slightly broader left- and right-hand margins than the rest of the narrative as well as by empty space between the units. Arguably, though not overwhelmingly so, these layout units are furthermore distinguished from each other by means of differences in their perceived texture which here stems from typographi-cal factors such as the different size and slope of the typeface employed in the text blocks.[5] Other layout units of significance to our visual decod-ing of the text are the small text fragments – just above and below the larger text blocks in italics – which are probably quickly recognized as the conventional size and placement of respectively the date of a letter, the salutation and the complimentary close.

In rounding off the discussion of framing, attention may be drawn to the difference in meaning created by different aspects of the framing by white space we see on the two-page spread of Kostova's novel. While the framing discussed above plays a part in the multimodal construction of narrative meaning (i.e., the construction of the meaning of 'letter'), closer scrutiny soon reveals that although the frame of the bottom mar-gin on p. 562 visually divides the first letter into two parts, readers are unlikely to decode this visual frame as indicative that this is what the let-ter looks like, that is, that it consists of two pages, for instance. Instead, the standard frames around the text of each page, that is, the standard margins, are meanings articulated at the stratum of production with a view to distribution (and, more specifically, to consumption). Rather than belonging to (and constructing) meanings articulated at the level of the fictional micro cosmos, the standard margins are motivated by factors such as technological affordances and a concern for readability.

Another mode of significance to the multimodal creation of the meaning of 'letter' is that of typography. Typography is the visual side of written verbal language which may be meaningful in itself as well as in multimodal interaction with wording. A fruitful way of teaching typographic meaning-making within a multimodal framework is to look at the semiotic principles involved in typographic semiosis. Inspired by van Leeuwen (2005a, b) and Mollerup (1999), it has been argued elsewhere (e.g., Nørgaard 2009; 2010a) that typographic meaning-making may be described and categorized in terms of four general semiotic principles: *symbol, icon, index* and *discursive import*, of which symbol, icon and discursive import will be dealt with here, while indexical meaning shall be discussed in Section 4. *Symbol, icon* and *index* are borrowed from Peirce (in Mollerup 1999); *discursive import* springs from the work done on typography by van Leeuwen (2005a: 26–45, 2005b, 2006).

According to Peirce, a symbol is an arbitrary sign with no natural relationship between the signifier and the signified. Although the plain black typography we see in most literary texts (including Kostova's novel discussed here) may, strictly speaking, be motivated naturally by the technological affordances of the printing industry through history, most readers today are probably likely to consider the relationship between such typographic signifiers and that which is signified an arbitrary one. Consequently, plain black typography is arguably best categorized as symbolic meaning in Peirce's terms.

An icon, on the other hand, is a sign which resembles or imitates that which it signifies. On a very basic level, the visual difference between the text in regular type and the text in italics in the pages discussed above may be seen as iconically signifying difference in terms of meaning, thus visually constructing the meaning of 'different text'. The typographic contrast between regular and italics hence visually mirrors – and helps construct – the contrast between the narrative presented in the first person by the main character of the novel and the different voice of the letters which are inserted into that narrative. There may, however, also be another sense in which the choice of italics may be seen as iconic here, since the sloping nature of the typeface may seem to imitate the sloping nature of (much) handwriting.

At this point of the analysis, it might be fruitful to introduce an additional tool for dealing with typographic meaning-making. With the aim of approaching typography as systematically as linguists approach verbal language, van Leeuwen (2006) suggests that typographic signifiers can be described in terms of a number of *distinctive features*. His preliminary list consists of the following features which will help analysts understand and describe how one typeface stands out from another: *weight* (light[6] ↔ bold), *expansion* (narrow ↔ wide), *slope* (sloping ↔ upright), *curvature* (angular ↔ rounded), *connectivity* (connected ↔ disconnected), *orientation* (horizontal orientation ↔ vertical orientation) and *regularity* (regular ↔ irregular). While the sloping nature of Kostova's use of italics in the pages discussed above may thus be seen to iconically imitate the sloping nature of handwriting, another distinctive feature, that is, *regularity*, somewhat undermines the mimesis, since the typeface is clearly far more regular than what could have been produced by human hand. An additional concept to introduce here is that of *modality*, which, while borrowed from linguistics, is regarded as a multimodal principle by Kress and van Leeuwen (e.g., 1996: 159–80).[7] According to Halliday, linguistic modality concerns interpersonal 'colouring' in terms of speaker commitment to what is uttered through the modal categories of probability, usuality, obligation and inclination. Similar interpersonal 'colouring' is found in other modes where modality is defined as the question of 'as how true' or 'as how real' something is represented. In other words, high modality creates the sense that 'what we see is what we would have seen if we had been there' (van Leeuwen 2005a: 160). If we introduce the concept of modality for the analysis of Kostova's two-page spread, the sloping of the typeface that helps construct the meaning of 'letter' – and, more specifically, 'handwritten letter' – will be categorized visually as high modality, whereas its regularity is an example of low visual modality.

If we finally zoom in so that the text becomes readable, we quickly see how wording also plays a part in constructing the meaning of 'letter'. First of all, the experiential meaning of the surrounding narrative concerns a number of postcards that the protagonist finds in her father's room. The wording thus confirms our initial hunch that what we see is some kind of letter, and even specifies the nature of the letter to that of a postcard. Secondly, the text of the three small layout units aligned with respectively the right- and left-hand margins of the layout units in italics is easily recognizable as belonging to the genre of the letter: 'May 1962', 'My beloved daughter' and 'Your loving mother, Helen Rossi'. Altogether, the meaning of 'letter' (or 'postcard') created in Kostova's pages must be seen to be a multimodal construct, of which visual modes such as layout and typography play a significant role in addition to, and combination with, wording. It should be noted, however, that it is through wording that the more specific nature of the letter is constructed such as for example, the establishment of experiential meaning (what the letter is about) and interpersonal relations between the sender and the intended addressee.

A final look at the two-page spread from the *Historian* reveals that one more element stands out in terms of typography, namely the typeface selected for the chapter headings which are set in Blackletter type. In this example, typographic meaning appears to be created through the semiotic principle of *discursive import*. According to van Leeuwen (2005b: 139), a typeface which is typically associated with one domain may be employed in a different domain into which it thus discursively imports associations from the domain to which it originally belonged. Blackletter is an old style of typeface and hence not likely to be what readers generally expect to encounter in a contemporary novel. If asked what associations the typeface creates when used for Kostova's chapter headings, students regularly suggest meanings such as 'old', 'ancient' and perhaps even 'gothic', and it is thus easy to see how this particular typographical choice imports meaning which adds visually to the gothic contents of Kostova's vampire novel.

To provide students with an awareness of the importance of taking context into consideration in our analysis, it might briefly be mentioned how the meaning of Blackletter is likely to differ in a German context where, unlike the rest of the Western world, Blackletter type was used well into the twentieth century. As a consequence, Blackletter is perhaps not (yet) as prone to mean quite as 'ancient' and 'gothic' in a German context, but may, on the other hand, construct the meaning of 'German' or 'German-ness' in certain other contexts.

4   Extending the concept of 'the text'

While the aim of the analysis above was to help students realize how much can be said about the multimodal meaning-making even of a passage which is as multimodally inconspicuous as the extract from Kostova's novel, the aim of the present section is to spark considerations about what it is that constitutes our object of stylistic analysis and how a multimodal approach may help us cope analytically with an extended notion of 'the text' as, for instance, in the case of the novel. Where more traditional stylistic approaches – with their concern with wording – for obvious reasons tend to focus their analysis on the written verbal text, from the first word of Chapter 1 to the final full stop, a multimodal approach more easily accommodates meanings created by elements such as for example, the book cover of a given novel. A useful introductory exercise in this respect is to put the cover of a novel on display and ask students *what* meanings are created, and *how*, even before they have started reading (the verbal text of) the novel.[8] An illustrative example to employ for this purpose is Mark Haddon's novel, *The Curious Incident of the Dog in the Night-Time* (2004 [2003]; henceforth *Curious Incident*) displayed in Illustration 11.1.

First of all, the wording of the title clearly plays a role in encoding meaning on the book cover with its reminiscences of the mystery story. Some readers may even catch the intertextual reference to Conan Doyle's stories about Sherlock Holmes – whether in general terms, or to

Illustration 11.1 The Curious Incident of the Dog in the Night-Time (cover I[9]). 'Vintage Book Cover' copyright © 2004 by Vintage Books, a division of Random House, Inc., from THE CURIOUS INCIDENT OF THE DOG IN THE NIGHT-TIME by Mark Haddon. Used by permission of Doubleday, a division of Random House, Inc.

the specific story, 'The Adventure of Silver Blaze' (Doyle 1986 [1892]: 282–3), in which the famous phrase occurs.

As for the more specific nature of the 'curious incident' of Haddon's story, this meaning is partly disambiguated on the cover through the mode of visual images which consists of a blue background, two clouds, a moon, six stars, a dog and a garden fork. While the blue background, the moon and the stars experientially construct the circumstantial information of 'night', which is thus represented visually as well as by wording, the meaning constructed by the participants of the dog and the garden fork clearly extends the meaning of 'curious incident' to involve the information of the dog having been killed by somebody planting a garden fork in its chest. Notice in passing how the absence in both the visual and the verbal mode of the participant who killed the dog contributes to the construction of 'mystery'. This is a good place to draw students' attention to the fact that different modes carry (or construct) different information, and that the meaning constructed by the text as a whole (in this case, the book cover) is a result of the complex interaction of different modes. The title says one thing, the visual images another, yet with a certain overlap such as for example, the visual and verbal representation of 'dog' and 'night'. By being part of the same text, different modes combine into meaning that is more comprehensive than each of the modes taken alone.

A very salient feature of Haddon's book cover is the typography of the title which looks as if it has been produced by human hand – and, more specifically, by the hand of a child. If we inquire further into the typographic meaning-making by considering in more detail exactly what elements of the visual side of the title create this meaning, the distinctive feature of irregularity proves central in several respects. Not only do we see a marked irregularity of the individual letters, but also of the way they have been positioned in the layout of the cover, and of the inconsistent use of majuscules and minuscules. The visual look of the title is thus very different from – and forms a distinctive contrast to – the factual information above the title that the book is the 'winner of the Whitbread book of the year' which is set in a typeface that is clearly produced by technological means. In addition to this, the letters seem drawn rather than written, with surfaces which indicate that the reader also sees the top and the sides of some of the letters, thus apparently attempting to create a sense of three-dimensionality which may be seen as quite typical of children's playful writing. In terms of the semiotic typographical principles listed in Section 2, the typography of the title of Haddon's novel is thus likely to be interpreted as an *indexical* marker of a child (just as the archetypal example of a footprint is seen as an indexical marker of the person who made the footprint), and expectations that a child will be central to the ensuing narrative are not unlikely to arise. As we start reading the narrative proper, the expectations set up by the typography are soon fulfilled, since the story is narrated from the first-person perspective of an autistic boy. In addition to the indexical nature of the typography (i.e., of the letterforms being seen as an indexical marker of a child), there may furthermore be a sense in which meaning is imported discursively by the use of this particular typography. As a matter fact, playful irregular handwriting like that of Haddon's novel must statistically be seen as a relatively uncommon choice for the book cover of books for adults. The typographic signs are thus arguably imported into a context where they did not previously belong along with their associated meanings, most prominently that of 'child'.

The meanings created typographically by the somewhat clumsily drawn lettering of the title are matched by the mode of visual images in that the image of the dog is a drawing, that is, a visual mode often associated with children, and a drawing with some inconsistency at that. Closer scrutiny thus reveals that although the moon is situated to the top right of the image and the garden fork and the dog in the middle, the shadows cast by the garden fork and the dog are placed to the right of the dog rather than to the left.

As an aside, one might at this point play an extract from the audio book version of Haddon's novel to make students reflect on the different affordances of different modes and media. While the visual images of the book cover as well as those inserted into the narrative itself can obviously not be created sonically, the nature of the audio book enables – and enforces – the sonic realization of the narrative voice. In the case of Haddon's novel, the narrative is recorded by a boy, thereby sonically reflecting the meaning that is created visually by the typography employed for the title of the novel.

If we extend the notion of the text to also encompass, for example, the book cover when analysing a novel, we obviously encounter the challenge of coping with objects of analysis which are less stable than when focusing more conventionally on the written verbal text of the novel from Chapter 1 to the final full stop. To exemplify this, the cover of a different edition of Haddon's novel may be presented and the students asked to make a comparative multimodal analysis of the two covers. The cover used to this end here is that of the First Vintage Contemporaries edition displayed in Illustration 11.2. In the following, I shall refer to the two covers as 'cover I' and 'cover II'.

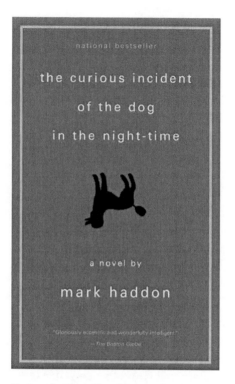

Illustration 11.2 Curious Incident, First Vintage Contemporaries edition (cover II), Vintage 2004. Used by permission of The Random House Group Ltd.

In contrast to cover I, where the blue colour of the background is likely to be decoded as an iconic construction of 'night' (in combination with the stars, the moon and the verbally realized 'night-time' of the title), the red background of cover II must be seen as a far more arbitrary choice of colour. On cover II, the meaning of 'night' is instead constructed by means of a slim black edge with a number of scattered white stars at the right-hand side of the cover – in addition, of course, to the meaning created by the wording of the title. The most marked difference between the two covers concerns the construction by cover I of the indexical meaning of 'child' which is completely absent from cover II. Unlike the (seemingly) hand-drawn nature of the typography of cover I, the plain grotesque typeface employed for cover II clearly has its origins in technological means of production. Nor does the visual image of the dog of cover II appear to be produced by human hand, let alone by a child, but consists of a black silhouette of a poodle which has been turned upside down. As for the visual disambiguation of the nature of the 'curious incident' of the title, the visual meanings of cover II are rather vague in experiential as well as interpersonal terms. Experientially, the fact that the garden fork is not represented on cover II makes this cover notably less informative than cover I as regards the question of what has happened to the dog. Interpersonally, the modality involved in the representation of the dog as an abstract silhouette rather than a drawing with more (realistic) detail, furthermore, makes it far less obvious that the dog is dead, even if its being turned upside down may indicate that something is not quite right.

To sum up, the meanings constructed by the two covers of *Curious Incident* differ in rather significant ways – and there are, in fact, more editions of the book to investigate for those who wish to extend the exercise. A logical consequence of this would be to consider to what extent the book cover is part of the meaning of a novel. While some analysts may wish to disregard the book cover in their analysis to avoid the possible instability of meaning involved by different editions of the novel, others, including the author of the present chapter, will claim that the meanings created by the book cover may well be seen as a not entirely insignificant part of the meaning of a given novel. In particular, the meanings created by the book cover seem to play a certain role in our decoding of the text when we first pick up the book and start reading it. The meanings created by the cover clearly give rise to expectations which are later fulfilled, disappointed or simply adjusted when we read the narrative proper. Some may argue that because the book cover is typically not created by the author, the meanings constructed may be a far cry from those intended by the author. However, from a multimodal perspective, which acknowledges the semiotic potential of discourse, design, production and distribution, the meanings constructed by the book cover must be seen as a valid part of the meaning of the novel, even if the author dislikes it no end.

In rounding off the analysis of the book cover of *Curious Incident*, further insights about multimodal meaning-making may be obtained by presenting students with the book cover of Haddon's next novel, *A Spot of Bother* (2007 [2006]) displayed in Illustration 11.3. Interestingly, the typographic- and visual discourses employed here are similar to those of cover I analysed above, but unlike *Curious Incident*, the main character and all-important focus of *A Spot of Bother* is the retired life – and fear of dying – of a 57-year-old man. If the visual side of the book cover spurs initial expectations in the reader similar to those of *Curious Incident*, such expectations are quickly eliminated by the text on the back of the

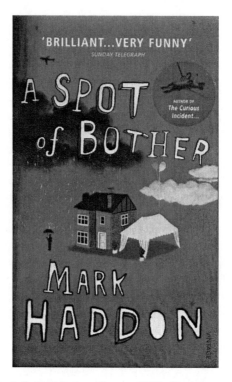

Illustration 11.3 A Spot of Bother, Vintage 2007. Used by permission of The Random House Group Ltd.

book ('At fifty-seven, George is settling down to a comfortable retirement') and the first paragraphs of the novel which concern the funeral of George's squash partner. What seems to be at play here in semiotic terms is the discursive import of the typography and visual style of Haddon's bestseller (i.e., *Curious Incident*) to create the meaning of 'Mark Haddon' for his succeeding novel. This meaning is further supported (and constructed) by the sticker placed next to the title, with its easily recognizable image of the dog with a garden fork planted solidly in its chest, the blue background and the written verbal text 'AUTHOR OF *The Curious Incident...*'. That the typographic and visual style of *Curious Incident* has, in fact, turned into a kind of visual identity for Mark Haddon's writings is further supported by the fact that the same visual discourse is presently employed on the publisher's website for Haddon's books (www.aspotofbother.co.uk/virtualtour). It might finally be noted in passing that an extra bit of meaning appears to be constructed typographically in the title of *A Spot of Bother* in that the broken cross bar of the 'T' may be decoded as an iconic representation of the 'bother' promised by the title.

5   Conclusion

Even though multimodal analysis ideally involves the constant analysis of the interaction of all semiotic modes employed in a given text, the complexity of multimodal semiosis typically leads to mode-by-mode analyis in practice. As teachers of multimodal stylistics we probably have to acknowledge the pragmatic necessity of such an approach, but should at the same time aim to make our students aware of the importance of the *interaction* of the modes involved in a given text.

While the practical analytical exercises suggested above introduce different aspects of multimodal stylistic analysis such as typography, layout, framing, distinctive features, modality and so on, none of these aspects is treated in detail, but they are intended as appetisers to the field of multimodal stylistics. Since *the* book on multimodality or multimodal stylistics does not yet exist, it is up to the teacher to select the most suitable texts for his or her course. Among the (largely 'monomodal') grammars and articles in the field today, I find the following particularly useful for courses on multimodal stylistics. On visual analysis: *Reading Images* (Kress and van Leeuwen 1996, 2006). On typography: 'Typographic meaning' (van Leeuwen 2005b); 'Towards a semiotics of typography' (van Leeuwen 2006); 'A Multimodal Approach to Meaning-Making in Trademarks' (Johannessen 2008). On layout: *Multimodality and Genre* (Bateman 2008). On colour: 'Colour as a Semiotic Mode' (Kress and van Leeuwen 2002). On multimodality: *Introducing Social Semiotics* (van Leeuwen 2005a); *Multimodal Transcription and Text Analysis* (Baldry and Thibault 2006); *Multimodal Discourse* (Kress and van Leeuwen 2001); 'Mastering Multimodal Complexity' (Boeriis 2008). On sound – a mode less central to literary analysis, yet of great relevance to those who wish to conduct multimodal stylistic analyses of, for example, film, television or drama: *Speech, Music, Sound* (van Leeuwen 1999). Since the specialized field of multimodal stylistics is very new, the critical output in the field is still sparse – exceptions being 'Integrating multimodal analysis and the stylistics of drama' (McIntyre 2008); '"I contain multitudes": Narrative multimodality and the book that bleeds' (Gibbons 2010); 'The Semiotics of Typography in Literary Texts' (Nørgaard 2009); 'Multimodality: Extending the stylistic tool kit' (Nørgaard 2010b).

As for the selection of suitable material for analysis, any book goes, though the selection of explicitly multimodal texts is, of course, likely to spur most interest as well as analytical output. Two novels of particular interest are, in my opinion, Lawrence Sterne's *The Life and Opinions of Tristram Shandy* (1992 [1759–67]) and Jonathan Safran Foer's *Extremely Loud and Incredibly Close* (2005). If equally interested in experimenting with the multisemiotic potential of their novels, the different results of the technological affordances of text production, printing and publishing available to Sterne and Foer at the respective time of publication would be an interesting topic to study. Another type of material for analysis is that of poetry and the ways in which poetic meaning-making can be seen as multimodal – in iconic poetry like, for example, Herbert's 'Easter Wings' (1986 [1633]) as well as in more 'conventional' poetry. Altogether, multimodal stylistics may open up to analysis of a broad range of texts – be it novels or musical performances, commercials or bus time-tables, posters or websites – and may hence help promote the stylistic analysis of literature to a more central position in the students' universe.

Notes

1. I follow here Halliday's (e.g., 1994) use of 'wording' which refers to the combination of the lexis and grammar of verbal language.
2. Strictly speaking, the focus of Kress and van Leeuwen (1996) and O'Toole (1994) is visual social semiotics rather than multimodality, yet these works implicitly involve multimodal thinking and incontestably make up the foundation of the multimodal paradigm.
3. An alternative term is *ideational meaning*.
4. In multimodal analysis, *compositional meaning* corresponds to Halliday's *textual meaning*.
5. In other examples, such differences in perceived texture may be more pronounced.
6. Strictly speaking, van Leeuwen's terms are 'regular ↔ bold' here, but to enable description of typefaces whose strokes are thinner than 'regular', I have substituted 'light' for 'regular'.
7. In spite of the implicitly multimodal orientation of their exploration of modality in visual communication, Kress and van Leeuwen (1996) do not use the term 'multimodality' here. Van Leeuwen's later take on modality (2005a: 160–77) is explicitly multimodal.
8. In the case that some respondents already know the novel in question, it is important to ask those who possess this knowledge to pretend that they do not and to keep their knowledge to themselves for the sake of the experiment.
9. Photographic reproductions of the book covers analysed in this chapter can all be accessed on the internet – simply do a 'google image' search or check for example, www.amazon.com.

References

Baldry, A. and Thibault, P. J. (2006) *Multimodal Transcription and Text Analysis*. London: Equinox.

Bateman, J. A. (2008) *Multimodality and Genre: A Foundation for the Systematic Analysis of Multimodal Documents*. Basingstoke: Palgrave Macmillan.

Boeriis, M. (2008) 'Mastering multimodal complexity', in Nørgaard, N. (ed.), *Systemic Functional Linguistics in Use. Odense Working Papers in Language and Communication* 29: 219–36.

Doyle, A. C. (1986 [1892]) 'The Adventure of Silver Blaze', in *The Complete Illustrated Sherlock Holmes*, pp. 271–86. London: Omega Books.

Foer, J. S. (2005) *Extremely Loud and Incredibly Close*. London: Hamish Hamilton.

Gibbons, A. (2010) '"I contain multitudes": Narrative multimodality and the book that bleeds', in Page, R. (ed.), *New Perspective on Narrative and Multimodality*, pp. 99–114. Abingdon: Routledge.

Haddon, M. (2004 [2003]) *The Curious Incident of the Dog in the Night-Time*. London: Vintage.

Haddon, M. (2004 [2003]) *The Curious Incident of the Dog in the Night-Time* (First Vintage Contemporaries Edition). New York: Vintage.

Haddon, M. (2007) *The Curious Incident of the Dog in the Night-Time*. Audiobook narrated by Ben Tibber. London: Random House Audiobooks.

Haddon, M. (2007 [2006]) *A Spot of Bother*. London: Vintage.

Halliday, M. A. K. (1994) *An Introduction to Functional Grammar*, 2nd edn. London: Arnold.

Herbert, G. (1986 [1633]) 'Easter Wings', in *The Norton Anthology of English Literature*, Volume 1 (5th edn). New York and London: Norton.

Johannessen, C. M. (2008) 'A multimodal approach to meaning-making in trademarks', in Nørgaard, N. (ed.), *Systemic Functional Linguistics in Use. Odense Working Papers in Language and Communication* 29: 460–80.

Kostova, E. (2006 [2005]) *The Historian*. London: Time Warner Books.

Kress, G. and van Leeuwen, T. (1996) *Reading Images: The Grammar of Visual Design*. London: Routledge.

Kress, G. and van Leeuwen, T. (2001) *Multimodal Discourse: The Modes and Media of Contemporary Communication*. London: Arnold.

Kress, G. and van Leeuwen, T. (2002) 'Colour as a semiotic mode: Notes for a grammar of colour', *Visual Communication* 1(3): 343–68.

Kress, G. and van Leeuwen, T. (2006) *Reading Images: The Grammar of Visual Design*, 2nd edn. London: Routledge.

McIntyre, D. (2008) 'Integrating multimodal analysis and the stylistics of drama: A multimodal perspective on Ian McKellen's *Richard III*', *Language and Literature* 17(4): 309–34.

Mollerup, P. (1999) *Marks of Excellence*. London: Phaidon.

Nørgaard, N. (2009) 'The semiotics of typography in literary texts: A multimodal approach', *Orbis Litterarum* 64: 141-60.

Nørgaard, N. (2010a) 'Multimodality and the literary text: Making sense of Safran Foer's *Extremely Loud and Incredibly Close*', in Page, Ruth (ed.), *New Perspectives on Narrative and Multimodality*, pp. 115–26. Abingdon: Routledge.

Nørgaard, N. (2010b) 'Multimodality: Extending the stylistic tool kit', in McIntyre, D. and Busse, B. (eds), *Language and Style*, pp. 433–48. Basingstoke: Palgrave Macmillan.

O'Halloran, K. L. (2005) *Mathematical Discourse: Language, Symbolism and Visual Images*. London: Continuum.

O'Toole, M. (1994) *The Language of Displayed Art*. London: Leicester University Press.

Sterne, L. (1992 [1759–67]) *The Life and Opinions of Tristram Shandy*. Oxford: Oxford University Press.

Van Leeuwen, T. (1999) *Speech, Music, Sound*. Basingstoke: Palgrave Macmillan.

Van Leeuwen, T. (2005a) *Introducing Social Semiotics*. London: Routledge.

Van Leeuwen, T. (2005b) 'Typographic meaning', *Visual Communication* 4(2): 137–43.

Van Leeuwen, T. (2006) 'Towards a semiotics of typography', *Information Design Journal + Document Design* 14(2): 139–15.

12
Teaching Cognitive Stylistics

David West

Editors' preface

In this final chapter, David West challenges literary studies to accept the importance of language in literary criticism, and the consequent central role of stylistics in interpreting literature. West demonstrates that a cognitive stylistic approach can account for the linguistic features of a text and how real readers might respond to them.

What is cognitive stylistics?

Cognitive stylistics is an approach to literature which focuses upon the dynamic relationship between the literary text, as a complex linguistic phenomenon, and the cognitive processes that underlie, make possible, and are manifested in our interpretation or reading of the text.[1] It is an approach that is based upon the earlier approach of stylistics in its principled and systematic focus upon literature *as language*. However, it also moves beyond stylistics in its insistence that the linguistic phenomena identified in a literary text have psychological reality; in other words, that they do not exist independently of the reader, and in particular of the cognitive processes – for example, attention, expectation, memory, categorization, analogical reasoning – that the reader inevitably and unconsciously brings to the text. Thus, the meaning of a text resides not in the text itself but in the interplay between the words on the page and the reader's cognitive processes, and it is this interplay that is the focus of cognitive stylistics. This is what Peter Stockwell means by *texture*.[2] For example, to be able to understand a statement such as 'Juliet is the sun' requires us to recognize it as a metaphor, and to recognize it as a metaphor requires us to draw upon our fundamental cognitive ability first to categorize objects in the world (according to what is human and what is not human) and second to transfer (some of) the properties of one category (the non-human sun) to the other category (the human Juliet). This is a remarkably complex act of meaning-making that is performed effortlessly, instantly and unconsciously, and it is the task of cognitive stylistics to uncover the processes that make such acts possible. In short, it is to expose what we do with a text when we read it, to slow the reading process down so that we can make visible and conscious what is normally invisible and unconscious.

Cognitive stylistics, then, is not so much interested in individual texts or writers or periods or genres, but in literature *per se*, and in particular in the nature of the text-reader interaction. It is therefore an approach which asks the fundamental questions, such as: How do we understand or make sense of a literary text? Why do we gain pleasure from literature? What accounts for the (sometimes overwhelming) emotions that we experience when we read literature? What effects does a literary text have upon us, and what effects do we have upon the literary text? Cognitive stylistics, then, is rooted in linguistics in its focus upon the text's language; and it is rooted in cognitive science (in particular, cognitive psychology) in its focus upon the reader's cognitive processes. It is an approach not without precedents: in its focus upon the text, it has commonalities with formalism (and, indeed, with post-structuralism); in its focus upon the reader, with reader-response criticism. Where it differs from both, though, is in its grounding in cognitive psychology and its systematic relating of the text's style to the reader's cognition.

Finally, cognitive stylisticians may argue that an explanation of literature is only truly valid if it is grounded in an understanding of linguistics and cognitive psychology, but, as Stockwell (2002a: 6) argues in his introduction to the field,[3] that does not mean to say that they see literature as offering simply another set of data for these two master disciplines – cognitive stylistics is not simply the handmaiden of linguistics, or cognitive psychology, or the discipline that unites the two, cognitive linguistics. It is important to stress that cognitive stylisticians see literature as peculiar language,[4] as a discourse field that pushes ordinary language to its limits; and that they therefore see literature also as peculiar cognition, as a phenomenon that pushes human cognition to its limits. I do not want to argue here for the modularity of literature; literature is quite clearly embedded in everyday language and in everyday cognition. It is produced and read by language-using, cognitive human beings, and we do not cease being human when we put pen to paper to write a poem or when we open a novel to read it. Nonetheless, we should also not lose sight of the remarkable, and unique, things that literature can do: we are often highly motivated to seek it out and read it; we can read and re-read the same literary text; a literary text can give us the kind of pleasure that no other piece of writing can come near to giving us; the effects that a literary text can produce in us – empathy, anger, ecstasy, grief – are effects that no other kind of text can produce. These are things that mark literature out, and indeed that enable us to recognize a category – fuzzy though it may be – called *literature*. Therefore, we need to recognize the singular power of literature while recognizing also that this power derives from cognitive capacities which are common to us all as human beings.

The consequence of such a dual recognition is an approach that sees literature as not only being illuminated by linguistics and cognitive psychology, but also as illuminating these two disciplines. It is no coincidence that cognitive linguistics effectively began in the late 1970s with work on that most literary of tropes, metaphor.[5] Nor that the most prominent cognitive linguists have either had a background in literature or developed an interest in literature arising from their work in cognitive linguistics.[6] It seems, then, that literature is peculiarly amenable to a cognitive and linguistic approach. Indeed, we could surmise that the fundamental principle of literature, its defining feature, lies in the very way that it deals centrally with, or foregrounds, language and cognition, and that, in other words, language and cognition are the essence of literature.

In this chapter, I want to give an idea of what a cognitive-stylistic approach might look like in the classroom, before outlining some of the implications of such an approach for students, teachers and the subject of English.

Teaching cognitive stylistics in practice: attention

In reality, the cognitive processes that we are born with, and that mark us out as the human species, are not discrete, but work together seamlessly to help us to negotiate the world in which we live. It is these processes that enable us to perform such apparently diverse tasks as tying our shoe laces, riding a bike, and reading or writing a sonnet. Nonetheless, it is useful to consider them for our purposes as having a degree of modularity, as long as their essential intertwinedness is borne in mind. In this section, I want to focus upon, or attend to, the cognitive process of *attention* to illustrate how it underlies our engagement with literature, and to exemplify how we might teach literature from a cognitive-stylistic perspective. I have chosen to focus upon *attention* because it is quite a well-researched area both in cognitive psychology (it is one of the areas that the *Gestalt* psychologists investigated in the early twentieth century) and in cognitive linguistics.[7] It is also an area that cognitive stylisticians have tended to focus upon.[8] I want to take the three steps that I normally take when I focus upon the concept of *attention* in a cognitive-stylistics class: first, to establish *attention* as a cognitive phenomenon, as something that can be seen at work outside language and literature; second, to establish the presence of *attention* in language in general; third, to apply the concept to our reading of literature.

First, then, look at the sheet of paper before you and consider what you see. I would expect that your answer would be something like: *words* or *words on a page* or, simply, *black marks*. These are the kinds of answers that students always, without fail, give. What we all quite clearly see *are* words or black marks on a page; this seems so obvious as to require no comment or explanation. Yet, what we see does *not* correspond with what is really there; or, rather, what we see only *partially* corresponds with what is really there. Between the eye and the page falls our mind, which makes us see what is before us in a particular way. Thus, what we are looking at, in truth, are black marks (i.e., the letters) and white shapes between the black marks (i.e., the page). Indeed, the space occupied by the white shapes is probably greater than the space occupied by the black marks, so one would think that it would be the white space, as the object that fills more of our perceptual field, that would attract most attention. What is astonishing, however, is that we never see the white shapes – it would require an enormous effort of will for us to see the white shapes and not the black marks, and indeed no student has ever given *white shapes* as an answer. What accounts for this remarkable phenomenon?

In our every moment of sensory experience – visual, auditory, olfactory, haptic, gustatory – we are automatically and unconsciously organizing and selecting the data that we receive in such a way that we attend to or foreground certain things and ignore or background others. What we give primary attention to in the perceptual field is referred to in cognitive science as the *figure*, and what we give secondary attention to is referred to as the *ground*. Thus, in our example, the *figure* would be the black marks or the words, and the *ground* would be the white shapes or the page.

The example that I have given is extreme in the sense that we always see the black marks and never the white shapes, so that it would be almost impossible to switch between the two. A less extreme example is the famous image created by the Danish *Gestalt* psychologist Edgar Rubin in 1915, an image which allows us to see either a black vase against a white background, or two white faces in profile against a black background.[9] With Rubin's image, we can switch our attention so that we can see either one or the other, but the crucial point is that we cannot see both simultaneously, despite the fact that both images, quite clearly, are there before us. The reason that we cannot switch our attention so easily with the extreme example of the black marks and the white shapes is primarily because it is, of course, the black marks that we are (hopefully) interested in. We know that the black marks are words, and that the words are meaningful, and our perception makes us attend to what is more salient and to ignore what is less salient. This saves us a lot of cognitive effort, since we do not have to process everything in the perceptual field. Such an unconscious and automatic process of attending to what is important might even save our lives one day, as it is this process that enables us to attend to or notice on the horizon a lion moving towards us. It is the same process that leads us to notice immediately a scratch on a table or a speck of dirt on a floor.

The cognitive process of *attention*, like all cognitive processes, is automatic, omnipresent, inevitable, innate – and therefore invisible and unconscious. One of the ways that we can make visible and become conscious of the workings of attention is through looking at language, for one of the fundamental tenets of a major branch of cognitive science, cognitive linguistics, is that our cognitive processes shape, and are manifested in, the patterns that we can perceive in language – in particular, its semantic, syntactic (or grammatical) and phonetic/phonological features. To illustrate this in terms of syntax, look at the following pairs of noun phrases and join them with an appropriate preposition – you can swap the order of the noun phrases as you see fit.

1. the ring / her finger
2. the stirrup / her foot

I would suggest that the following solutions are possible:[10]

1(a) the ring on her finger	1(b) her finger in the ring
2(a) the stirrup on her foot	2(b) her foot in the stirrup

Theoretically, there are two possible solutions for each pair, which means that each possible solution has a 50 per cent chance of being chosen. What is remarkable is that 1(b) and 2(a) are *never*[11] chosen – indeed, native speakers would probably judge these as being wrong. Yet, what we see is just as much *her finger in the ring* as *the ring on her finger*, and just as much *the stirrup on her foot* as *her foot in the stirrup*. Again, what can account for this remarkable phenomenon? Why do we switch the syntactic pattern from *the ring on her finger* (preposition *on* and human body part in end position) to *her foot in the stirrup* (preposition *in* and human body part in initial position)? If we can say *her foot in the stirrup*, then why can't we say *her finger in the ring*? .

The answer, of course, is *attention*. What we can notice with this set of data is that the two objects automatically chosen to occupy initial position in the noun phrase – *the ring* and *her foot* – share certain features in relation to the two objects chosen to occupy end position: namely they are smaller (at least, the portion of her foot that is in the stirrup is small in relation to the stirrup) and more mobile (we move a ring towards a finger and not *vice versa*, and we move a foot towards a stirrup and not *vice versa*). Both objects are also the more important in each pair: the ring signifies her married status, whereas her finger signifies, in itself, nothing; her foot is significant because it is a part of her body, whereas the stirrup is just a piece of metal, indistinguishable from all the other stirrups in the world. It is no coincidence, argue cognitive linguists, that the more salient object in each pair, the *figure*, should precede syntactically the less salient object, the *ground*. In other words, there is a clear correlation between the position of the object in the noun phrase and the importance that we give to it in our attention: the *figure* precedes the *ground* syntactically because it is the more important. This explains also, to return to our first example, why we say *the words on the page* rather than *the page under the words* – it is simply the words that we are interested in and not the page, and we represent this bias of interest iconically, by placing the object of most importance in initial position. What comes first syntactically is what we attend to first and is of greatest importance.

For cognitive linguists, the application of the notion of *attention* is not restricted to how we arrange the constituents of noun phrases in relation to each other. On the contrary, attention is a cognitive process that affects and is manifested in all aspects of language. For example, in using the passive rather than the active voice in *Our house is being renovated* (rather than *Builders are renovating our house*), we are attending to *our house* (the semantic patient, i.e., the thing being acted upon) rather than *builders* (the semantic agent, i.e., the thing doing the acting). The house then becomes the figure and the builders become the (invisible) ground – we know when we say *Our house is being renovated* that somebody is doing the renovating, but the passive construction allows us to omit the semantic agent. These examples could be multiplied *ad infinitum*.[12] The crucial point is that *Our house is being renovated* may mean the same thing – in the sense of referring to the same state of affairs in the world – as *Builders are renovating our house*, but they are in actual fact very different because each encodes a particular pattern of attention.

Thus, language is not a transparent window on to the world, but a reflection of our cognitive relation with the world, which means that when we look at language we are looking first and foremost at our cognitive processes, at the pattern of our minds. This makes language itself the central focus of attention, because language – each word, phrase, clause, syntactic relation – is fraught with significance. This obviously has – or, at least, should have – major implications for literature and for our teaching of the subject of English.

So far, I have established, I hope, the fact that the cognitive process of attention can be seen at work in sensory perception. I have also established that, like all other cognitive processes, attention shapes language and is manifested in language. It would be curious to say the least to assume that literature – which is, after all, made of language and is written and read by cognitive beings – can be a separate, discrete module, one not subject to, and therefore one not explicable in terms of, the same set of cognitive processes. And, indeed, what we find is that the cognitive process of attention, along with other cognitive processes, is one of the fundamental principles of literature: put simply, when writers write, they attend to certain things and ignore or give less prominence to others; they use an array of devices to focus readers' attention now on one thing and now on another; and readers, reading, necessarily attend to certain things in the text and barely notice others. All of this takes place largely automatically and unconsciously: we don't notice what or how we notice. It is the primary function of teaching cognitive stylistics, I would argue, to make what is invisible and unconscious visible and conscious. How might this be done?

To begin with, put yourself in the position of a potential murder victim. You are lying supine on a sofa. There is a person moving towards you. Of the following objects, which one would you notice first?

an arm   a clenched hand   a carving knife

The chances are that you would notice first the carving knife – this is what students almost always tell me, in any case. Clearly, it is for you at this particular instance (you are in a murder scene and not sitting down to a Sunday roast) by far the most important object in the room. Moreover, a carving knife has similar features to the other figures discussed earlier: like the ring and the foot, the carving knife in the murder scene is (relatively) small and mobile. This is why we would be more likely to say *the carving knife in her clenched hand* than *her clenched hand around the carving knife*; and it is also why we would be more likely to say *a clenched hand at the bottom of her arm* than *an arm at the top of her hand*. In other words, there is a clear hierarchy in the order of our attention, from carving knife to clenched hand to arm. Moreover, we would expect this to be reflected in language (this is what is meant by *iconicity*), with the object of primary importance (the carving knife) preceding syntactically the two objects of secondary importance (the clenched hand and the arm). Thus, we would expect a sentence such as: *the carving knife in her clenched hand at the end of her arm.*

Now read the following sentence, which is taken from Conrad's novel *The Secret Agent* (1907), and consider what you notice:

> He saw partly on the ceiling and partly on the wall the moving shadow of an arm with a clenched hand holding a carving knife.
>
> (Conrad 1947: 262)

What should now be immediately apparent is that the normal order of attention has been reversed. What is attended to first in the long noun phrase which acts as the object of the sentence is 'the moving shadow of an arm', and second 'a clenched hand', and third 'a carving knife'. We experience these three objects temporally in our processing of the noun phrase, from arm to hand to knife, and this also is the order in which we attend to the objects. The reversed order is also the order in which the character whose perception we share at this particular moment, Verloc, attends to the objects: he perceives the scene in its entirety (from his supine position on the sofa), but he makes into the figure of the noun phrase the object of least importance ('an arm') and relegates to the ground the object of most importance ('a carving knife'). This would be akin to saying: *I saw under the sky a tree in front of which was a lion coming towards me with its mouth open and its teeth bared.* By the time I have processed all the perceptual data, and decided that my attention should focus first upon the sky and last upon the lion's teeth, those said teeth will be around my throat. Verloc's reversed order of attention has the same fatal consequences, for at the beginning of the next paragraph we read that the carving knife has already been sunk into his side.

What we are doing as readers here is gaining a glimpse into the cognitive processes of the novel's main character: what Verloc attends to is what we attend to, as we are placed temporarily into his mental world. By being placed into an aberrant mental world, one in which the sequence of attention has a strange order, our attention is drawn to the very process of attention. Writing in the preface to his short novel *The Nigger of the 'Narcissus'* (1897), Conrad (1950: x) defined his central task to his readers as being 'to make you hear, to make you feel – it is, before all, to make you *see*'. Thus, what we see is seeing itself. Moreover, as readers, our attention in this particular sentence is focused upon the object at the end of the long noun phrase (the carving knife), precisely because it is in the wrong position. We would expect the information given in the sentence to correspond to how we would normally experience the scene, and we would therefore expect the carving knife to precede the clenched hand, which in turn would precede the arm. The fact that Conrad's narrator's sentence runs against the texture of our expectations means that the carving knife is given even greater prominence in our attention. To say *the ring on her finger* or *her foot in the stirrup* would not be particularly noticeable, but to say *her finger in the ring* or *the stirrup on her foot* would clearly be. Similarly, we could pass over a sentence with the noun phrase *the carving knife in her clenched hand at the end of her arm* with relative equanimity, but not the one that Conrad's narrator gives us. I often ask my students several weeks after we have looked at the paragraph as a whole describing Verloc's murder for details of the murder, and they forget certain details (e.g., where Verloc is lying, which room the murder takes place in), but they always know that it is a knife, and a carving knife, that is used. This would suggest that what we pay particular attention to has a greater permanence and prominence in long-term memory.[13]

We could discuss this particular sentence in much more detail – for example, we could draw attention to the way in which the head of the long noun phrase is not even a concrete object at all but a 'moving shadow'; and we could observe that the long noun phrase is the syntactic object of the sentence, and that it is preceded by an adverbial ('partly on the ceiling and partly on the wall'), which has the effect of disassociating the act of perception encoded by the verb ('saw') from the object of perception ('the moving shadow', etc.). We could then relate this particular sentence to the paragraph as a whole in which it appears, and see whether the same patterns of attention are noticeable in the rest of the paragraph. What we would then notice is the way in which the attention of the unnamed first-person narrator (the narrator appears once only as 'I', at the beginning of the second chapter) works metonymically. For example, the murderer (Mrs Verloc) is seen in terms of her body parts – 'her right hand', 'her face', 'the lower lip', 'the eyes' – rather than as a whole; and certain events are described in terms of their end state rather than in their entirety, as can be observed in the following sentence:

> Her [Mrs Verloc's] right hand skimmed slightly the end of the table, and when she had passed on towards the sofa the carving knife had vanished without the slightest sound from the side of the dish.
>
> (Conrad 1947: 262)

What we see is that the carving knife has vanished; we don't see it being seized by Mrs Verloc. What we see is Mrs Verloc having already walked towards the sofa; we don't see her walking there.

Such an approach would begin by establishing how the cognitive process of attention works and the way in which the process manifests itself in language. It would then explore the applicability of the notion of *attention* to key extracts from a handful of literary texts, with the emphasis being on the devices that a writer uses to attract and distract a reader's attention, and the patterns of attention that can be identified in a reader's engagement with the text. Potentially, that would be more or less a whole semester's teaching in itself, although a consideration of other cognitive processes could also be integrated. For example, with the Conrad passage, what is quite clearly also important in producing the effect of suspense in the reader is *expectation*, or the reader's projection into the future based on past and present experience. The fact that the carving knife has already been mentioned in the paragraph, and then as the grammatical subject (it 'had vanished'), means that when we see 'the moving shadow of an arm', and then 'the clenched hand', we are projecting forward – and our expectations are confirmed (at last!) when we see the carving knife.

Some objections and implications

There are perhaps three objections to such an approach, and I wish to foreground and counter these objections explicitly, before moving on in my final section to an outline of some of the implications of teaching cognitive stylistics. The first objection might be that such a fine-grained, language-obsessive approach, in which a single sentence can be discussed for the entire duration of a two-hour class, cannot possibly be used when it comes to discussing whole novels, let alone whole genres or periods or *oeuvres*. Such an objection is justified if this is what we think teaching literature means, if we think that it means dealing with a novel a week (*Bleak House* this week, *Middlemarch* the next) or a whole period in a semester (the nineteenth-century novel). However, to teach literature in this way might give students a spurious knowledge of a particular writer or genre or period, but it does not enable them to develop the skills necessary to read, appreciate and understand literature in itself. Teaching cognitive stylistics means enabling students to read very slowly, so that they begin to notice what they are doing when they read. In doing so, it develops students' capacities to read independently all literature from all genres and periods; what is relevant in a discussion of a Shakespeare sonnet is relevant also in a discussion of a Roddy Doyle novel. In short, it is the only approach that enables students to read literature.

The second objection might be that such an approach may well work with a writer like Conrad, who, as a modernist writing at the time of the birth of cognitive science in the late nineteenth and early twentieth century, was peculiarly interested in his writing in exploring human cognition, but that it is irrelevant in a discussion of other writers from other periods. It is certainly true that nothing interesting can be said about Conrad (or, indeed, about literary modernism in general) without placing his work against the background of the rise of cognitive science. However, the approach of cognitive stylistics is thoroughly relevant for all writers from all periods because what it deals with are the general cognitive processes that underlie the writing and reading of texts, and these cognitive processes have not changed significantly in the last few thousand years. Thus, I have discussed in depth with students the notion of *attention* in relation to sonnets of the English Renaissance. In particular, I have investigated with students how Sidney and Spenser control the focus of our attention through building up and confounding our expectations through metrical, syntactic and semantic deviation.

The third objection might be that such an approach, in its focus upon the words on the page and their relationship with the essential biological fact of human cognition, lacks any social, historical or political dimension. Yet, what is clear is that human cognition, because it is fundamental to how we interact with our environment and therefore with others, is peculiarly vulnerable to social, historical and political forces. Thus, cognitive processes may be biological at root (in the sense that attention, for example, works in the same way for all human beings), but how these processes actually work themselves out in every second of our waking lives is heavily influenced by our social experience. To give just one example very quickly with regard to attention: in Kate Chopin's second and final novel *The Awakening* (1899), the main character, Edna, gives a dinner party to celebrate her separation from her husband. What is noticeable is the frequent use of the passive voice throughout the passage, the effect of which is to foreground, or turn into the figure, the food brought to the table, and to background, or turn into the ground, the actual people who cook and serve the food – the overwhelming majority of whom were, at this particular time in postbellum America, black servants. The following sentence is typical:

> All her interest seemed to be centered upon the delicacies placed before her.
>
> (Chopin 1969: 971)

This contrasts very sharply with Chopin's other novel, *At Fault*, published in 1890, and many of her short stories published in the early and mid-1890s (e.g., 'La Belle Zoraïde' and 'Désirée's Baby'), which have very strong black presences, either as characters or narrators. Thus, an understanding of *attention* and its linguistic encoding allows us to notice an ideological shift in Chopin's writing, a shift in which black people move from being the figure in the early 1890s to the (invisible) ground in the late 1890s. Thus, a cognitive-stylistic approach does not preclude an approach that sees the ideological or political or historical significance of literature; indeed, a cognitive-stylistic approach can be the basis of our understanding of a text's context.

From the perspective of students, cognitive stylistics is empowering because the focus in a cognitive-stylistics class is the student's reading of a text. Thus, the teacher no longer has a natural advantage gained simply through having read more and having developed a better understanding of the text's social or political context. Moreover, doing cognitive stylistics is intrinsically enjoyable, interesting and meaningful, for both students and teachers, simply because dealing with literature in such a way affords us a glimpse of what we are as human beings, of how we experience, interpret and construe the world around us. All that cognitive stylistics does is make conscious and visible through its dealings with literature those cognitive processes which are unconscious and invisible. Thus, cognitive stylistics is rooted in the ordinary, and enables students to make connections between what they do when they read literature and what they do in every second of their everyday lives. In this way, doing literature becomes intrinsically meaningful and relevant again.

In a review of the 2006 volume *English: The Condition of the Subject*, a collection of essays from the 2003 English Subject Centre annual conference, Vicky Greenaway (2007: 33) celebrates 'the relativism and fragmentation of the discipline and its practitioners in its current state'.[14] It is certainly true that the subject of English is characterized by its relativism and fragmentation, but, far from seeing these as positive attributes, we should question why we have allowed the subject to fall into such a critical condition. English is a fragmented subject because it lacks a set of aims, methods and assumptions, and we should lament this state of affairs rather than celebrate it. It is a subject without a centre or a soul. Different scholars approach literature from wildly different perspectives, so that there is very little common ground between them: a scholar specializing in Shakespeare, for example, would claim not to be in a position to teach contemporary fiction. I do not want to offer here cognitive stylistics as simply another approach to literature, as simply another fragment. Rather, I want to argue that it is an approach that can unite the discipline because it goes to the heart of what literature is: a complex linguistic phenomenon in which the workings of our cognition are foregrounded and manifested.

Cognitive stylistics is not new. As I have already mentioned, it has commonalities with formalism and with reader-response criticism. Most intriguingly, it was a form of cognitive stylistics that I. A. Richards was working towards at Cambridge in the 1920s and 1930s.[15] It is an approach that was resurrected in the 1990s by Mark Turner in *Reading Minds* (1991) and popularized by Peter Stockwell and others in the Poetics and Linguistics Association (PALA) in the early 2000s.[16] Indeed, much of the work in stylistics produced by the international community of PALA scholars during the last decade can be seen as fundamentally cognitive in the sense that it relates a text's language to the reader's meaning-making processes. It is also an approach that has some empirical substance to it.[17] Thus, teachers of English should not shy away from the approach. To begin teaching cognitive stylistics requires some knowledge of cognitive linguistics,[18] but teachers of English have drawn upon sociology and history and politology and psychoanalysis in their teaching of the subject, so to develop an understanding of this field should not prove too arduous. Indeed, if we want to make our subject relevant and important again, we have no choice.

As it is currently taught, English, with its diversity and fragmentation, is, in Widdowson's terms, simply a *subject* and not a *discipline* (Widdowson

1975: 2) since it lacks completely a set of theoretical requirements. As a consequence, it is possible for those teaching English at schools and universities to get away with doing more or less whatever they want, however bizarre and outrageous that might be; indeed, the more bizarre and outrageous, it often seems, the better. For the subject to reclaim its rightful place at the centre of the humanities, it has to reground itself upon the recognition of literature as a human achievement. Cognitive stylistics is able to reorientate the subject precisely because it sees literature as a human achievement, as something rooted in our fundamental human cognitive capacities. It is time that we take the cognitive turn in our discipline.

Notes

1. Cognitive stylisticians tend to distinguish between *interpretation* and *reading*. For example, Stockwell (2002b: 75) reserves '*interpretation* for the initial readerly sense of the work, and *reading* for its conscious and perhaps socially uttered expression'. It is a distinction that I find dubious, since it introduces an unnecessary hierarchy in readerly response.
2. See Stockwell 2009.
3. Stockwell's introductory book is titled *Cognitive Poetics*. The field has three nomenclatures which are more or less interchangeable: *cognitive poetics*, *cognitive stylistics* and *cognitive rhetoric*. Stockwell (2009) has recently added a fourth, *cognitive aesthetics*.
4. The term is taken from the title of Derek Attridge's book *Peculiar Language* (1988). As a post-structuralist, Attridge is interested in language but not cognition; he is therefore not a cognitive stylistician.
5. In effect, cognitive linguistics was launched with the publication in 1980 of Lakoff and Johnson's *Metaphors We Live By*.
6. I am thinking in particular of the cognitive linguists George Lakoff, Mark Turner and Raymond Gibbs, who have all authored or co-authored major books on literature. See in particular Lakoff and Turner 1989; and Gibbs 1994.
7. For an overview of the cognitive treatment of attention in psychology and linguistics, see Ungerer and Schmid 2006: 163–206.
8. See, for example, Stockwell 2002a: 13–25, and Stockwell 2003: 13–25.
9. The famous image first appeared in Rubin's 1915 Danish-language book *Synsoplevede Figurer* (*Visual Figures*). For an interesting account which places Rubin's work in the context of *Gestalt* psychology, see Hochberg 1964: 82–94.
10. For the sake of clarity, I am ignoring *the stirrup around her foot* as a possibility.
11. Or hardly ever. A student with an overactive imagination and a peculiar penchant for crime fiction once chose *her finger in the ring*, but he meant by that that her body part was lying in the boxing ring, an interpretation which would also fit the usual figure-ground configuration of smaller, mobile object preceding larger, immobile object.

12. More examples of how the figure-ground configuration is manifested in language are given in Radden and Dirven 2007: 28–30.
13. Experiments on memory, in which respondents were given short literary texts and asked for their recollections, were conducted by Bartlett at Cambridge in the 1910s and 1920s, and reported on in Bartlett 1932.
14. I have written about this elsewhere. See West 2008.
15. See in particular Richards's *Principles of Literary Criticism* (1924) and *Practical Criticism* (1929). The importance of Richards's work for cognitive stylistics is the focus of West (forthcoming).
16. I am thinking in particular here of the following introductory books: Gavins and Steen 2003; Semino and Culpeper 2002; Stockwell 2002a.
17. See in particular van Peer 1986, and van Peer, Hakemulder and Zyngier 2007.
18. An excellent introduction to cognitive linguistics is Evans and Green 2006.

References

Attridge, D. (1988) *Peculiar Language: Literature as Difference from the Renaissance to James Joyce*. London: Routledge.

Bartlett, F.C. (1932) *Remembering: A Study in Experimental and Social Psychology*. Cambridge: Cambridge University Press.

Chopin, K. (1969) *The Awakening*, in Seyersted, P. (ed.), *The Complete Works of Kate Chopin*. Baton Rouge: Louisiana State University Press.

Conrad, J. (1947) *The Secret Agent*. London: J. M. Dent.

Conrad, J. (1950) *The Nigger of the 'Narcissus'*. London: J. M. Dent.

Evans, V. and Green, M. (2006) *Cognitive Linguistics: An Introduction*. Edinburgh: Edinburgh University Press.

Gavins, J. and Steen, G. (eds) (2003) *Cognitive Poetics in Practice*. London: Routledge.

Gibbs, R. (1994) *The Poetics of Mind: Figurative Thought, Language, and Understanding*. Cambridge: Cambridge University Press.

Greenaway, V. (2007) Review of Martin, P. (ed.) (2006) *English: The Condition of the Subject*, English Subject Centre Newsletter 13: 33–4.

Hochberg, J. (1964) *Perception*. Englewood Cliffs, NJ: Prentice-Hall.

Lakoff, G. and Johnson, M. (1980) *Metaphors We Live By*. Chicago: University of Chicago Press.

Lakoff, G. and Turner, M. (1989) *More Than Cool Reason: A Field Guide to Poetic Metaphor*. Chicago: University of Chicago Press.

Martin, P. (ed.) (2006) *English: The Condition of the Subject*. Basingstoke: Palgrave Macmillan.

Radden, G. and Dirven, R. (2007) *Cognitive English Grammar*. Amsterdam: John Benjamins.

Richards, I. A. (2001 [1924]) 'Principles of Literary Criticism', in Constable, J. (ed.), *I. A. Richards Selected Works 1919–1938*. London: Routledge.

Richards, I. A. (2001 [1929]) 'Practical Criticism: A Study of Literary Judgement', in Constable, J. (ed.), *I. A. Richards Selected Works 1919–1938*. London: Routledge.

Semino, E. and Culpeper, J. (eds) (2002) *Cognitive Stylistics: Language and Cognition in Text Analysis*. Amsterdam: John Benjamins.

Stockwell, P. (2002a) *Cognitive Poetics: An Introduction.* London: Routledge.

Stockwell, P. (2002b) 'Miltonic texture and the feeling of reading', in Semino, E. and Culpeper, J. (eds), *Cognitive Stylistics: Language and Cognition in Text Analysis.* Amsterdam: John Benjamins.

Stockwell, P. (2003) 'Surreal figures', in Gavins, J. and Steen, G. (eds), *Cognitive Poetics in Practice.* London: Routledge.

Stockwell, P. (2009) *Texture: A Cognitive Aesthetics of Reading.* Edinburgh: Edinburgh University Press.

Turner, M. (1991) *Reading Minds: The Study of English in the Age of Cognitive Science.* Princeton, NJ: Princeton University Press.

Ungerer, F. and Schmid, H. (2006) *An Introduction to Cognitive Linguistics,* 2nd edn. London: Longman.

Van Peer, W. (1986) *Stylistics and Psychology: Investigations of Foregrounding.* London: Croom Helm.

Van Peer, W., Hakemulder, J. and Zyngier, S. (2007) *Muses and Measures: Empirical Research Methods for the Humanities.* Cambridge: Cambridge Scholars Publishing.

West, D. W. (2008) 'Changing English: A polemic against relativism and fragmentation', *Changing English: An International Journal of English Teaching* 15(2): 137–43.

West, D. W. (forthcoming) *I. A. Richards and the Rise of Cognitive Stylistics.* London: Continuum.

Widdowson, H. G. (1975) *Stylistics and the Teaching of Literature.* London: Longman.

APPENDIX 1: CHRONOLOGY OF KEY EVENTS IN STYLISTICS

Cross references to works in stylistics listed and annotated in Appendix 3 are indicated by an arrow within brackets.

Date	Event
Early 20th century	Members of the Moscow Linguistic Circle initiate a critical movement which is to become known as Russian Formalism and which attempts to locate the source of literariness in the language of texts.
	Roman Jakobson identifies the poetic function of language as distinct from other communicative functions.
	Victor Shklovsky develops the concept of defamiliarization, a forerunner to foregrounding theory, as a defining feature of literature (⇨Shklovsky 1990).
	Jakobson works on uncovering linguistic patterning (parallelism) as a trigger for defamiliarization.
1920	Jakobson emigrates to Prague and works with Jan Mukarovský and others on the distinction between poetic language and the standard language (⇨Mukařovsky 1964).
1926	Jakobson and Czech colleagues establish the Prague Linguistic Circle.
1929	Jakobson coins the term 'structuralism' to reflect the structural interrelations between linguistic units.
1941	Jakobson settles in America thereby transferring formalist and structuralist ideas to the West (⇨Jakobson 1987).
Post-war	The New Criticism (USA) and Practical Criticism (UK) movements develop under the influence of Russian Formalist ideas.
	In Austria, Leo Spitzer rejects impressionistic criticism in favour of a principled text-based approach to literary analysis (⇨Spitzer 1948).
1950s	The French tradition of *analyse de texte* develops out of the work of Spitzer, Auerbach, Bally and Guiraud.
Early 1960s	In a series of articles and exchanges, the linguist Roger Fowler and the literary critic F. W. Bateson debate the relative merits of linguistic and literary criticism (⇨Fowler 1971).

(continued)

Continued

Date	Event
1960s – early 1970s	Chomskyan principles begin to be applied to stylistic analysis (⇨Freeman 1971; Levin 1965).
1964	The Brown corpus, the first electronic corpus of American English, is developed at Brown University, USA. This opens up possibilities for establishing quantitative norms for language against which foregrounding can be measured.
Late 1960s	The rise of linguistics as a discipline leads to an interest in non-literary stylistics (⇨Crystal and Davy 1966; Enkvist 1973).
1969	Publication of Leech's *A Linguistic Guide to English Poetry* takes stylistics beyond formalism by making explicit the connection between form and function (⇨Leech 1969).
Early 1970s	Halliday's work on functional grammar develops and is applied to literary texts (⇨Halliday 1971).
	Work on cognitive stylistics begins (⇨Tsur 1992).
1979	The Poetics and Linguistics Association (PALA) is established in the UK, initially as an offshoot of the Linguistics Association of Great Britain.
1981	Leech and Short's influential *Style in Fiction* is published, offering a rigorous and objective approach to the analysis of prose fiction (⇨Leech and Short 2007).
1980s	The development of pragmatics as a sub-discipline of linguistics revolutionizes work on the stylistics of drama (⇨Short 1981)
1986	The first electronic corpus of British English, the Lancaster-Oslo-Bergen corpus (LOB), is developed as a parallel to the Brown corpus. Stylistic analysis that uses a corpus linguistic methodology becomes increasingly possible.
	Van Peer's *Stylistics and Psychology* finds empirical evidence for foregrounding theory (⇨van Peer 1986).
Mid–late 1980s	Interest develops in the cognitive aspects of text comprehension, leading to work on reader-responses to literary texts (⇨Short 1989).
Late 1980s–90s	Advances in pragmatics and their concern with context facilitate a renewed interest in non-literary stylistics (⇨Carter and Nash 1990; Simpson 1993).
1997	Emmott's *Narrative Comprehension* is published, setting out a comprehensive account of the cognitive processes involved in text comprehension (⇨Emmott 1997).

(continued)

Continued

Date	Event
1996	Scott's concordancing software, *WordSmith Tools*, is released, facilitating work in corpus stylistics (⇨www.lexically.net).
2000s	Corpus stylistics grows as a result of an increase in availability of specialist software and corpora which is enabled by the increased processing power and storage of computers.
	Growth of work in cognitive stylistics (Semino and Culpeper 2000, Stockwell 2002).
2005	Leech and Short's *Style in Fiction* wins the 25th anniversary PALA prize for best stylistics book since PALA was founded.
2010	Thirtieth anniversary of PALA is celebrated at the annual conference at the University of Genoa, Italy.
	Mick Short's contribution to stylistics is recognized by the publication of a *festschrift* (⇨McIntyre and Busse 2010).

APPENDIX 2: LIST OF KEY WORKS IN STYLISTICS

Burton, D. (1980) *Dialogue and Discourse: A Socio-Linguistic Approach to Modern Drama Dialogue and Naturally Occurring Conversation*. London: Routledge & Kegan Paul.

Carter, R. and Nash, W. (1990) *Seeing Through Language: A Guide to Styles of English Writing*. Oxford: Blackwell.

Crystal, D. and Davy, D. (1966) *Investigating English Style*. London: Longman.

Emmott, C. (1997) *Narrative Comprehension: A Discourse Perspective*. Oxford: Oxford University Press.

Enkvist, N. E. (1973) *Linguistic Stylistics*. The Hague: Mouton.

Fowler, R. (1986) *Linguistic Criticism*. Oxford: Blackwell.

Freeman, D. C. (ed.) (1971) *Linguistics and Literary Style*. New York: Holt, Rinehart & Winston.

Halliday, M. A. K. (1971) 'Linguistic function and literary style: An inquiry into the language of William Golding's *The Inheritors*', in Chatman, S. (ed.), *Literary Style*, pp. 330–65. Oxford: Oxford University Press.

Jakobson, R. (1960) 'Closing statement: Linguistics and poetics', in Sebeok, T. A. (ed.), *Style in Language*, pp. 350–77. Cambridge, MA: MIT Press.

Jakobson, R. (1987) *Language in Literature*. Cambridge, MA: Harvard University Press.

Jeffries, L. (1993) *The Language of Twentieth Century Poetry*. Basingstoke: Macmillan – now Palgrave Macmillan.

Jeffries, L. and McIntyre, D. (2010) *Stylistics*. Cambridge: Cambridge University Press.

Leech, G. (1969) *A Linguistic Guide to English Poetry*. London: Longman.

Leech, G. (2008) *Language in Literature: Style and Foregrounding*. London: Pearson Education.

Leech, G. and Short, M. (2007) *Style in Fiction: A Linguistic Introduction to English Fictional Prose*, 2nd edn. London: Pearson Education.

Levin, S. R. (1965) 'Internal and external deviation in poetry', *Word* 21: 225–37.

Mukařovsky, J. (1964 [1932]) 'Standard language and poetic language', in Garvin, P. (ed.), *A Prague School Reader on Esthetics, Literary Structure, and Style*, pp. 17–30. Washington, DC: Georgetown University Press.

Sebeok, T. A. (ed.) (1960) *Style in Language*. Cambridge, MA: MIT Press.

Semino, E. (1997) *Language and World Creation in Poems and Other Texts*. London: Longman.

Semino, E. and Culpeper, J. (eds) (2000) *Cognitive Stylistics: Language and Cognition in Text Analysis*. Amsterdam: John Benjamins.

Short, M. (1981) 'Discourse analysis and the analysis of drama', *Applied Linguistics* 11(2): 180–202.

Short, M. (ed.) (1989) *Reading, Analysing and Teaching Literature*. London: Longman.

Short, M. (1996) *Exploring the Language of Poems, Plays and Prose*. London: Longman.

Simpson, P. (1993) *Language, Ideology and Point of View*. London: Routledge.

Sinclair, J. (1966) 'Taking a poem to pieces', in Fowler, R. (ed.), *Essays on Style and Language*, pp. 68–81. London: Routledge.

Spitzer, L. (1948) *Linguistics and Literary History*. Princeton, NJ: Princeton University Press.

Stockwell, P. (2002) *Cognitive Poetics: An Introduction*. London: Routledge.

Toolan, M. (2001) *Narrative: A Critical Linguistic Introduction*, 2nd edn. London: Routledge.

Tsur, R. (1992) *Toward a Theory of Cognitive Poetics*. Amsterdam: Elsevier.

Van Peer, W. (1986) *Stylistics and Psychology: Investigations of Foregrounding*. London: Croom Helm.

Verdonk, P. and Weber, J. J. (eds) (1995) *Twentieth Century Fiction: From Text to Context*. London: Routledge.

Wales, K. (2001) *A Dictionary of Stylistics*, 2nd edn. London: Longman.

Werth, P. (1999) *Text Worlds: Representing Conceptual Space in Discourse*. London: Longman.

APPENDIX 3: AN ANNOTATED BIBLIOGRAPHY OF FURTHER READING AND RESOURCES IN STYLISTICS

Books, chapters and journal articles

Brown, P. and Levinson, S. C. (1987) *Politeness: Some Universals in Language Usage.* Cambridge: Cambridge University Press. [Develops Goffman's concept of face by introducing the notion of positive and negative face threatening acts.]

Burton, D. (1980) *Dialogue and Discourse: A Socio-Linguistic Approach to Modern Drama Dialogue and Naturally Occurring Conversation.* London: Routledge & Kegan Paul. [First significant study of dramatic discourse from a pragmatic perspective.]

Busse, B. (2006) *Vocative Constructions in the Language of Shakespeare.* Amsterdam: John Benjamins. [Studies Shakespeare from a corpus stylistic perspective.]

Carter, R. (2004) *Language and Creativity: The Art of Common Talk.* London: Routledge. [Argues that creativity is not restricted to literary writing but is a common feature of everyday speech.]

Carter, R. and Nash, W. (1990) *Seeing through Language: A Guide to Styles of English Writing.* Oxford: Blackwell. [Covers literary and non-literary stylistics and discusses the concept of literariness from a variety of perspectives.]

Crystal, D. and Davy, D. (1966) *Investigating English Style.* London: Longman. [Rigorous study of a range of non-literary registers.]

Culpeper, J. (2000) *Language and Characterisation.* London: Longman. [Introduces a model of the cognitive processes by which readers comprehend dramatic characters.]

Culpeper, J., Short, M. and Verdonk, P. (eds) (1998) *Exploring the Language of Drama: From Text to Context.* London: Routledge. [Collection of essays on cognitive and pragmatic approaches to analysing dramatic texts; includes advice for students on writing an essay on the stylistics of drama.]

Douthwaite, J. (2000) *Towards a Linguistic Theory of Foregrounding.* Alessandria: Edizioni dell'Orso. [Comprehensive survey of the history and development of foregrounding theory.]

Ehrlich, V. (1965) [1955] *Russian Formalism: History and Doctrine.* The Hague: Mouton. [Survey of one of the most significant critical movements underlying contemporary stylistics.]

Emmott, C. (1997) *Narrative Comprehension: A Discourse Perspective.* Oxford: Oxford University Press. [Sets out a model of how readers process narrative texts.]

Emmott, C., Sanford, A. J., and Dawydiak, E. J. (2007) 'Stylistics meets cognitive science: Studying style in fiction and readers' attention from an interdisciplinary perspective', *Style* 41(2): 204–24. [Tests Emmott's model of narrative comprehension through interdisciplinary experimentation.]

Enkvist, N. E. (1973) *Linguistic Stylistics.* The Hague: Mouton. [Study of non-literary style markers.]

Forceville, C. (1996) *Pictorial Metaphor in Advertising*. London: Routledge. [Applies cognitive metaphor theory to visual images.]

Fowler, R. (1971) *The Languages of Literature*. London: Routledge & Kegan Paul. [Collection of essays focusing on the linguistic analysis of literature, including the articles that arose from the infamous debate between Fowler and F. W. Bateson.]

Fowler, R. (1977) *Linguistics and the Novel*. London: Methuen. [Applies stylistic methods to the analysis of prose fiction.]

Fowler, R. (1986) *Linguistic Criticism*. Oxford: Blackwell. [Outlines a model of point of view based on the categorization of narrators.]

Freeman, D. C. (ed.) (1971) *Linguistics and Literary Style*. New York: Holt, Rinehart & Winston. [Collection of essays that makes the case for using linguistics in literary criticism.]

Gavins, J. and Steen, G. (eds) (2003) *Cognitive Poetics in Practice*. London: Routledge. [Companion volume to Stockwell (2002) in which key ideas in contemporary cognitive stylistics are explored.]

Halliday, M. A. K. (1971) 'Linguistic function and literary style: An inquiry into the language of William Golding's *The Inheritors*', in Chatman, S. (ed.), *Literary Style*, pp. 330–65. Oxford: Oxford University Press. [Early exploration of what Fowler was later to call *mind style*; applies functional grammar to account for Golding's presentation of a Neanderthal world view.]

Hoover, D. (1999) *Language and Style in The Inheritors*. Lanham, MD: University Press of America. [Comprehensive study of text style in Golding's novel *The Inheritors*.]

Hoover, D. (2004) 'Altered texts, altered worlds, altered styles', *Language and Literature* 13(2): 99–118. [Uses Pope's concept of *textual intervention* to reflect on the creation of particular stylistic effects in prose writing.]

Jakobson, R. (1960) 'Closing statement: linguistics and poetics', in Sebeok, T. A. (ed.), *Style in Language*, pp. 350–77. Cambridge, MA: MIT Press. [Important manifesto for the future development of stylistics.]

Jakobson, R. (1987) *Language in Literature*. Cambridge, MA: Harvard University Press. [Collection of Jakobson's most important work in stylistics.]

Jeffries, L. (1993) *The Language of Twentieth Century Poetry*. Basingstoke: Macmillan – now Palgrave Macmillan. [Applies stylistic tools to characterize the distinctive features of twentieth-century poetry.]

Jeffries, L. (2001) 'Schema theory and White Asparagus: Cultural multilingualism among readers of texts', *Language and Literature* 10(4): 325–43. [Debates Cook's and Semino's application of schema theory to the definition of literariness.]

Jeffries, L. (2009) *Critical Stylistics*. Basingstoke: Palgrave Macmillan. [Applies systematic stylistic methods to critical discourse analysis.]

Jeffries, L. and McIntyre, D. (2010) *Stylistics*. Cambridge: Cambridge University Press. [Comprehensive account of the principles, practice and scope of stylistics from its inception.]

Lakoff, G. and Johnson, M. (1980) *Metaphors We Live By*. Chicago: Chicago University Press. [Influential introduction to cognitive metaphor theory.]

Lambrou, M. and Stockwell, P. (eds) *Contemporary Stylistics*. London: Continuum. [Collection of essays on stylistic approaches to prose, poetry and drama.]

Leech, G. (1969) *A Linguistic Guide to English Poetry*. London: Longman. [Illustrates a key stage in the development of stylistic description; focuses particularly on the relationship between form and function.]

Leech, G. (2008) *Language in Literature: Style and Foregrounding*. London: Pearson Education. [Collection of Leech's key articles on stylistics, focused particularly on the concept of foregrounding.]

Leech, G. and Short, M. (2007) *Style in Fiction: A Linguistic Introduction to English Fictional Prose*, 2nd edn. London: Pearson Education. [Second edition of the book voted by PALA to be the most influential work in stylistics since 1980.]

Levin, S. R. (1965) 'Internal and external deviation in poetry', *Word* 21: 225–37. [Develops the concept of foregrounding through deviation.]

Louw, B. (1993) 'Irony in the text or insincerity in the writer? The diagnostic potential of semantic prosodies', in Baker, M., Francis, G. and Tognini-Bonelli, E. (eds), *Text and Technology: In Honour of John Sinclair*, pp. 157–76. Amsterdam: John Benjamins. [Demonstrates how semantic prosodies arise out of collocational tendencies.]

Macleod, N. (2009) 'Stylistics and the analysis of poetry: A credo and an example', *Journal of Literary Semantics* 38(2): 131–50. [Argues from an analytical and theoretical perspective for stylistics to reassert its relevance to the study of literature in the face of its dismissal by the literary establishment.]

Mahlberg, M. (2007) 'Clusters, key clusters and local textual functions in Dickens', *Corpora* 2(1): 1–31. [Demonstrates the stylistic effects of clusters and key clusters in a corpus of Dickens's novels compared against nineteenth-century fiction generally.]

Mandala, S. (2007) *Twentieth Century Dramatic Dialogue as Ordinary Talk: Speaking Between the Lines*. London: Ashgate. [Rigorous demonstration of the application of linguistic techniques in the analysis of drama.]

McIntyre, D. (2004) 'Point of view in drama: A socio-pragmatic analysis of Dennis Potter's *Brimstone and Treacle*', *Language and Literature* 13(2): 139–60. [Argues for the importance of point of view in the analysis of dramatic texts as well as prose fiction.]

McIntyre, D. (2006) *Point of View in Plays: A Cognitive Stylistic Approach to Viewpoint in Drama and Other Text-types*. Amsterdam: John Benjamins. [Uses developments in cognitive linguistics to account for point of view effects in drama.]

McIntyre, D. (2008) 'Integrating multimodal analysis and the stylistics of drama: A multimodal perspective on Ian McKellen's *Richard III*', *Language and Literature* 17(4): 309–34. [Demonstrates how the multimodal analysis of film drama can be undertaken in a rigorous fashion.]

McIntyre, D. and Busse, B. (eds) (2010) *Language and Style*. Basingstoke: Palgrave Macmillan. [*Festschrift* for Mick Short celebrating his influence on stylistics.]

Montgomery, M. (2004) 'The discourse of *war* after 9/11', *Language and Literature* 14(2): 149–80. [Application of stylistic techniques in non-literary analysis.]

Mukařovsky, J. (1964 [1932]) 'Standard language and poetic language', in Garvin, P. (ed.), *A Prague School Reader on Esthetics, Literary Structure, and Style*, pp. 17–30. Washington, DC: Georgetown University Press. [Significant discussion of ideas at the time concerning the formal distinction between poetic language and standard language; now superseded by notions of prototypicality and functionality.]

Nørgaard, N. (2009) 'The semiotics of typography in literary texts: A multimodal approach', *Orbis Litterarum* 64(2): 141–60. [Demonstrates how the rigorous techniques of stylistics can be applied to understand the multimodal effects of typography.]

Nørgaard, N., Busse, B. and Montoro, R. (2010) *Key Terms in Stylistics*. London: Continuum. [Encyclopaedic reference book focusing on key concepts and key figures in stylistics.]

O'Halloran, K. A. (2007) 'Corpus-assisted literary evaluation', *Corpora* 2(1): 33–63. [Demonstrates how large reference corpora can be used to support the stylistic analysis of short texts.]

O'Halloran, K. A (2007) 'The subconscious in James Joyce's "Eveline": A corpus stylistic analysis which chews on the "Fish hook"', *Language and Literature* 16(3): 227–44. [Presents a corpus-based analysis of a short story in order to address and dismiss Fish's criticisms of stylistics.]

Pope, R. (1994) *Textual Intervention: Critical and Creative Strategies for Literary Studies*. London: Routledge. [Introduces a pedagogical technique for understanding stylistic effects by altering original texts.]

Ryder, M. E. (2003) 'I met myself coming and going: Co(?)-referential noun phrases and point of view in time travel stories', *Language and Literature* 12(3): 213–32. [An examination of the relationship between syntax and style.]

Sebeok, T. A. (ed.) (1960) *Style in Language*. Cambridge, MA: MIT Press. [Classic collection of early essays in stylistics.]

Semino, E. (1997) *Language and World Creation in Poems and Other Texts*. London: Longman. [Applies cognitive linguistic insights to the interpretation of poetry.]

Semino, E. and Culpeper, J. (eds) (2000) *Cognitive Stylistics: Language and Cognition in Text Analysis*. Amsterdam: John Benjamins. [Collection of essays delimiting the state-of-the-art in cognitive stylistics.]

Shklovsky, V. (1990 [1923]) *Theory of Prose*, trans. Benjamin Sher. Normal, IL: Dalkey Archive Press. [Seminal work of Russian formalism in which the concept of defamiliarization is explained.]

Short, M. (1981) 'Discourse analysis and the analysis of drama', *Applied Linguistics* 11(2): 180–202. [Applies pragmatic principles in the analysis of dramatic texts; argues that stylistics should focus on text not performance.]

Short, M. (ed.) (1989) *Reading, Analysing and Teaching Literature*. London: Longman. [Collection of essays on pedagogical stylistics.]

Short, M. (1996) *Exploring the Language of Poems, Plays and Prose*. London: Longman. [Classic introduction to the techniques of literary stylistics.]

Simpson, P. (1993) *Language, Ideology and Point of View*. London: Routledge. [Introduces a modal grammar of point of view.]

Simpson, P. (2004) *On the Discourse of Satire*. Amsterdam: John Benjamins. [Develops a model of satirical discourse using stylistic techniques.]

Simpson, P. and Montgomery, M. (1995) 'Language, literature and film: The stylistics of Bernard MacLaverty's *Cal*', in Verdonk, P. and Weber, J. J. (eds), *Twentieth Century Fiction: From Text to Context*, pp. 138–59. London: Routledge. [Extends stylistic analysis to take account of the multimodal aspects of film drama.]

Sinclair, J. (1966) 'Taking a poem to pieces', in Fowler, R. (ed.), *Essays on Style and Language*, pp. 68–81. London: Routledge. [Analysis of a poem using linguistic stylistic techniques; often criticized for its focus on linguistic description to the exclusion of literary interpretation.]

Spitzer, L. (1948) *Linguistics and Literary History*. Princeton, NJ: Princeton University Press. [Outlines the importance of objectivity and rigour in literary analysis.]

264 *Appendix 3*

Stockwell, P. (2002) *Cognitive Poetics: An Introduction*. London: Routledge. [Survey of developments in cognitive science and how these can be applied in stylistic analysis.]

Stubbs, M. (2005) 'Conrad in the computer: Examples of quantitative stylistic methods', *Language and Literature* 14(1): 5–24. [Demonstrates the techniques of corpus stylistics.]

Toolan, M. (2001) *Narrative: A Critical Linguistic Introduction*, 2nd edn. London: Routledge. [Comprehensive account of techniques of narrative analysis.]

Tsur, R. (1992) *Toward a Theory of Cognitive Poetics*. Amsterdam: Elsevier. [Overview of Tsur's distinct conception of cognitive poetics.]

Van Peer, W. (1986) *Stylistics and Psychology: Investigations of Foregrounding*. London: Croom Helm. [Reports the findings of experiments to establish the empirical foundations of foregrounding theory.]

Verdonk, P. (ed.) (1993) *Twentieth Century Poetry: From Text to Context*. London: Routledge. [Collection of essays applying stylistic techniques in the analysis of poetry.]

Verdonk, P. and Weber, J. J. (eds) (1995) *Twentieth Century Fiction: From Text to Context*. London: Routledge. [Collection of essays applying stylistic techniques in the analysis of prose fiction.]

Wales, K. (1992) *The Language of James Joyce*. Basingstoke: Macmillan – now Palgrave Macmillan. [Extensive study of the authorial style of James Joyce.]

Wales, K. (2001) *A Dictionary of Stylistics*, 2nd edn. London: Longman. [Comprehensive reference book explaining key terms in stylistics and related fields.]

Watson, G. and Zyngier, S. (2006) *Literature and Stylistics for Language Learners*. Basingstoke: Palgrave Macmillan. [Collection of essays focusing on pedagogical stylistics in terms of its application to the teaching of literature; includes a special focus on EFL and ESL language classroom situations.]

Werth, P. (1999) *Text Worlds: Representing Conceptual Space in Discourse*. London: Longman. [An account of Werth's significant contribution to the understanding of how readers construct mental representations of texts as they read; published posthumously.]

Widdowson, H. (1975) *Stylistics and the Teaching of Literature*. London: Longman. [Makes the case for stylistics as a pedagogical middle ground connecting linguistic and literary studies.]

Websites

IALS (http://literarysemantics.wordpress.com/) [Website of the International Association of Literary Semantics.]

IGEL (http://www.psych.ualberta.ca/IGEL/) [Website of the International Society for the Empirical Study of Literature.]

Language and Style (http://www.lancs.ac.uk/fass/projects/stylistics/index.htm) [A free web-based interactive stylistics course.]

Oxford Text Archive (http://ota.ahds.ac.uk/) [Access to a wide variety of electronic literary and linguistic resources and advice on the creation and use of such resources.]

PALA (www.pala.ac.uk) [Website of the international Poetics and Linguistics Association; includes free access to conference proceedings, occasional papers and the PALA stylistics bibliography of the twentieth century.]

REDES (http://www.letras.ufrj.br/redes/) ['Research and Development in Empirical Studies'; website of a inter-institutional project aimed at promoting the scientific study of literature and culture from a multi-cultural perspective.]

WordSmith (www.lexically.net) [Website for Scott's concordancing software, *WordSmith Tools*, facilitating work in corpus stylistics.]

APPENDIX 4: LIST OF KEY STYLISTICIANS AND THEIR CONTRIBUTIONS TO THE DISCIPLINE

This is a necessarily selective list, for which there were a number of contenders for inclusion. We have tried to focus on those stylisticians who have had most influence on work that is ongoing today. Full references for publications mentioned below can be found in Appendix 3.

Ronald Carter

Carter's work in stylistics has focused on uncovering creativity in non-literary, particularly spoken, everyday language. He has contributed to the debate about whether literary style is distinct from other styles (see Carter and Nash 1990) and produced evidence against their differentiation. More recently his work has concentrated on using corpus techniques in the pursuit of these ends (see, for example, Carter 2004). He is Professor of Modern English Language at the University of Nottingham.

Roger Fowler

Fowler is most well known for his work on point of view and his development of the concept of mind style (see Fowler 1977, 1986). He developed the concept of critical linguistics from his consideration of ideology in news discourse and this has had a significant impact on the development of critical discourse analysis. He was Professor of English and Linguistics at the University of East Anglia.

Roman Jakobson

Jakobson could legitimately be called the founder of stylistics. He was central to the activities of the Russian formalist school of criticism as well as the Prague Linguistic Circle, which introduced the concepts of defamiliarization, standard language and poetic language (see Jakobson 1987). His necessarily nomadic lifestyle before and during the Second World War led to the cross-fertilization of ideas between East and West. He held a number of posts and was latterly Professor of Slavic Languages and Literature and General Linguistics at Harvard University.

Geoffrey Leech

Leech's work in stylistics has encompassed the full range of methods and genres, from qualitative studies of poetry to the corpus analysis of prose fiction. He has contributed significantly to the development of the theory of foregrounding (see Leech 1969) and, with Mick Short, co-authored *Style in Fiction* (2nd edition, Leech and Short 2007). He is Emeritus Professor of English Linguistics at Lancaster University.

Mick Short

Short's major contribution to stylistic theory is his model of speech and thought presentation which posits the existence of a cline of narrator interference along which a variety of discourse presentation categories offer varying degrees of faithfulness to a perceived original statement or thought. With colleagues at Lancaster University, he has tested this model on a range of written and spoken data using corpus-based techniques, and has refined the model as a result. The co-author of *Style in Fiction* (2nd edition, Leech and Short 2007), he is Professor of English Language and Literature at Lancaster University.

Paul Simpson

Simpson's development of a modal grammar of point of view refined a number of aspects of narratological theory and demonstrated the shared interests of critical discourse analysis and stylistics (see Simpson 1993). More recently, he has applied the techniques of stylistics to the study of humour and has developed a theory of satirical discourse (Simpson 2004). He is Professor of English Language at Queen's University, Belfast.

Willie van Peer

Van Peer's work has concentrated on the empirical study of literature, including literary style, reader response and pedagogical applications of stylistics. His major contribution to stylistics is the evidence he produced in support of foregrounding theory (see van Peer 1986). His recent work has focused on the use of empirical techniques in the Humanities generally. He is Professor of Literary Studies and Intercultural Hermeneutics at the University of Munich.

Peter Verdonk

Verdonk's work in stylistics has focused on the detailed analysis of literary genres, the importance of context to interpretation and the application of stylistics in teaching English syntax. He has edited a series of three books focusing on the relationship between language and context in poetry, prose and drama (Verdonk 1993, 1995; Culpeper, Short and Verdonk 1998). He is Emeritus Professor of Stylistics at the University of Amsterdam.

Katie Wales

Wales is best known for her dictionary of stylistics which has been significant in establishing the field as a recognized discipline (2nd edition, Wales 2001) and which has proved an invaluable resource for both students and academics. Her work in stylistics has also encompassed an extensive study of the language of James Joyce (Wales 1992). She is Special Professor in the School of English, University of Nottingham.

Paul Werth

Werth's major contribution to stylistics was the development of his theory of text worlds, which explains the processes by which readers develop mental representations of fictional worlds as they read (Werth 1999). He was Professor of English Linguistics at the University of Amsterdam.

Henry Widdowson

Widdowson's work in stylistics has focused particularly on its applications in Applied Linguistics. He has specialized in examining the ways in which stylistics can be used in the teaching of language and literature (see Widdowson 1975). He is Emeritus Professor of Education, University of London.

APPENDIX 5: A SURVEY OF CURRENT PROVISION OF POSTGRADUATE COURSES IN STYLISTICS IN THE UK AND US

Below is a selection of UK and US institutions offering MA courses with significant stylistics components and opportunities for doctoral research in stylistics. All can be found on the web.

Aston University, UK (http://www1.aston.ac.uk/)
MA Applied Linguistics
MPhil/PhD

University of Birmingham, UK (http://www.bham.ac.uk/)
MA Literary Linguistics
MPhil/PhD

University of Central Lancashire, UK (http://www.uclan.ac.uk/)
MA English Language and Literature
MPhil/PhD

University of East Anglia, UK (http://www.uea.ac.uk/)
MA Literary Translation
MPhil/PhD

University of Glasgow, UK (http://www.gla.ac.uk/)
MA English Language and English Linguistics
MPhil/PhD

University of Huddersfield, UK (http://www.hud.ac.uk)
MA Modern English Language
MA Language in Conflict
MPhil/PhD
Professional Doctorate in Applied Linguistics (including taught component)

Northern Illinois University, USA (http://www.niu.edu/index.shtml)
MA Linguistics/Stylistics
PhD

Lancaster University, UK (http://www.lancaster.ac.uk/)
MA Language Studies
MA Discourse Studies
MA English Language and Literary Studies
MPhil/PhD

University of Leeds, UK (http://www.leeds.ac.uk/)
MA English Language
MPhil/PhD

University of Nevada, Reno, USA (http://www.unr.edu/)
MA English
PhD

New York University, USA (http://www.nyu.edu/)
MA English
PhD

University of Nottingham, UK (http://www.nottingham.ac.uk/)
MA Literary Linguistics
MPhil/PhD

Queen's University, Belfast, UK (http://www.qub.ac.uk/)
MPhil/PhD

University of Sheffield, UK (http://www.shef.ac.uk/)
MA English Language and Literature
MPhil/PhD

Index